6

THE GREAT GAME

AFGHANISTAN

OBERON BOOKS
LONDON

This collection first published in 2009 by Oberon Books Ltd
521 Caledonian Road, London N7 9RH
Tel: 020 7607 3637 / Fax: 020 7607 3629
e-mail: info@oberonbooks.com
www.oberonbooks.com

Reprinted with the addition of *Wood for the Fire*, 2010, 2011

Introduction © Nicolas Kent 2009, 2010

Individual copyright and licensing information can be found at the beginning of each play.

A catalogue record for this book is available from the British Library.

ISBN: 978-1-84002-922-2

Cover photograph by Zahra Qadir

Printed in Great Britain by CPI Antony Rowe, Chippenham.

Contents

Introduction

For much of the last fifteen years Iraq has been the big story for the world's media. For a short period in the Autumn of 2001, just after 9/11, Afghanistan took centre stage. But after the fall of the Taliban both Bush and Blair ensured that the world's attention moved swiftly back to Iraq.

Iraq was in the headlines almost every day, and artists, writers, film-makers and theatres produced much work about the invasion and its aftermath. The Tricycle, in common with many other London theatres, mounted a number of plays on the subject – indeed, in 1993, the first of our 'Tribunal plays' was a dramatisation of Lord Scott's 'Arms to Iraq' inquiry.

In the middle of the present decade no one paid much attention to the war in Afghanistan, and even Defence Secretary John Reid, whilst committing British troops to ISAF forces in Helmand province, was quoted as saying: 'We would be perfectly happy to leave in three years and without firing one shot because our job is to protect the reconstruction'.

However in early 2008, less than two years after that statement, I began to notice that world's political focus was very slowly but inexorably swinging back towards Afghanistan. The insurgency was strengthening, increasing numbers of British soldiers had been killed and injured, and the West looked dug in for the long haul.

Afghanistan was surely going to be the main focus of British, European and American policy for at least the next decade. But still early last year, not only was there almost no public debate about this, there was very little reporting and almost no artistic response – except a handful of novels including the work of Khaled Hosseini.

I knew vaguely about the three Anglo-Afghan wars, the British and Russian imperialist 'Great Game' manoeuvres, and something about the factions of the Mujahideen fighting the civil war after the Soviet withdrawal. But there were huge gaps in my knowledge of Afghanistan's history, and the causes of where we are now. And I was sure I was not alone in this ignorance.

Information sparks debate, and theatre can often be the catalyst, but how to tackle Afghanistan?

Well, two experiences came to my aid – some years ago we had produced a trilogy, *Love Song for Ulster* by Bill Morrison, which looked at Northern Ireland's politics, and from that experience I knew that day-long theatre events could be both exciting and stimulating – this feeling was reinforced last April by seeing the RSC's 'Histories' season at the Roundhouse. The other experience was a response we had to the Darfur crisis when, two years ago, the Tricycle commissioned six dramatists from our Bloomberg Playwrights group to come up with ten minute plays, and all the writers rose enthusiastically to the challenge. The resulting evening played to a week of full houses.

So I had my template – a day-long event using a number of playwrights, but where to start? Initially I did a trawl for writers, including novelists, from the sub-continent, but apart from Siba Shakib I met with little success. Next I turned to 'political' writers working here or in America. David Edgar's play *Testing the Echo* was on at the Tricycle at that time so who better to get the ball rolling, and Ron Hutchinson's play *Topless Mum* was the next play in that Summer, so he, too, was quickly enlisted. I must, also, thank Jack Bradley, the Tricycle's literary adviser, who as well as deploying his excellent dramaturgical skills, suggested other writers, as did Purni Morell of the National Theatre Studio. Literary agents Mel Kenyon, Rose Cobbe and Alan Brodie were all important keys to the project.

All the writers have embraced *The Great Game* with huge enthusiasm – some of them have chosen their own subjects, and some have been 'coerced' into periods of Afghan history about which they knew nothing, and have now become expert. I am incredibly grateful to them for these wonderful plays. As I am to my co-director Indhu Rubasingham for her invaluable advice and support; as well as to our two assistants Zoe Ingenhaag and Rachel Grunwald, our designer Pamela Howard, and the actors, who have all greatly helped to make this project a reality.

Nicolas Kent
24th March 2009

On the 23rd July 2010 *The Great Game* was remounted at the Tricycle Theatre before going on a U.S. Autumn tour, which included the Shakespeare Theatre in Washington, The Guthrie Theater in Minneapolis, The Berkeley Rep, and The Public Theater in New York. J.T. Rogers unilaterally withdrew his play from this revival and the U.S. tour, but we were delighted to commission Lee Blessing and his play *Wood for the Fire* replaces it, and is printed here.

Performed between the plays in Parts 1 & 2 of the Trilogy were some specially commissioned monologues by Siba Shakib, and between the plays in Parts 1 & 3 the actors took the roles of some of the main players in the current Afghan conflict for verbatim interviews specially edited for the production by Richard Norton-Taylor

Nicolas Kent
21st June 2010

The Great Game

'The Great Game' was a term used for the strategic rivalry and conflict between the British Empire and the Russian Empire for supremacy in Central Asia. The classic Great Game period is generally regarded as running approximately from the Russo-Persian Treaty of 1813 to the Anglo-Russian Convention of 1907. Following the Bolshevik Revolution of 1917 a second, less intensive phase followed. The term 'The Great Game' was introduced into mainstream consciousness by British writer Rudyard Kipling in his novel *Kim* (1901).

The Tricycle

The Tricycle Theatre has established a unique reputation for presenting plays that reflect the cultural diversity of its community; in particular plays by Black, Irish, Jewish, Asian and South African writers, as well as for responding to contemporary issues and events with its ground-breaking 'tribunal plays', and political work.

In 1994 it staged the first of its *'Tribunal Plays': Half the Picture* by Richard Norton-Taylor and John McGrath (a dramatisation of the Scott Arms to Iraq Inquiry), which was the first play ever to be performed in the Houses of Parliament. The next, marking the fiftieth anniversary of the 1946 War Crimes Tribunal, was *Nuremberg*, which was followed by *Srebrenica* - The 1996 UN Rule 61 Hearings, which later transferred to the National Theatre and the Belfast Festival. In 1999, the Tricycle's reconstruction of the Stephen Lawrence Inquiry, *The Colour of Justice*, transferred to the West End & the National Theatre. In 2003 *Justifying War* - Scenes from the Hutton Inquiry opened at the Tricycle. *Bloody Sunday* - Scenes from the Saville Inquiry followed in 2005 and was also performed at the Abbey in Dublin, Belfast and Derry - it received an Olivier Award for Outstanding Achievement. More recently *Called to Account* - the indictment of Tony Blair for the crime of aggression against Iraq - a hearing was staged at the Tricycle with evidence from Richard Perle, the Chilean Ambassador to the U.N. and ex-Cabinet Minister Clare Short. All of these plays have been broadcast by the BBC on radio or television, and have together reached audiences of over 30 million people worldwide.

In 2004, the critically acclaimed *Guantanamo - Honor Bound to Defend Freedom*, written by Victoria Brittain and Gillian Slovo from spoken evidence transferred from the Tricycle to the West End and New York (where Archbishop Tutu appeared in the production). In 2006 the Tricycle presented a performance of the play at the Houses of Parliament and on Washington's Capitol Hill. It has since been performed around the world and in the US through the 'Guantanamo Reading Project', which develops community productions of readings of the play. Twenty-five of these have already been held in cities across America. Notable theatre productions staged at the Tricycle have included the British premiere of *The Great White Hope* by Howard Sackler (later re-staged for the Royal Shakespeare Company), the world premiere of *Playboy of the West Indies* by Mustapha Matura, which subsequently received more than twenty productions all over the world, and was televised for BBC Television.

West End transfers from the Tricycle also include *The Amen Corner* by James Baldwin, the Fats Waller musical *Ain't Misbehavin'*, *The Price* by Arthur Miller; and transfers to Broadway: the South African musical *Kat and the Kings* (winning two 1999 Olivier Awards for Best New Musical and Best Actor – awarded to the entire cast), *Stones in His Pockets* by Marie Jones, and *39 Steps* adapted by Patrick Barlow (both won Olivier awards in the West End for Best New Comedy). In November 2006, the Tricycle was proud to win a Special Award at the Evening Standard Theatre Awards for 'its pioneering political work'.

In 2005/6 the Tricycle pioneered a black ensemble company in three British premieres of African-American plays chronicling the black experience of the last hundred years: *Walk Hard* by Abram Hill, *Gem of the Ocean* by the late August Wilson and *Fabulation* by Lynn Nottage. The Tricycle has also premiered six of August Wilson's decalogue chronicling the African-American experience of the twentieth century plays. In 2009 the Tricycle staged a a trilogy of full length plays by Roy Williams, Kwame Kwei-Armah & Bola Agbaje, in the season entitled 'Not Black and White', looking at 21st century London from a black perspective. In 2010, following the General Election, the Tricycle presented a season of fourteen new plays entitled 'Women, Power and Politics' which examined both the history of women's role in politics and the complex issues surrounding women's participation and roles in contemporary governments.

The Tricycle and Bloomberg LP have, for the last ten years,

collaborated in working with 18 emerging and leading Black and Asian writers, all of whom have now had their work professionally produced on the London stage. The writers enjoy an annual series of weekend workshops and retreats to develop and support their writing.

Education and community activities are an integral part of the artistic output of the Tricycle. Last year there were more than 40,000 attendances by young people to see films and plays, or to take part in workshops. The Tricycle's home in the London borough of Brent comprises a theatre, cinema, art gallery, café and bar, and it is open all year round.

PART ONE
INVASIONS AND INDEPENDENCE
1842-1930

BUGLES AT THE GATES OF JALALABAD

by Stephen Jeffreys

First production

The Tricycle Theatre, London, 17 April 2009

The following cast performed in the remount in July 2010 at the Tricycle Theatre prior to the USA tour:

Characters / Cast

LADY FLORENTIA SALE (a General's wife, 50s)	Jemma Redgrave
McCANN (a corporal, 30s)	Daniel Betts
DICKENSON (a private, late 20s)	Tom McKay
HENDRICK (a private, 30s)	Rick Warden
WINTERFLOOD (a private, early 20s)	Karl Davies
AFZAL (about forty)	Nabil Elouahabi

Director	Indhu Rubasingham
Designer	Miriam Nabarro
Lighting	James Farncombe
Sound	Tom Lishman

Setting

The play is set outside the Kabul gate of Jalalabad after midnight on January 13th 1842 during the First Afghan War.

Lights up on one small, separate area of the stage, either elevated or to the side. This is the station of LADY FLORENTIA SALE, a General's wife in her mid-fifties. She speaks with an eye-witness's authority.

The other characters do not hear her, but she is aware of the other characters and is usually motivated to speak because of what they say and do. Mostly she shares her memories and insights with the audience: occasionally she speaks directly to the four soldiers, apparently believing that she can influence their actions, which she can't. Perhaps she moves among them, though she is never visible to them.

LADY SALE: It is easy to argue on the wisdom or folly of conduct after the catastrophe has taken place.

Lights up on the main stage area.

Before the Kabul gate of Jellalabad.

Four BUGLERS enter. They form a line facing out front.

McCANN: He prophesied it, our Brigadier.

DICKENSON: He did, in the morning.

HENDRICK: The morning of the thirteenth of January 1842.

WINTERFLOOD: Brigadier Dennie, speaking to the General, it was the talk of the regiment.

McCANN: Standing on the ramparts, here in Jalalabad –

HENDRICK: – yesterday morning, the thirteenth of January 1842 –

WINTERFLOOD: Turned to the General and prophesied: 'They are all massacred, every soul –'

DICKENSON: Every poor bugger that started on the retreat from Kabul –

WINTERFLOOD: Running from the enemy! Running, the British Army!

DICKENSON: Running rather than make a stand against the Afghan uprising –

McCANN: 'Every soul but one. And he shall come to bring news of the death of every other soul'

WINTERFLOOD: Sixteen thousand souls –

HENDRICK: All dead but one, and he will bring the news –

McCANN: The tidings –

WINTERFLOOD: And so we watched all through the day, us sentries –

McCANN: Sentinels! Sentinels on the ramparts of Jalalabad –

WINTERFLOOD: – held our watch through the long cold day until we saw it, a speck –

HENDRICK: – not even a speck –

WINTERFLOOD: – a dot –

HENDRICK: – not even a dot

WINTERFLOOD: – a pinpoint

HENDRICK: – a pinpoint growing into a dot, growing into a speck –

McCANN: at which juncture, speaks up the Brigadier: 'Behold. This speck is the messenger I foretold.'

DICKENSON: And we waited and watched until the speck becomes a man on a pony –

HENDRICK: – a yaboo –

WINTERFLOOD: – a ragged figure, an officer on a yaboo –

DICKENSON: – near to death the yaboo

WINTERFLOOD: – near to death the officer –

HENDRICK: – and the Brigadier smiles –

DICKENSON: – the smug fucker –

HENDRICK: – because he has been proved right.

McCANN: The speck is Doctor William Bryden a medical officer with the Fifth Native Infantry and he brings indeed the tidings prophesied.

WINTERFLOOD: Sixteen thousand: soldiers, men, women, children, camp followers –

DICKENSON: Fucking camp followers –

McCANN: Not a soul alive –

WINTERFLOOD: Frozen, starved or cut to bits on the retreat from Kabul.

McCANN: Who is to blame?

HENDRICK: The politicians who put them there –

DICKENSON: The dithering, numbskull Generals –

WINTERFLOOD: The cowards in the ranks –

McCANN: The bloodthirsty, deceitful enemy.

DICKENSON: Blame one, blame all, the upshot is the same:

WINTERFLOOD: One soul alive, the rest of sixteen thousand stretched out in the snow: dead as mutton.

McCANN: Then pipes up the General:

HENDRICK: He may not be the last. There may be more, skulking close to our walls, late at night, reluctant to approach for fear of Afghan marauders.

WINTERFLOOD: And so comes the order. Four buglers to stand beyond the ramparts of the Kabul gate of Jalalabad, and every ten minutes to sound the Advance –

HENDRICK: – so that any straggler from the retreat might approach with confidence –

WINTERFLOOD: – to be snatched from the jaws of death.

McCANN: Jaws of death, just so. Four buglers.

LADY SALE: I kept the anniversary of my marriage to General Sale by dining with the ladies of Mahommed Shah Khan's family, a very stupid entertainment, not at all appropriate to the wife of a General in the British Army on active service overseas. They were largely formed, and coarsely featured. The favourite wife, and the best dressed, was attired in a common Cabul silk, with a rough piece of chintz inserted behind, for economy's sake. Her dress resembled a night-dress; with pieces of silver or gold, including coins, tacked on to it all over the sleeves, the front and sides, from the shoulders to the feet. The Cabul women are much addicted to the use of both white and red paint; and they colour not only the nails, as in Hindostan, but the whole hand up to the wrist, very disgusting to our ideas as it looks to have been plunged in blood.

McCANN: Squad, as a squad, to position.

The men become a unit. They step forward, dress, raise their bugles and stand perfectly still.

On a signal from the Corporal they play the 'Advance'. It should sound shatteringly loud.

They drop the bugles to their sides. They peer into the darkness, even the most cynical believing for a moment that the power of their call will bring forth the living.

Then HENDRICK draws away. He sits apart from the others who continue to scan the horizon.

HENDRICK: There's no-one there.

WINTERFLOOD: How do you know?

HENDRICK: There's no-one there.

WINTERFLOOD: If it was you out there, cold, starving, wounded, you would want a comrade at least to try.

HENDRICK: I know there's no-one there.

WINTERFLOOD: Would want a comrade to act like a comrade.

HENDRICK produces a clay pipe and lights it.

HENDRICK: Cold, starving, wounded, you said it. You could not, in these conditions, survive.

DICKENSON: Bryden survived.

HENDRICK: Through several strokes of improbable good fortune.

LADY SALE: A copy of Blackwood's Magazine stuffed in his forage cap cushioned a blow from an Afghan blade. The pen, for once, is mightier than the sword.

HENDRICK: The chances of a similar survivor appearing twelve hours later in the middle of the night are nil.

DICKENSON: Close to nil.

DICKENSON relaxes his guard a little and moves closer to HENDRICK.

WINTERFLOOD: As long as there is a chance we should remain watchful. Is that not correct, Corporal?

McCANN: That is correct, Private Winterflood. Foolish, but correct.

WINTERFLOOD: I stand by my comrades. Nothing foolish in that.

McCANN: The British Army relies on the enlistment of a high proportion of fools. I'm glad to have you numbered amongst us.

WINTERFLOOD ignores this and watches.

LADY SALE: Snow all day. We are starving. My horse gnaws voraciously at a cartwheel. Nothing is satisfied for food except the pariah dogs who are gorged with eating dead camels and horses. Even some of the gentlemen are eating camel, particularly the heart. I was never tempted by these choice viands so cannot offer an opinion.

DICKENSON: What a fucking business.

Everyone knows what he's talking about but no-one wants to engage. Eventually:

McCANN: Did you speak to him?

DICKENSON: What?

McCANN: Did you, Private Dickenson, in person, hear the testimony, given after his ordeal, by Dr William Bryden, the sole survivor of the retreat.

DICKENSON: Everyone has heard.

McCANN: Very few have heard! Those who have not heard have picked up scraps from those who have. Picked up, each eager ignoramus, a fragment of the true cross from an original disciple. And each ignoramus has proceeded to fashion it into his own ark of the covenant, crafted to his own peculiar fears and phantasies, that he might more easily pass these garrison days in a funk of his own devising.

DICKENSON: We know the truth.

LADY SALE: We were hacked to pieces.

DICKENSON: They were hacked to pieces.

McCANN: So it is alleged.

DICKENSON: We know the Afghan! When we have fought fair, he has descended to the depths, when we have killed like gentlemen, he has hacked and dismembered, carried off the heads of our officers and envoys and paraded them in public.

LADY SALE: Colonel Mackrell, emerging from the Rikabashees' fort to see if relief was on its way, was wounded and fell and the enemy cavalry cut him up dreadfully. He was wounded in both legs, one below the knee, the other on the thigh; he had three cuts in his back, two toes cut off and three or four cuts on the arm, which was taken off immediately after he was brought in. He said: 'This is not battle, it is murder.' To persons accustomed to civilised warfare, these details must be revolting. Even a dead enemy is never passed without a cut at the body. They cry 'Aman' themselves, but never show mercy to us Kaffirs.

HENDRICK: The desperation of men fighting on their own territory.

This angers DICKENSON.

DICKENSON: If you was fighting in England, would you carve the dead and dying?

HENDRICK: Personally I would not. But I cannot speak with confidence of my comrades of whom I have no high opinion. As to the Afghans: we have not dealt fairly with them.

DICKENSON: They promised us safe conduct! Then the tribesmen who were supposed to be our look-outs fell upon us!

HENDRICK: Because we double-crossed them. That's why we're in our present wretched state.

McCANN: Our state is not wretched.

HENDRICK: This country is a death-trap for foreign armies. The narrow defiles, the paths through the mountains. Sixty Afghan tribesmen, hiding on the tops of ridges with their long rifles can take out a battalion. So we bribed them –

McCANN: We paid them subsidies –

HENDRICK: We bribed them, the Gilzye, to look after the defiles for us. Not a single man was killed in the mountain passes, not one letter was lost in three years. Then someone in London, says it's costing too much. We must make economies. We halve the bribes to the tribal chiefs, and, in doing so, we break our word. They no longer wish to provide protection. The narrow defiles, our lifelines, suddenly are blocked. And we wake up to the fact that we are stuck in a country we do not understand upholding a puppet king nobody wants.

DICKENSON: What has this to do with chopping bits off of the dead?

HENDRICK: We did not play fair. That is why we are all going to die here.

McCANN: Private. We have heard enough from you.

LADY SALE: The road was covered with mangled bodies, all naked: I counted fifty-eight Europeans in the riverbed; the natives innumerable. Numbers of camp followers, still alive, frostbitten and starving; some perfectly out of their senses and idiotic. I recognised Major Ewart of the 54th, and Major Scott of the 44th, as we passed them. The smell of the blood was sickening and the corpses lay so thick it was impossible to look away, because I needed to guide my horse from treading upon the bodies. But it is unnecessary to dwell on such a distressing and revolting subject. Certain it is that we have very little hope of saving our lives.

WINTERFLOOD has been spooked by the talk.

WINTERFLOOD: We will not, will we, Corporal? Die here?

HENDRICK: Sixteen thousand dead on the march. No garrison in Kabul to defend us. They will come for us.

McCANN: This is a fortress. We are trained soldiers with cannon. They are tribesmen with knives.

DICKENSON turns his attention away from HENDRICK, seeing a chance to get a rise out of WINTERFLOOD instead.

DICKENSON: Knives though. Handy at close range, handy in the dark.

WINTERFLOOD: I will not let any Gilzye get so close he can use a knife.

DICKENSON: Gets the fear running in your guts though, doesn't it, Winterflood?

WINTERFLOOD: I'm not afraid.

DICKENSON: Middle of the night. Snow and darkness. Away from everything you understand.

McCANN: Fear. Double dealing. They have no relevance. We are Christians. We make our stand for what we believe. If we are scythed down, it is the Lord's will and we shall profit everlastingly. We call them Infidel and they say the same of us. But who is the infidel here? Which is the side of no faith? Let it not be us. It is time again. Squad, as a squad, to position.

As before, the SOLDIERS form a line for the bugle call. HENDRICK does this with a discernible weariness, though just short of insubordination.

Once again, they blow the call. HENDRICK returns to his pipe as soon as decency allows.

The other three peer into the night. Then DICKENSON turns away.

DICKENSON: It was the fault of the camp followers. Sixteen thousand on a retreat. Of whom only four thousand are soldiers. It doesn't make sense. Soldiers can move at speed, whatever the terrain. A column moves at the speed of its slowest marcher.

Servants? Wives? Took the rear of the column all day just to get out of Kabul.

HENDRICK: And who are the camp followers?

DICKENSON: I said. Wives, servants.

HENDRICK: Precisely. And who's notion was it to bring them?

DICKENSON: The officers.

HENDRICK: Indeed. There was a Brigadier in our regiment came to the war with sixty camels bearing plate, bedding, dressing cases, Windsor soap and eau-de-cologne.

McCANN: It is easier for a camel to go through the eye of a needle than for a rich man to enter into the kingdom of God.

HENDRICK: What military insight can be expected of such an individual?

LADY SALE: Now that the time for action against the uprising is long past, one of our officers suggests we force our way into the Royal Palace. But how are we to get our ammunition in? Through the work of fairies in the night?

WINTERFLOOD: There's someone there.

HENDRICK: Is there fuck.

WINTERFLOOD: There was a movement. Against the snow.

McCANN advances ahead of WINTERFLOOD. DICKENSON is alert. Only HENDRICK stays where he is.

HENDRICK: (*Sings to himself.*) To heal my lovesick passion
If you'll consent with me to go
I'll roll you in my morning cloak
And bring you home to Easter Snow.

McCANN: Where, Private?

WINTERFLOOD points.

Your eyes are better than mine.

HENDRICK: It was a ghost. One of the sixteen thousand. Cannot rest till he has reached his destination.

LADY SALE: 'Few, few shall part where many meet
The snow shall be their winding sheet:
And every turf beneath their feet
Shall be a soldier's sepulchre.'

McCANN is suddenly energised. He raises his rifle.

McCANN: Stay there. Don't move.

LADY SALE stands, staring into the distance. HENDRICK leaps to his feet. Everyone stares in the same direction.

Hands in the air. Come to me slowly.

A figure, hands raised, comes towards the four men. The figure is a man dressed in a turban and long flowing robes. His name is MOHAMMED AFZAL. He is surprisingly relaxed, almost as if he were a ghost.

AFZAL: I thank you all very much for your music.

AFZAL drops his hands and smiles.

McCANN: Who are you?

AFZAL: I was not expecting a serenade. The bugle is a primitive instrument. Hence its popularity on the battlefield. One could not, of course, summon cavalry with counterpoint and quarter tones.

McCANN: Who are you?

AFZAL: The question is curious. You stand in a bright red coat in my country's customary snow and ask me who I am? But who are you?

McCANN: I am an admirer of simplicity. When I ask you who you are and I am the one with the rifle, you tell me.

AFZAL: A name? Is that what you require. Supposing I said my name was Mir Mahmud. Would that satisfy you?

McCANN: It would be a commencement.

AFZAL: But Mir Mahmud was the name of a military leader, over one hundred years ago. After defeating the Persians in battle, he invited their leaders to a banquet and then slaughtered them all. Who would name their child after a homicidal maniac? But, there again, perhaps someone would. Perhaps that is the custom of this country. After all, what do you know? You are strangers here.

WINTERFLOOD: It wouldn't surprise me.

AFZAL: An opinion, good. At least, the beginning of an opinion. It is, so often, the youngest who is the first to voice his opinion. To what do you refer, private?

McCANN: Say nothing, private.

But WINTERFLOOD is losing it.

WINTERFLOOD: You promised us safe conduct from Kabul. We gave you treasure and hostages. You killed us, stripped us and cut us to bits.

AFZAL: Your usage of the words 'you' and 'us' is extremely loose. You say I did these things, but I have already established that you don't know who I am.

WINTERFLOOD: Your people, our people.

McCANN: That's enough. Why are you here?

AFZAL: I was born here.

LADY SALE: I often hear the Afghans designated as cowards: they are a fine manly-looking set, and I can only suppose it arises from the British idea among civilised people that assassination is a cowardly act. The Afghans never scruple to use their long knives for that purpose, ergo they are cowards; but they show no cowardice in standing as they do against guns without using any themselves.

DICKENSON interrupts.

DICKENSON: Let him past. This is not our job. We are not sentries. There are sentries behind us. It is up to them whether he passes or not. Our job is bugling. Let us fucking bugle.

AFZAL: Another opinion. I am almost replete with opinions.

McCANN: As am I! I am the corporal here and my opinion is the only one that counts. My authority is vested in me by my superior officers and comes through them by the grace of God.

DICKENSON: Steady, steady, you're only a corporal.

AFZAL: The grace of God. So you are Kitabi.

McCANN: Kitabi?

AFZAL: A Christian. One of the book.

McCANN: Yes I am. I am 'of the book'.

AFZAL: Then for you, because you are Kitabi I have respect. For you (*DICKENSON.*) because you wish to let me pass I have respect. For you (*WINTERFLOOD.*) because you are the first to give me an opinion I have respect. But for you (*HENDRICK.*) because you have offered me nothing I have nothing.

HENDRICK: I am one of those – you have surely met one before – who wants nothing.

AFZAL:Ah hah!

HENDRICK: And I have nothing to offer you except my pipe. And I shall not be offering that.

LADY SALE: As always in this country, the waiting. But within the waiting, within every second, the whole weight of ones existence. As if you are permanently at the ready, on the instant, to drop from the edge of a cliff to your death.

AFZAL:A question for you all and I shall be on my way to my interview with the sentries at the Kabul gate of Jalalabad. Tell me, each of you, first the corporal whose authority comes from God, tell me, each one, what you think you are doing here.

McCANN: God's will.

AFZAL:Excellent answer. You. (*DICKENSON.*)

DICKENSON: Killing savages.

AFZAL:Excellent again. Economy and clarity. You. (*WINTERFLOOD.*)

WINTERFLOOD: I am here because of my country. And what is happening. The Russians. Keeping them out of India. And to stop this. All this not fighting fairly. Your cruel ways.

AFZAL:Oh. A disappointment. Confusion, excessive emotion, a lack of grasp. You, (*HENDRICK.*) why are you here?

HENDRICK: Orders.

AFZAL:More.

HENDRICK: Many years ago, I was left with a dwindling stock of choices. So I joined the army.

AFZAL:That is too personal.

HENDRICK: My life has been personal.

AFZAL:You know more than you are saying.

A pause. LADY SALE is alert, ready for something.

LADY SALE: One's whole life held in tension in a single moment.

HENDRICK: I am here, we are all here, because of a mistake. It is our job to fight cheap wars so that our people back home can live expensive lives. There was a mistake. It has been an expensive war.

WINTERFLOOD: This is how he talks. The whole time. Not a man in the company will listen to him.

AFZAL: Silence! (*To HENDRICK.*) What will happen now?

HENDRICK: The war will become more expensive. We, here in Jalalabad, must be relieved. Then our enemy must be punished.

WINTERFLOOD: You listen to him, you listen to a drivelling fool.

HENDRICK: Then all us soldiers must be got out, evacuated. Leaving the country in a worse state than we found it.

AFZAL:So. The one who at first gave me nothing now gives me the most of all.

WINTERFLOOD: And you are a fool to listen.

AFZAL:(*To HENDRICK.*) Thank you.

Suddenly WINTERFLOOD rushes at AFZAL, pushing and dragging him towards the city.

WINTERFLOOD: I don't want to hear any more. Get on your way to the gate!

There's an untidy scrimmage as AFZAL tries to repel WINTERFLOOD. McCANN and DICKENSON jump in to keep WINTERFLOOD and AFZAL apart. HENDRICK watches. WINTERFLOOD lands a punch on AFZAL who goes down. DICKENSON pulls him away.

Everyone breathes heavily. It seems to be over. McCANN helps AFZAL to his feet. Then WINTERFLOOD draws his bayonet.

LADY SALE gasps.

WINTERFLOOD goes berserk and plunges the bayonet into AFZAL. AFZAL goes limp and falls to the ground.

A moment as they all stare. AFZAL is dead.

I meant something else. I meant something else.

Everyone looks at him. Then McCANN takes control.

McCANN: Dickenson. Hendrick. Get rid of this. Out there. In the snow. At the double. Mark the spot. Discreetly. At the double!

DICKENSON and HENDRICK pick up the body and carry it away into the snow.

Faster. Two minutes before bugle call. Faster!

WINTERFLOOD is trembling.

It did not happen. There will be more snow tomorrow and we will bury him further. He is one among thousands.

WINTERFLOOD: Yes, corporal.

McCANN: And call to mind his beliefs. You have, by his lights, granted him a boon.

WINTERFLOOD: Yes, corporal.

LADY SALE: In Afghanistan the English act as they do in all other countries. They visit, keep to themselves and generally employ only servants brought with them. There was more than one survivor. I and two score others were taken prisoner and remained captives for eight months. I lost everything except the clothes I wore and, kept in a small bag tied around my waist, my diary.

DICKENSON and HENDRICK return.

DICKENSON: We took him –

McCANN: I don't wish to know. The bugle call. Squad, as a squad, to position.

They line up again. They play the call. They peer into the night. HENDRICK gets his pipe going again. Hands it to DICKENSON.

LADY SALE: Snow all day. Snow all day. As to the justice of dethroning one ruler, and setting up another in his place, I have nothing to say: nor regarding our policy in attempting to keep possession of a country of uncivilized people, so far from our own; whence all supplies of ammunition and money, must be obtained. Let our Governors-General and Commanders-in-Chief look to that whilst I knit socks for my grand-children.

McCANN: Any one out there, soldier?

WINTERFLOOD: Can't. Can't see, corporal.

McCANN: Keep looking.

WINTERFLOOD: Yes, corporal.

McCANN: Keep looking and you will see.

Slow fade to

BLACKOUT

Note: The Advance is played as follows:

DURAND'S LINE

by Ron Hutchinson

First production

The Tricycle Theatre, London, 17 April 2009

The following cast performed in the remount in July 2010 at the
Tricycle Theatre prior to the USA tour:

Characters / Cast

SIR HENRY MORTIMER DURAND (Foreign Minister of British India 1885-94)	Michael Cochrane
ABDUR RAHMAN (Amir of Afghanistan 1880-1901)	Raad Rawi
THOMAS SALTER PYNE (Engineer to the Amir)	Rick Warden
SERVANT	Danny Rahim

Director	Nicolas Kent
Designer	Pamela Howard
Lighting	James Farncombe
Sound	Tom Lishman

Setting

The play is set in a guest house owned by the Amir in Kabul
in 1893.

Her Majesty's Indian Foreign Secretary, SIR HENRY MORTIMER DURAND faces AMIR ABDUL RAHMAN in a room strewn with maps and charts of every size and littered with surveying equipment. They're in a house provided for DURAND in Kabul which shows some homely English touches such as a piano and table set with lace and tea-cakes. These sit incongruously alongside the tribal rugs and cushions which are the chief decor.

DURAND has the politesse of the British Imperial administrative class but his patience is clearly wearing a little thin –

DURAND: At some point one stops beating about the bush and gets down to brass tacks, Amir. We've been pushing these maps and counter maps around for long enough. Now I respectfully submit that it's time for business.

Her Majesty's Government regards the immediate establishment of a fixed, settled and permanent border to your country to be essential to the defence of British India.

He pushes a map across –

You will see our proposals – our final proposals – for its disposition – a disposition which will make clear to the Russians that they have gone as far as they can; that they must come no nearer to Hindustan than where they are now.

RAHMAN doesn't even glance at the map – he's a despot, used to command, more than able to hold his own against his interlocutor –

RAHMAN: The cucumbers – did you receive them?

DURAND: Yes but –

RAHMAN: How did you find them?

DURAND: Excellent.

RAHMAN: And the apricots?

DURAND: Remarkable – but to return to the reason I have been sequestered here for the past weeks –

RAHMAN: You are comfortable here? You feel safe?

DURAND: (*Deadpan.*) With your men surrounding my house and watching my every move, how could I not be?

RAHMAN: They make you nervous?

He indicates the door –

Perhaps it would be better to postpone this to another day. We will meet again in the Valley, perhaps? In Peshawar?

DURAND: I'm very fond of Pesh. Reminds me of the best of Surrey. But we have to thrash this out here and now.

Back to the map –

The sticking point seems to be the question of the Waziris and the Pushtun area in general –

RAHMAN: A hornet's nest. Perhaps you had better leave it alone.

DURAND: The facts of physical geography make that impossible. We cannot have wild men like that unsupervised.

RAHMAN: Then give them to me. Draw the line of my country so that it includes them, for me to deal with.

DURAND: Would you succeed?

RAHMAN: Unlikely –

A teasing smile –

But these are only imaginary lines on paper, after all.

DURAND: Not when backed by the actions of the finest army in the world.

RAHMAN: You will fight for these imaginary lines?

DURAND: If we have to.

RAHMAN: How many men are you willing to lose?

DURAND: As many as it takes – and we will win in the end. I'm not one of those who think that the laws of military conflict are mysteriously suspended when one reaches Central Asia.

RAHMAN: But does it not feel as if you are fighting the wind?

DURAND: I'm not a soldier. There's been too much bleating by the chaps in uniform who keep trying to find excuses why they can't bring things to a close. It all needs picking up and shaking by the scruff of the neck.

RAHMAN: Am I one of those to be shaken?

There's steel in his voice and DURAND reacts diplomatically –

DURAND: You don't want the Russians here any more than we do, Amir. They're a threat to you as well as to us.

RAHMAN: And you would rather fight them here than across the mountains. On our territory instead of yours.

DURAND: We won't have to fight them if we can establish you as a sovereign and stable country between them and us.

RAHMAN: Which makes me what? An ear of grain between two millstones?

DURAND: Waziristan and the Pushtuns are in the wrong place, we can all see that. In some ways, your entire country is.

RAHMAN: How thoughtless of Providence to put us in the wrong place.

DURAND stabs his finger at the map –

DURAND: The narrative of the pacification of the Waziris, who are the key to Afghanistan and thus to the region is to be read here – here – here – and here –

RAHMAN: Regardless of the Waziris themselves?

DURAND: They are a piece with their land. They have been regarded as wild and ungovernable as it. We will change that.

RAHMAN: With ink?

DURAND: It's easy to mock and look for flaws in a scheme – far easier than to do but we're about doing.

We will be defining the Western border of India for the first time, which means we will be, in effect, creating a new country on the other side of it. The only matter between us is –

RAHMAN: Who gets what. Isn't that what all these imaginary lines on paper really mean?

DURAND: You seem to think, Amir, that a map has no physical reality beyond what it's drawn on. But take my country –

He grabs a pen and draws on a piece of paper –

Scotland – Wales – England –

RAHMAN: I have heard of these tribes.

DURAND: More than tribes. Nations. Comprised of men who know that one side of the line they are one thing – native, at home – on the other – *other*. I daresay we began much as you and the Waziris did, feeling we had loyalty only to the tribe. Over the years we understood we were something larger.

RAHMAN: The map told you?

DURAND: To look at one is to give shape to the world; to put one outside of oneself; from which comes wisdom.

RAHMAN claps his hands and a SERVANT hurries in with bowed head, hands RAHMAN an envelope before hurrying out again –

RAHMAN: This is a letter from a Colonel Vannovsky; he has been sent to Roshan. Why should I not invite him to Kabul to share *his* wisdom?

DURAND: Because you know that what we want is a state between us and the Russians. They want to annex you, lock, stock and barrel in order to threaten us directly.

He waits until the SERVANT has left before lowering his voice

I'll sweeten the deal – I'll increase the subsidy we pay you and give you the monopoly of the opium trade. You'll retain a free hand to run your affairs as you wish and we'll help you to get your hands on more up to date weapons, especially artillery –

He presses the bell and THOMAS SALTER PYNE appears.

Pyne is currently licensed by us to make copies of European artillery pieces for you. He will explain the deficiencies of the current arrangements and what I'm willing to propose.

When PYNE speaks it's in a self assured Cockney accent –

PYNE: We have to keep up with the times, Amir. Unless I'm allowed to get my hands on what Le Creuset and Krupps and Vickers are up to, you're sunk. Sir Mortimer is prepared to give me carte blanche to bring your artillery up to modern standards – as good as anything even the Rooskies could throw at you –

DURAND: – but it needs an agreement on where we draw the border.

Before RAHMAN can answer –

We were talking of maps, Mr Pyne. My belief is that they allow one to turn the world inside out, as it were – one takes the internal *you* and places it here – or here – or here –

PYNE: I wouldn't know about that –

DURAND: – which in turn leads one to realize – yes – this is where I am in relation to the larger whole – this piece fits here – that piece fits there – it leads us from wish, if you will, to event – and event is what I have been sent here to achieve.

RAHMAN pulls the map across –

RAHMAN: By retaining the Wakhan Range for yourselves?

DURAND: What better Southern border for the Russian bear than that impassable massif?

RAHMAN: Impassable, perhaps, but also a dagger aimed at their heart; the point of a spear held in a British hand.

DURAND: With all respect, Amir – that's poetry, it will get us nowhere. Take a tip from Pyne here, a man of prose if ever I met one.

RAHMAN: If they go to war over where you have drawn the line?

DURAND: Then how much more will you be in need of the very best that Mr Pyne's ordnance works can give you? The key to which Her Majesty's government holds –

He sits back, knowing that the trap has been sprung –

This is God's sketch for a country, not mine. We want order for it, Amir. That's all. Order. It seems a small enough thing but nothing good can happen here without it.

RAHMAN: (*Needling.*) Such as civilization? Or what you mean by it?

DURAND: You have as ancient a one as any.

RAHMAN: But as rich?

DURAND: How could that be? With unbridled brigandage for centuries – which we are here to put a stop to.

RAHMAN: What if that *is* our civilization?

He turns to PYNE –

You must have sometimes thought that in the time you have been here, Mr Pyne, the things you have seen.

PYNE: Engineer, Amir. No interest in anything outside the workshop, me.

DURAND: We will not let there be a hole in the world. We will not allow a nation without law to threaten the rest of us.

RAHMAN: What is your law? How do you express your civilization? You raid our villages, burn our crops, take reprisals, execute hostages.

He turns back to PYNE –

You are from London, I believe, Mr Pyne? Can you tell me in what way London is under threat from us? By what right war is made on us?

DURAND doesn't let PYNE answer –

DURAND: Whatever actions we take, Amir, will be taken in concert with you. Our safety and security will be the best guarantee of yours.

RAHMAN: I hang with you or I hang alone?

DURAND looks as if he's about to lose it –

DURAND: We must *get on*, Amir. A decision must be made. The pace of these negotiations would fit the perfumed indolence of an Eastern Court –

He indicates the cushions and rugs –

– not the modern state we are trying to help you bring about here – and a state must have a border.

RAHMAN: The other map again –

He reaches for the sheet of paper that DURAND sketched the British Isles on –

Hmmm. England is too big, I think. Wales – this is Wales? – too small.

He draws a line on it –

There –

He looks at it critically –

This is Scotland at the top? I think I will split it in two and make another country – so –

He draws another line –

I will call it Durandistan. The people this side of the line will be Scottish and the other not. Shall we call them Durandistanis? If they protest, they will be pacified with ink.

Before PYNE or DURAND can respond –

Are there mountains in this Scotland?

PYNE: The Highlands, yes –

He sketches on the map –

RAHMAN: That is inconvenient. My map would look much better without them.

He scribbles on the map –

There. They are gone. They were only lines on a map. But because a pen has magic powers no doubt the real mountains have disappeared, too – as have any troublemakers who lived there.

He pushes the map towards DURAND –

There is your map. Take good care of it. The lines on it may be imaginary but the problems they cause only too real. You will be fighting because of them for many years.

DURAND: Entertaining. Very. Make a grand music hall turn, that. The fact is –

RAHMAN: The fact is that you are from a very small country which needs firm borders to stop you and your neighbours being forever at each other's throats. To impose such a thing on a land as vast as this, which has never had them, is to invite endless trouble.

He tosses the map back, his voice suddenly harsh –

Perhaps, Sir Mortimer, you just do not understand us. What you see as perfumed indolence may be a recognition of the dangers of thoughtless change.

DURAND looks stung –

DURAND: Not understand? Pyne may be from London, I was born in Bhopal. I'm a man of the East more than the West. I know as much as any man about how all the pieces fit together in this part of the world. I've helped put some of them in place and I intend to make this one fit.

RAHMAN: With me or without me?

DURAND: May I remind you that we made you Amir in the first place.

RAHMAN: You need me.

DURAND: We need someone to negotiate with.

RAHMAN: Or you will replace me with someone else?

He turns to PYNE –

That unfortunate may not even know he has been chosen, of course. They declared me Amir without me even being there.

DURAND: It could be done again.

RAHMAN: Is that a threat?

DURAND: It is a statement of fact.

RAHMAN: Perhaps this Colonel – what is his name? –

He makes a show of looking at the letter again –

Vannovsky – would have better terms for me.

DURAND: The Russians would use you to kick us out, then put a bullet in you.

RAHMAN: And if I don't agree to your terms, the bullet would be an English one?

They're nose to nose and PYNE heads to the piano, clears his throat and sings, accompanying himself –

PYNE: 'Pale hands I loved beside the Shalimar,
Where are you now? Who lies beneath your spell?
Whom do you lead on Rapture's roadway, far,
Before you agonize them in farewell?'

He turns towards DURAND –

Would you mind turning the page, Sir Mortimer?

As DURAND leans over the piano to turn the page PYNE speaks sotto voce *to him –*

Take care. He'll turn on the charm when he has to but he's an old ruffian at heart. He's boiled people alive and blown them from cannons.

He sings again –

'Oh, pale dispensers of my Joys and Pains,
Holding the doors of Heaven and of Hell,
How the hot blood rushed wildly through the veins
Beneath your touch, until you waved farewell.'

He nods for DURAND to turn the next page and again speaks to him sotto voce *–*

They've cut up entire armies here. What do you think our chances would be of getting out in one piece if he turned against us?

He sings again –

*Pale hands, pink tipped, like Lotus buds that float
On those cool waters where we used to dwell,
I would have rather felt you round my throat,
Crushing out life, than waving me farewell!*

RAHMAN claps politely –

RAHMAN: Your own, Pyne?

PYNE: No, sir. Memsahib I knew in India.

RAHMAN: Perhaps that is what you are in love with too, Sir
  Mortimer? A dream of the East? Not the real thing at all?

DURAND: I think I have my feet on the ground.

RAHMAN: It is a kind of magic that you believe in, with these maps.

  Before the irritated DURAND can respond –

  You are a complicated man. I respect that in you. But I beg you
  not to try to force the world into a shape it cannot take.

DURAND: You're not a simple man yourself, Amir.

RAHMAN: I am a thistle blown by the wind –

DURAND: Poetry again.

  He looks levelly at the Amir, as if about to go on the attack

  I studied you up on my way here. Wanted to take the measure
  of the chap I'd be dealing with. A man who on the one hand
  could build a pile of his enemy's heads but who was also a man
  of letters –

RAHMAN: You flatter me too greatly on both accounts –

DURAND: I know soldiers. You're one of the best. But soldiers are
  ten a penny out here. What really interested me was that travel
  book of yours –

RAHMAN: A slight thing for my own amusement

DURAND: Did you know he wrote a book, Pyne?

PYNE: (*Evasive.*) Heard good things about it but not had the time
  to –

DURAND: It's a rum go, some of it. Hodge podge, in some ways – I
  know you won't mind me observing that, Amir, you're a man of
  action, not some thin skinned pansy of a writer. It's like a fairy
  tale about this country – even more than that song Pyne was
  murdering.

  It's about the Silk Road and Samarkand and peculiar goings-
  on that make you wonder if that actually happened or the fella
  wasn't just – well, *dreaming* – like in his head he was making up a
  place that wasn't really there –

RAHMAN: As with your – (*Mocking.*) Afghanistan –

DURAND: If that's a dream, let's dream it together.

There's passionate urgency in his voice as he holds out the map –

There it is. A thing few men have been given. A moment that comes once in five hundred, a thousand years. To birth a country. To call a nation into being at the very centre of the world. In the end this isn't about Delhi or London or Moscow and their endless scraps and intrigues. It's about the reach of a man's imagination and how wide is his soul.

Beat –

And the monopoly of the opium trade, too.

He indicates the map again –

See where you sit – astride the route which the Russians must take to threaten India; the path whereby East could hurl itself on West; where North and South collide; you play a role in the fortunes of a dozen of nations and two entire continents and you will not sign? Sign and have this new thing spring from the brow of History? With your name forever on it?

RAHMAN: The Rahman Line? Or the Durand?

DURAND: No more cat and mouse, Amir. Action. Deed. Prose.

RAHMAN turns to PYNE –

RAHMAN: A persistent man, Sir Mortimer. Fearless. You hear how he talks to me when the last time an envoy from your country came to Kabul to make demands he was torn to pieces by the mob?

PYNE: (*Uncomfortable.*) Engineer. Workshop. Have to be getting back –

He makes to leave but RAHMAN signals him to stay –

RAHMAN: His father, Sir Henry, fought in what I suppose we must call the First Anglo-Afghan War. How many are we on now?

PYNE: The Second or Third – depending how you count them.

DURAND: (*Stiffly, to RAHMAN.*) To a gentleman – and I know you to be one – a man's family should be out of bounds.

RAHMAN: Your father – what a loss that he was not able to bring his talents and energy to bear on these matters

Smoothly he turns to PYNE –

Such a tragic end. Not untouched by elements of farce, of course –

DURAND: *Farce?*

RAHMAN: I have the wrong word?

Pretending to turn anxiously to PYNE –

A thing that is unlikely, extravagant, impossible – this is the meaning of farce, yes?

PYNE: One of them – but Engineer, me. Worlds of things. Not words.

With an innocent expression RAHMAN turns back to DURAND –

RAHMAN: To fall from an elephant, that is all those things, would you not say? To be one moment lord of all one surveys and the next dashed to the ground, hurled to the dust –

He turns to PYNE –

Do you know the full story, Mr Pyne? How Sir Henry was warned that he should dismount and enter the city he was to receive the honours to on foot but felt – one understands his position – that to do so would be to risk his prestige in the eyes of the onlookers – most of them, no doubt, natives of the meanest sort? How he refused to listen to the warnings that the roof of the gate he had to enter under was too low and pressed ahead, regardless – showing, one might say, that kind of determination which has won for your country possession of so much of the world – but, alas, paid the price when the warnings proved true and –

He gestures at the ground –

Landed at the feet of the very people he meant to overawe; carried away with a broken back through the crowds he had meant to impress and died – no doubt lamented by all of them but there is also no doubt that some of them would have – unfairly of course – blamed his death on pride; regarded it – shame be on their heads – as a punishment; drew from it – people being what they are – the lesson that a foolish attention to one's dignity and a refusal to heed reasonable warning will lead to disaster.

DURAND: It was an accident, pure and simple.

RAHMAN: Of course –

DURAND: A moment's misjudgment –

RAHMAN: (*Piously.*) May Providence protect us from our own –

DURAND: He was right, in principle.

RAHMAN: The principle being that to enter on foot, in the dust, would be to suggest he was only a man and not The British Empire in miniature?

PYNE: (*Uneasily.*) I do think, Amir, that how a man's father met his end –

RAHMAN: Is instructive?

PYNE: That wasn't what I –

RAHMAN: That it foreshadows the son? That you fear similar stubborn, wilful, wrongheadedness about these maps? That Sir Mortimer is powerless to help himself?

PYNE: I – er – no –

He turns to DURAND, confused –

That is –

DURAND is glaring at RAHMAN as if he is having difficulty controlling himself –

DURAND: If I thought for a moment that you were mocking my father's death –

RAHMAN: I would not presume even to point a moral from it.

PYNE: I think I'll turn in for the night –

RAHMAN: Do stay, Mr Pyne. You have another piece for us? One could get used to what passes for music in the West, in time –

PYNE: No I think I'll –

He's anxious to get out of the door he's edging towards –

Early start tomorrow –

RAHMAN: You are sure? Sir Mortimer, I think, would like to hear your honest opinion of his map and what his real motives are in fighting for it so hard –

PYNE: No personal opinions one way or the other –

PYNE moves quickly to the exit, leaving the two men facing each other –

DURAND: My father –

RAHMAN: Your father was part of the first British army to invade us. Truly, I sometimes think you look on us as your family business.

DURAND: My father –

RAHMAN: (*Smoothly ignoring it.*) Before that, I believe, he was caught up in the Sepoy Rebellion –

DURAND: We call it the Mutiny –

RAHMAN: Where his reputation never completely recovered from the suggestion that he ran from his post –

DURAND: Poppycock. He ended up as Governor of Punjab.

RAHMAN: But were there not those who said he had let the side down?

DURAND: I make it a practice to confront those who spread such lies.

RAHMAN: You British and we – we understand honour; I understand why a man who heard that said behind his back would refuse to do the sensible thing, bow his head and dismount; how his son would want to make his own mark on history –

DURAND: Word-play. Clever-dickery.

RAHMAN: How he would refuse to leave things as they are when that would be for the best –

DURAND has just about had enough –

DURAND: The war we just finished here solved nothing. It's not even clear what number war it was. Those puffed up fools of Generals were fought to a standstill by men who made their own weapons out of scrap and whose wives and children went into battle alongside them. The nineteenth century was caught by the heel by the downright medieval. We didn't have a victory here and yet we weren't beaten, either. If anything is to be salvaged from it I must do it –

RAHMAN: Sir Henry's son? Fighting his own Afghan war – this one with pen and paper?

DURAND: The Durands have given our blood to Asia. My father served it, I serve it, my son is headed for Sandhurst, he will serve it too in his turn and you and I must come to an arrangement.

RAHMAN: What if whatever arrangement we come to will be worse than none?

DURAND: (*Totally perplexed.*) What if what?

RAHMAN: Is there not a case for leaving the exact borders undefined for now?

DURAND: (*Even more perplexed.*) A thing has to be defined – Good
God, that's what this whole century has been about. A disease,
a law of science, an international border – they need defining;
progress flows from the act of it.

RAHMAN: But to define a country? Where there have been only
tribes?

DURAND: What a glorious thing.

RAHMAN: Or recipe for disaster.

DURAND: The way forward to the modern age.

RAHMAN: Or endless conflict in which you will shed more blood.

Before DURAND can answer –

You want order – this is how to get its opposite.

DURAND: My head spins. It does. *Any arrangement worse than none?
Order is its own opposite?* You make no sense. You're like a
German philosopher.

He brandishes the map, passionate –

There is no government without a map. You can put it on a wall,
stick pins in it, point at it, make policy about it, if you have to
go to war over it see what you've won and what you've lost. It is
the abstract of decision, it is fact unvarnished. Absent it, there's
nothing there, the world has no shape and that which has no
shape has no meaning.

RAHMAN: If it leads to greater problems than it pretends to cure?

DURAND: We'll fix those in turn.

RAHMAN: If it leads to endless war?

DURAND: Then we'll fight it.

RAHMAN: It *is* a kind of magic with you –

Almost wonderingly he passes a pencil across a sheet of paper.

To believe that it is not the map which describes the world but
which brings it into being. As if just to wish a thing – is that
what you said you are here to do? – is to secure event. But what
of fact? The reality of the exterior world? The rude awakening
when – say – you fall off the elephant?

DURAND takes a deep breath, controls himself –

DURAND: Not my strong suit that. Poetical speculation. Plain
man. Tweed, not silk. Here to give Whitehall what it wants.

Resolution. A way forward. A barrier to Russian ambition. Protection to you. Something that says this is why we fought the Second Afghan War – or the Third, if that's what it was.

RAHMAN: If it also says it will lead to a Fourth and Fifth and how many more? To endless conflict?

Another deep breath from DURAND, using all his will power to keep himself in check –

DURAND: You will be good enough to signal your assent to these proposals or see if you can get better terms from the Russians.

RAHMAN: In which case you will seek to bring your masters my head?

DURAND: Don't want your head. Wouldn't know what to do with it. Preposterous idea. Wilful exaggeration. Sort of thing said in a pantomime.

Another deep breath –

Comes an end to everything, Amir.

To an elaboration of delay; artful procrastination; the tropes of the East where history has hung fire for so long even men of affairs see negotiation as an endless circling of the same fixed point; comes an end even to the patience of a man like me who enjoys up to a point the to and fro of treaty work such as we have been engaged on here; comes at last instead, inevitability; comes fact and map; submission.

His thumb stabs at the map –

We take Roshan and Shignan East of the Oxus. You retain Chaman and Kafir. We hold the Wakhan Corridor and the passes of the Sulieman Mountains and we partition the Waziris as herein shown with no further delay or amendment –

RAHMAN: Or else?

DURAND: What was that Russian's name? Vannovsky? You'd take your chances with him and Moscow. Of course, before then, you might no longer be Amir; I'm sure Whitehall would have something to say about that.

RAHMAN: I'm to choose between the embrace of the Bear and the claw of the Lion?

DURAND: There you go again. The fantastical. The metaphorical. It won't answer. Not in 1893. The world's been mapped, all of it, defined, parcelled out, even the odd bits and ends snapped up. This is the biggest odd and end left.

Your country, I firmly believe, is in the wrong place but there's nothing can be done about that. What we can do is tidy it up a little; make sure it's known where it begins and ends, a country should be a country, after all – not a question mark.

He rings the bell again –

Pyne! – Pen! – Ink! –

PYNE enters, carrying an ink well and pen. Avoiding RAHMAN's eye, he sets it on the table, dips the nib in the ink, stands back. DURAND picks up the pen, holds it out to RAHMAN –

RAHMAN: What, I wonder, is the opposite to the – what was it again? – perfumed indolence of an Eastern court?

DURAND: I'll withdraw that remark.

RAHMAN: What would you say, Mr Pyne? The pointless industry of the modern world?

PYNE: Couldn't –

RAHMAN: – say. No. Engineer. Workshop.

He takes the pen –

I do wonder which of them may be the more dangerous to us all –

He leans over the map –

I sign because I must, Sir Mortimer but I think you make me sign because you must, too – and may your God and mine forgive us both...

He leans over the map and signs its fateful corner as PYNE sits at the piano and plays the melody of 'Pale Hands I Loved', as the lights fade on him, RAHMAN and DURAND...

– END –

CAMPAIGN

by Amit Gupta

First production

The Tricycle Theatre, London, 17 April 2009

The following cast performed in the remount in July 2010 at the Tricycle Theatre prior to the USA tour:

Characters / Cast

JAMES KITE	Tom McKay
TOM	Karl Davies
PROFESSOR KHAN	Raad Rawi
MARTIN SPEED	Daniel Betts

Director Nicolas Kent
Designer Pamela Howard
Lighting James Farncombe
Sound Tom Lishman

Setting

The play is set in the Foreign Office, Present Day.

A discreet but important room in the Foreign Office

A big oak desk – blood red leather chairs – bookshelves. Some more informal seating around a coffee table – A couple of seats placed at the back of the room

JAMES KITE – 37 – Neutral accent covering private school tracks – a spook with a bland job title, Sandhurst, Cambridge, capable, dangerous.

He is looking through a very thick document – half the size of a telephone book when there is a knock at the door.

    KITE'S 'secretary' – TOM APPEARS.

TOM: Professor Khan.

    Enter PROFESSOR TARIK KHAN – Fifties, Affable, but serious in the
    way of a Oxford don – led in by TOM – KITE'S Secretary.

    KITE comes out from behind his desk, carrying the document.

KITE: Professor Khan, James Kite.

    They Shake Hands.

KITE: A pleasure to meet you. Please sit down.

    KITE steers him towards the informal seating.

KHAN: Thank you.

    As KHAN sits and looks around the room, KITE remains standing and
    turns to the last page of document, scans over quickly. Without looking
    up, KITE speaks –

KITE: I had the desk moved. I prefer the light behind me. *(Looks up*
    at KHAN.) We didn't inconvenience you too much I hope?

KHAN: By saying that, it usually means that you know that you did.

    KITE smiles.

KITE: Indeed. *(Beat.)* Would you like some tea or a coffee?

KHAN: Tea, please.

KITE: English Breakfast, Earl Grey – I believe we even have
    Peppermint.

KHAN: Earl Grey, thank you.

KITE: I should have guessed, a Royalist of course, you being an Oxford man. And your suit should have signalled the absurdity of offering you something herbal.

KHAN: *(Firm.)* Actually, sometimes I drink camomile. With honey.

KITE: Really?

TOM leaves sits opposite KHAN and places the document onto the coffee table.

Pause.

KHAN: Is the Minister on his way?

KITE: *(Suspicious.)* Why do you ask that?

KHAN: The message I received – it said he wanted to see me.

KITE: He does and he is on his way. *(Edges forward.)* I thought we'd talk first, get him up to speed when he arrives, if that's alright with you?

KHAN: I'm familiar with the procedure.

KITE: You came in a year ago.

KHAN: A little over. To see your predecessor, Mr. Hawk. *(Beat.)* That's a peculiar coincidence.

HAWK: What is?

KHAN: Hawk, now Kite. Both birds of prey.

KITE: *(Ruffled feathers.)* Technically Hawk isn't my predecessor.

KHAN: I assumed since you're in the same office…

KITE: It's not my office, just borrowing it and I'm not a politician. I'm the Special Adviser to the Minister, which allows me the luxury to look at a situation with a clarity and pragmatism that politics doesn't always permit. One of the advantages of the coalition is that ideology is, if not dead exactly, then certainly comatose and largely irrelevant.

KHAN: *(Amazed.)* You really believe that?

KITE: Don't you?

KHAN: It doesn't matter if I do, I don't work for the government.

KITE: Neither do I, I work for my country.

KHAN: I must say I'm surprised that you're comfortable to make such distinction.

KITE: You're not a journalist, so I'd like to be frank. Compromise is the paradigm for our age, a coalition affords us a certain room to manoeuvre.

KHAN: The left hand doesn't always know what the right hand's doing.

KITE: The left hand doesn't need or want to know what the right hand's doing, otherwise how does he deny knowledge later? It's one of the things I learnt spending time in your country – wipe your backside with one hand, eat with the other. I'm a great admirer of the Indian nation. Are you a cricket fan Professor?

KHAN: No.

TOM comes back in carrying a tray.

KITE: Tom, the Professor isn't a cricket fan.

TOM pauses, before serving tea.

KITE: This place would be unbearable without Test Match Special. *(Beat.)* Well that's a first for me. I've lived in a lot of places, met a great number of your countrymen and I've never met an Indian cricket agnostic.

TOM takes a seat at the back of the room – behind KHAN.

KHAN: You still haven't. I'm from Pakistan and with regards to sport, I'm a confirmed atheist.

KITE looks to TOM who takes out his phone – sends a text.

KITE: You're from Pakistan?

KHAN: I was born in India, but we moved after partition. Is that a problem?

Pause.

KITE: Quite the opposite. I think you'll see exactly where we're coming from.

KHAN: And where is that exactly? You haven't told me why I'm here.

TOM'S phone buzzes, he reads a message, stands up, looks to KITE, who nods. As TOM goes to open the door –

KITE: We're going to be joined by a colleague.

TOM opens the door – enter MARTIN SPEED

KITE: Professor, this is Martin Speed.

SPEED: *(American accent.)* Professor – don't mind me, I'm just here to observe.

As SPEED follows TOM to the seating behind KHAN, who looks Uncomfortable.

KITE: I was about to tell you why you're here.

KHAN: Er, yes, you were.

KITE: Well I have a specific remit. One of the elements of which is to revisit some of the more intriguing policy proposals the civil service explored, but were subsequently ignored by the previous administration. We came across a document and wanted to talk to you about it? Rather unhelpfully Mr. Hawk didn't leave much in the way of a report – a couple of cryptic asides, nothing more.

KHAN: A report? I don't know about any report. What do you want me to say?

KITE: I'd simply like you to talk through what you discussed when you came here last time.

KHAN: I signed the Official Secrets Act, I was told not to talk about it again.

Kite slides across a piece of paper.

KITE: This supercedes whatever you agreed to before.

KHAN: Just like that.

KITE: As if kissed and seized by fairies.

Pause as KHAN looks at the document, signs it.

KHAN: Now look, when I came in before I didn't discuss anything with Mr. Hawk, he just asked for a talk. He didn't tell me why!

KITE raises a calming hand,

KITE: That is absolutely our understanding and in fairness to Hawk, he probably didn't know why. He was only PPS to the Minister. I wouldn't be certain that the Minister knew what was going on. The previous PM liked to play his cards close to his chest, rejoiced in micromanagement.

KHAN: I have no idea what can I help you with.

KITE: It's very simple really. We – and by 'we', I mean the Minister, and in turn of course the present government, the nation – are considering an additional… *(Searches for the word very carefully.)* approach and require some input.

KHAN looks baffled.

KHAN: With regards to?

KITE: Before explaining, I should make something clear. The overall policy objectives of the British government remain the same as that of the US – there is however some latitude with regards to our tactics. *(Looks to the back of the room.)* Martin?

KHAN looks over his shoulder.

SPEED: A certain tactical latitude is one of the foundations of any successful alliance.

KITE: We're merely considering a supplementary plan that might be considered favourably.

KHAN: Mr. Kite, I'm afraid I have no idea what you're talking about, I'm a University Lecturer, that's all!

KITE: Who is a noted Islamic scholar and considered an authority on the history of Afghanistan – particularly the first half of the twentieth century – so I understand.

KHAN: It's an area I have a special interest in, but I wouldn't say I was an authority exactly.

KITE points at the document.

KITE: He would and does.

KHAN: Who?

KITE: Morris. Author of the report. Clever boy – Cambridge double First – Civil Service fast track, out to make a name for himself – not therefore prone to gaffes. He's now working with us. He suggested you as the man to talk to about King Amanullah and Mahmud Tarzi.

KHAN looks really confused.

KHAN: Amanullah and Tarzi, but why?

KITE: We will come to that – when the Minister arrives.

KHAN: What do you want to know?

KITE: About them – achievements, ideas, that sort of thing – as simple as you can make it. Assume we know absolutely nothing.

KHAN: You want the same talk I gave to Mr. Hawk? That may take some time.

KITE: That won't be necessary. Bullet points will be more than sufficient. Think of this as a briefing.

KHAN: You have researchers, there are any number of books available – mine included.

KITE smiles.

KITE: I understand this may seem an unusual request. But I have two problems. Hawk's notes, as I said, are brief and somewhat cryptic.

KHAN: I see.

KITE: And I believe in being thorough. A hangover from my army days no doubt.

Pause.

KITE: The predecessors in this department were often guilty of consulting the people who know or understand a situation, a country, a people, the history and then ignoring everything they were told. That's not a mistake we plan to repeat. We intend to cut through the red tape, play with a straight bat, that's why we asked you to come in.

KHAN: Alright.

KITE: There is a reason for this and what you tell me will help.

KHAN: Help what?

KITE: Our understanding. Which will in turn, I hope, aid the re-formulation of certain non-military counterinsurgency tactics and strategy in the region – in some ways in response to the President's re-formulation.

KHAN: I'm sorry, you lost me.

KITE: The cloud will lift – and believe me – I know this all might seem a little odd, but God is in the detail, Professor.

KHAN: *(Under his breath.)* I thought it was the Devil.

KITE gives KHAN a slightly harder look – before smiling.

KHAN: If it really helps

KITE: It will, I can assure you of that –

KHAN: – then of course, it's no problem.

KITE: Thank you.

TOM moves to the side of KHAN and takes out a notepad and pen.

KITE: As I said, assume I know nothing, this is just a briefing.

KHAN: Nothing?

KITE: Absolutely nothing.

Pause. KITE pours a cup of tea for KHAN and for himself.

KHAN: Thank you.

KHAN drinks some tea.

KHAN: Shall I start with the King?

KITE: From an Oxford man, I would expect no less.

KHAN: Is there anything in particular you want to know about?

KITE: Just an overview.

KHAN: An overview? *(Beat.)*

KITE: Exactly.

KHAN: OK. Well, you know Amanullah was King from 1919 to '29 – following the assassination of his father, Habibullah?

KITE: I do, but assume I know nothing else.

Pause as speed coughs – scribbles a note – hands it to TOM who passes it to KITE.

KITE: Was he involved, you think? In the assassination?

KHAN: Some believe he was – others blame the British, the Soviets, Habibullah's brother Nasrullah… there's nothing conclusive.

KITE: If your head was on the block?

KHAN: Amanullah was ambitious, maybe the best placed to seize power, that's all. Suspicion was always likely to fall on him.

KITE: But in your opinion, he wasn't involved?

KHAN: Yes that is my opinion and it's what I say in my book.

KITE: Good. Martin?

KITE looks to MARTIN SPEED who shakes his head.

KITE: Please continue Professor.

KHAN: Amanullah's first act as ruler was to declare his country an independent state with the right to conduct its own foreign affairs – something the British were very unhappy about and which led to the Third Anglo-Afghan War.

KITE: And what was the result?

KHAN: After a month's fighting and a bombing raid on Kabul – a peace treaty. The British cut off his finance but the King got his country's independence and his chance.

KITE: To do what?

KHAN: To modernise Afghanistan.

KITE: How exactly?

KHAN: By creating a major reform programme.

KITE throws a cold smile and looks to TOM and SPEED.

KITE: What kind of reforms?

KHAN: Bullet points?

KITE: Just the good stuff.

KHAN: The creation of the first written constitution, a Council of Ministers, reformed the legal structure, created an independent judiciary, established a number of secular schools, education for girls, enacted provisions to enhance the legal rights of women, identity cards

KITE: *(Surprised.)* Identity cards? And all these were passed as law?

KHAN: Not all of them.

KITE: Why?

KHAN: The tribal and religious leaders revolted in 1924.

KITE: But to be clear, he was trying to establish a *(Slowly and deliberately.)* secular liberal democracy?

KHAN: Given the period, that's precisely what he was trying to do.

Pause – KITE shifts in his seat. SPEED whispers something to TOM, who scribbles another note and hands it to KITE.

KITE: Can we talk about Tarzi?

KHAN: Tarzi's daughter, Soraya, was Amanullah's wife.

KITE: So he was the King's father in law.

KHAN: He was a great deal more than that – he was Amanullah's foreign Minister and mentor for a number of years.

KITE: And perfectly placed to whisper and nudge effectively.

KHAN looks irritated.

KHAN: Mahmud Tarzi was one of the great intellectuals of the 20th century. A thinker and reformer. We're talking about a man who spoke six languages and translated Jules Verne into Dari –

KITE: What about his politics?

KHAN: He was an Afghan nationalist, hated the British. He wanted closer ties with the Soviets or the Americans.

KITE: Why?

KHAN: He despised imperialism. He picked up a lot of his ideas from the Young Turks he met in Damascus during his family's exile – these were the same Young Turks who eventually overthrew the Caliphate... the Sultan.

KITE nods.

KHAN: And when King Habibullah, Amanullah's father, invited the Tarzis back to Afghanistan, Tarzi brought these ideas with him.

Another SPEED note – TOM whispers something to KITE –

KITE: What about his newspaper Professor?

KHAN: I thought you knew nothing?

KITE: I said 'assume' I do.

KHAN: The Seraj-ul-Akbar – Torch of News – he founded the paper in 1911. It was very influential in Afghan modernist thinking.

KITE: Anything else?

KHAN: About the Newspaper?

KITE: Yes.

KHAN: It was political – revolutionary – it attacked European imperialism as well as resistance to change by the orthodoxy.

KITE: Can you be more specific Professor?

KHAN: Tarzi contested the belief that Muslims could learn nothing from the West, which was, as it is now, an incredibly dangerous idea to propose.

KITE looks at SPEED, who nods a few times, very pleased.

KITE: What happened after the Tribal Chiefs revolted?

KHAN: Amanullah granted certain concessions – things looked to be settling down – but then he decided the way to get his reforms back on track was a shake up of the Cabinet.

KITE: How very British. And was Tarzi affected in this re-shuffle?

KHAN: He resigned in the middle of 1925. He had been trying to get the King to go more slowly with his reforms – Amanullah refused to listen.

KITE: A pragmatist as well as an idealist. There's a man you can hang your hat on.

KHAN: I'm sorry?

KITE: Nothing – what happened after that?

KHAN: Tarzi was quite ill – suffering from exhaustion – went away to Switzerland for treatment. When he returned he found that the King had planned a grand tour of major European cities, as well as Persia, Turkey, India – Tarzi tried to persuade him not to go.

KITE: Why?

KHAN: He could see that the concessions hadn't had any real effect – the tribal chiefs were still stirring and just waiting for an opportunity.

KITE: And the King didn't listen.

KHAN: No he didn't.

SPEED: And there gentlemen is the tragedy of Kings – like Caesar, they all eventually become deaf to those around them.

KHAN: Would that apply to Presidents and Prime Ministers too?

KITE: Certainly did for Gordon Brown.

SPEED: Dubya was all ears – just listened to the wrong people.

KHAN: And you gentlemen are the right people?

KITE: *(Icy.)* Our hearts and minds are in the right place Professor. *(Beat.)* So the grand tour?

KHAN: The King and Queen were feted across Europe – except by the British who were still resentful about independence.

KITE: I see.

KHAN: Whilst at home the Mullahs began a campaign – aided in some measure by the British – condemning his personal life and modernisation programs as anti-Islamic.

Pause.

KHAN: They even distributed photographs of Queen Soraya unveiled at European receptions – which just added fuel to the conservative flames.

KITE: And when they returned home?

KHAN: Amanullah was inspired by what he had seen and was more determined than ever to modernise.

KITE: What about Tarzi?

KHAN: He urged the King not to push social reform too quickly – at least not until he'd built up the army.

KITE: A shrewd man indeed.

KHAN: But Amanullah pushed even more radical reforms – minimum age for marriage, coeducational schools, forcing all Afghans in Kabul to wear Western clothes and all the men to cut their beards. The Queen Soraya pushed for further womens' rights and the banning of the veil.

KITE: Which I presume didn't go down very well with the tribal chiefs.

KHAN: You could say that.

TOM: *(Quietly.)* We should press on sir.

KITE nods.

KITE: So if we were to summarise – radical liberal reformer forced into exile by religious fanatics, backed by the British? That the way it is?

KHAN: Don't you mean the way it 'was'?

KITE smiles. The phone rings. TOM picks it up.

TOM: I'll pass you over.

TOM hands KITE the phone.

KITE: *(To KHAN.)* Excuse me. *(Hushed, into the phone)* He's here now – it has definite potential. *(Beat.)* No. Better to keep him… on the outside. No need for exposure on this.

KITE hangs up the phone.

KITE: *(To KHAN.)* Unfortunately the Minister is stuck on a bus with trailing reporters so he's not likely to risk a taxi and more expenses rage.

KHAN: He won't make it then?

KITE: I'm afraid not.

KHAN: So I suppose you're not going to…

KITE: Tell you what this is all about?

KHAN: Yes.

KITE: I'm a man of my word, you've signed the Official Secrets Act. *(Beat.)* And we do know where you live in any case.

KHAN looks uneasy.

KITE: Just a joke Professor.

KITE smiles – KHAN doesn't.

KITE: So, you see this document, Morris' document, is an idea. A proposal.

KITE hands the document to KHAN.

KHAN: *(Reading aloud.)* "The Historical Precedent for the Establishment of a Secular Liberal Democracy in Afghanistan by the People of Afghanistan." *(Beat.)* What does it propose?

KITE: Just that we should be engaged in reminding the Afghan people of their history. That a secular liberal democracy is something that was originally proposed and indeed pushed for by Afghans – not by the West.

KHAN thinks about this.

KHAN: I don't fully understand. What for exactly?

SPEED: Professor, as I'm sure you're aware, in the Pashtun area alone there are 57,000 madrasahs – the children are taught

Arabic and the Koran – and nothing about their own history. Not exactly what one might consider a secular education.

KITE: Morris suggests posters, statues of Tarzi – almost an advertising campaign – Che Guevara style.

KHAN: What?

SPEED: A more recent, maybe more relevant example might be what's happened with Massoud in Afghanistan since his assassination in 2001. He's been lionised – a cult figure – someone to look up to – an Afghan hero – who like Tarzi is not an Islamic fundamentalist.

KHAN: A campaign? But that

KITE: – might sound totally absurd, but

KHAN: *(Really frustrated.)* I think it's beyond that – what are you actually proposing?

KITE: The current military surge allows us a chance to push the non military counterinsurgency development programmes in some interesting ways. *(Beat.)* A strategic re-launch of the newspaper – the Seraj-ul-Akbar – Torch of News – that might have the desired effect –

KHAN: What effect? The newspaper was viciously anti-British!

KITE: Precisely.

KITE moves a little closer to KHAN.

KITE: Professor, can I speak candidly?

KHAN: I really wish you would.

KITE: The President has made it clear that the troop withdrawal from Afghanistan will start next year.

SPEED: Mid term elections demand(ed) it, the American people demand it.

KITE: As does economic necessity for all of the Allies.

KHAN: Isn't that what the Afghan people have been asking for, for some years now?

KITE: That's what it has to look like – but the Afghan government? You think Karzai flirting with the Taliban means he really wants to get into bed with them? He wouldn't last six months and the government…

KHAN: Which one?!

KITE: Our governments would prefer an exit strategy that doesn't appear to be an outright abandonment of the Afghan people.

KHAN: Doesn't appear to be…

KITE: It wouldn't be the British or the American thing to do. Start a war – not finish it – make a bit of a mess and go. But an Afghan nationalist campaign fuelled by the desire for a secular democracy? Now that would give us no choice. And we could go having left something behind, move on with a clear conscience to address the more critical problem.

KHAN: Which is?

SPEED: Pakistan. That's where the action's gonna be. That's where al-Qaeda is. That's where the threat to global security is now coming from. Pakistan's our theatre now, it's where we build our stage!

KHAN: You want to start another war?

SPEED: Start? Are you serious? Don't you know what's going on? The Pakistani government need us – it's a delicate, delicate situation, paranoia about India, nuclear weapons – it may be our last chance to keep them in the civilised fold.

KHAN shakes his head, astonished.

KHAN: The civilised fold? This is crazy, complete madness! *(Beat.)* Why did you want to speak to me?

KITE: Professor, you're an academic, a Muslim and an additional bonus, which admittedly we didn't know about – you're from Pakistan. Just by adding your name…

KHAN: You're insane if you think I'm having anything to do this.

KHAN stands up furious, moves to the door.

KITE: Professor, please, wait a second. *(Slowly.)* By rendering this small service, don't you know how much you could be helping aid the long term security and protection of your country and… family.

KHAN takes his hand off the door handle and turns back to look at KITE.

KITE: Good. Now do you want some more tea while we discuss details? *(Turns to TOM.)* Perhaps we can rustle up some camomile and honey for the Professor?

Lights Down.

NOW IS THE TIME

by Joy Wilkinson

First production

The Tricycle Theatre, London, 17 April 2009

The following cast performed in the remount in July 2010 at the Tricycle Theatre prior to the USA tour:

Characters / Cast

AMANULLAH KHAN (King of Afghanistan 1919-29, aged 36)	Daniel Rabin
THE DRIVER	Daniel Betts
MAHMUD TARZI (Amanullah's friend, aged 64)	Vincent Ebrahim
SOROYA TARZI (His daughter and married to Amanullah, aged 29)	Shereen Martineau

Director	Nicolas Kent
Designer	Pamela Howard
Lighting	James Farncombe
Sound	Tom Lishman

Setting

The play is set in the desert North of Kabul in 1929.

SCENE 1

Darkness. The sound of a car engine …

…cuts out. Lights up on a Rolls Royce somewhere outside Kabul, 1929.

AMANULLAH, SORAYA and TARZI sit in the back. The DRIVER sits in the front.

AMANULLAH: Why have we stopped?

DRIVER: Sorry, sir. I'll find out.

> *The DRIVER gets out.*

TARZI: The engine just died.

AMANULLAH: This is a Rolls Royce. The greatest engine in the world.

TARZI: A British engine.

AMANULLAH: We took our independence from them, Tarzi. We can at least take advantage of their nice motors. It's not the engine.

SORAYA: It could be a trap.

TARZI: Why would it be? The rebels got what they wanted. And we escaped.

SORAYA: We haven't escaped yet. What if they don't want us to?

> *She looks back, out of the rear window.*

AMANULLAH: There's no one out there, Soraya.

SORAYA: It could still be a trap. Who is that driver?

AMANULLAH: He came with the motorcar.

TARZI: He's British? You're sure we can trust him?

AMANULLAH: He's just the driver. Trust me.

SORAYA: I don't trust anyone any more. You have brought us to this, Amanullah.

TARZI: Soraya, be reasonable. A king can hardly help getting overthrown. He did everything he could. He negotiated. And when negotiations broke down, he got us out of there alive.

SORAYA: So far.

AMANULLAH: Charkhi is leading a Soviet force to meet us at the border and then we will march on Kabul, take on the tribal chieftains and take back my throne. You know we can trust Charkhi. He was my most loyal minister.

SORAYA: He was in Moscow most of the time. I don't trust the Soviets.

AMANULLAH: Put yourself in their place. It's not a matter of trust. It's expediency. Without me running things, tribal warfare will be inevitable, and just as inevitable will be the British stepping in to (*British accent.*) 'sort it all out' and then forgetting to go home afterwards. The Soviets can't risk that. They need me back in power, so that is what will happen.

SORAYA: And we will all live happily ever after.

AMANULLAH: Only if we stick together, Soraya, and stay strong. I know you are scared, but we cannot think of ourselves right now.

SORAYA: I'm not scared.

TARZI: I am, a little. And cold and hungry. What is that wretched man up to?

AMANULLAH takes a bag of dates from his pocket and gives them to TARZI.

AMANULLAH: Wait here. I'll talk to him.

He gets out. TARZI offers a date to SORAYA. She looks away.

TARZI: You must have times, like your mother and I had, when the decision to blaze a trail for monogamy seems to be an error. With many wives, I might have been less aware of one's particular faults. And I know your mother would have relished a break from my shortcomings. But I still believe she and I did the right thing, marrying for love and staying faithful no matter what. Whatever Amanullah's faults, he has been a loyal husband to you. And a good son-in-law to me.

SORAYA: And what kind of son was he to his own father?

TARZI: To his own…? Now, Soraya, we don't know –

SORAYA: You don't know – you don't know Amanullah's faults so don't tell me… Just don't tell me. You don't want to know.

TARZI: What? What is it, Soraya? Did something else happen, before we left?

SORAYA: Please, father, your breath makes the windows steam up.

She wipes a hole in the condensation to look back. TARZI finishes eating in silence.

Outside, AMANULLAH approaches the driver.

AMANULLAH: Is it the engine?

DRIVER: The engine? With respect, sir, she has the greatest engine in the world. It's not the engine.

AMANULLAH: No, I thought not. So what is it then?

DRIVER: Just the snow, sir. You can get back inside. I can dig her out.

The DRIVER starts digging the snow away with his hands.

AMANULLAH: It looks deep.

DRIVER: Yes, sir. It's deeper than it looks.

AMANULLAH looks back, troubled. He takes out his gun, checks that it's loaded, then puts it away quickly as TARZI gets out of the car.

AMANULLAH: It's just the snow. Wait inside.

TARZI: The snow?

AMANULLAH: We've run into a drift, but he can dig us out.

TARZI: Of every drift from here to the border?

AMANULLAH: Perhaps we can give him a hand.

DRIVER: That's alright, sir, I can manage.

TARZI: It will be dark soon. It will get colder.

AMANULLAH: It will be warmer in our motorcar than in any house you could walk to. But there'll be no need to walk, will there?

DRIVER: No, sir. I'll have her free in no time.

AMANULLAH: You can get back inside now, Tarzi, keep warm.

TARZI: Frostbite is warmer than Soraya's glance right now.

AMANULLAH: She's scared. You should reassure her.

TARZI: No, she is not scared. It's something else… Are you scared, Amanullah?

AMANULLAH: What, of certain victory?

TARZI: Of not reaching the meeting point. Of getting caught by the tribesmen or freezing to death courtesy of your driver and your delusions. Because unless this Silver Ghost spirits us to the border, we will stall and get stuck and its great British engine will get us killed.

Pause. AMANULLAH summons the DRIVER and writes a note as he speaks.

AMANULLAH: I need you to walk to the last town we passed and wire the Soviets. Get an update on Charkhi's position and have them send a mission direct to here, wherever here is.

The DRIVER takes the note.

DRIVER: Yes, sir. I'll find out exactly, sir.

TARZI: You think he will be safe?

AMANULLAH takes out his gun.

TARZI: I thought you weren't scared?

AMANULLAH: I'm not. (*Gives gun to the DRIVER.*) But if it helps him feel safer.

DRIVER: Thank you, sir. I'll be back directly.

The DRIVER goes.

AMANULLAH: A good job I got the telegraph system set up.

TARZI: A shame you didn't build your road.

AMANULLAH: My road?

TARZI: 'From the south to the north, from the mountains to the deserts, from the palace to…' I forget where. You forgot too.

AMANULLAH: I didn't forget. I've had one or two other problems to occupy me.

TARZI: No one can accuse you of not trying, Amanullah.

AMANULLAH: The tribal chieftains did. After all I've done for them.

TARZI: After all you've done for them.

AMANULLAH: I did not want to be king. I wept when my father was killed, cut down with a bullet like the beasts he was meant to be hunting. I wanted to run away, leave this place forever. But what did you say to me, Tarzi?

TARZI: Something, I forget.

AMANULLAH: You said: 'Do not cry, now is the time for action.' I dried my tears and I took your advice. I shook this ancient sand clock up until it knew it was the twentieth century and time to be free and equal.

TARZI: Yes, I remember you used to take my advice.

AMANULLAH: I always have. When the tribes rebelled, I tried to take things slower. But time doesn't run backwards, Tarzi. I don't. I had to keep going.

TARZI: And look where we've ended up. Nineteen-twenty-nine and this place hasn't changed since Allah created the world, from nothingness.

AMANULLAH: You want to know why my road isn't built? Modernising takes money. Money I turned down from the British when I turned them out of here. Money you were meant to get from the Soviets.

TARZI: I negotiated, at length. I gained their agreement.

AMANULLAH: You got a piece of paper. You got nothing. They took from us.

TARZI: If only the Americans –

AMANULLAH: Is that what keeps you awake at nights? It should send you to sleep. It's a pretty bedtime story. They ignored you, hoped you'd go away. And it worked. You went away, from all of us. You let me down, Tarzi. You let down your country.

TARZI: I could not think here. I needed time to think.

AMANULLAH: There was no time. There was too much to do.

TARZI: There is an infinite number of things to be done, always. But to know which to do now, and which will come undone, there must be thought.

AMANULLAH: A child could tell you what this place needs – teachers, guns, money –

TARZI: A child has much to learn, Amanullah.

AMANULLAH: I've had to do it all myself. Go begging at every table in Europe.

TARZI: Is that what you were doing, with your champagne and your dancing?

AMANULLAH: I've done everything I can for my country, so don't you dare accuse me of failing it.

TARZI: Perhaps you've done too much. That's what angers people.

AMANULLAH: You think too much and don't do enough. That's what angers me.

TARZI: I think too much. You do too much. You might expect us to have achieved more.

Pause.

AMANULLAH: It's not our fault. It's the British.

TARZI: The British and the Soviets.

AMANULLAH: And the Muslims.

TARZI: Ah yes, the Muslims.

AMANULLAH: And the Germans.

TARZI: All the Europeans, give or take.

AMANULLAH: And the Americans.

BOTH: If only the Americans.

    They laugh.

AMANULLAH: We will do better next time.

TARZI: What angers Soraya? I don't think I have ever seen her truly angry. Do you know what angers her, Amanullah?

AMANULLAH: (*Beat.*) Perhaps she preferred being queen to being stuck out here.

TARZI: She is still a queen, always has been. No tribesman could take that away, no man, except... What happened, Amanullah, in that room? What did you do?

AMANULLAH: You are thinking too much again, Tarzi.

    AMANULLAH starts digging. TARZI watches.

    SORAYA gets out of the car.

SORAYA: What are you doing?

AMANULLAH: There's no need to get out.

SORAYA: Where's the driver?

AMANULLAH: Gone to get help. He won't be long.

SORAYA: You said you'd get us out of here.

AMANULLAH: I just said, he's gone to get help. All we need to do is wait.

SORAYA: Then why are you digging?

AMANULLAH: Because I like my motorcar.

SORAYA: He's got the keys.

TARZI: He's also got his gun.

SORAYA: He took your gun?

AMANULLAH: I gave it to him.

TARZI: Amanullah is not scared.

SORAYA: Perhaps he was scared that I might use it.

AMANULLAH: I'm not scared. I know what I'm doing, Soraya.

SORAYA: I wish I knew what you were doing, Amanullah. I used to, without you needing to say a word. But now the more you say…

AMANULLAH: Why don't you wait in the warm?

SORAYA: It's not warm. The longer I sat there, the longer I wondered if I was still alive. If I hadn't been left for dead in that room with the tribes, and this was just cold hell. For god's sake, will you stop digging?

AMANULLAH: A king shouldn't be too proud to get his hands dirty.

SORAYA: You are no longer a king. And your hands could turn this entire whiteness to dirt. To blood.

TARZI: Someone's coming.

They stop still, turn to look back.

Now I am scared.

AMANULLAH: It will be the driver, coming back.

SORAYA: Not so soon. Not unless…

AMANULLAH: You should both get in the car. Soraya, you should put on a veil.

SORAYA: A veil? Why should I?

AMANULLAH: It could be someone local. I'm only thinking of your safety.

TARZI: He's right, Soraya, it would be safer.

SORAYA: A veil isn't bullet-proof. But it would stop you having to see my face.

TARZI: What does she mean, Amanullah?

AMANULLAH: She's just scared.

SORAYA: Why aren't you scared? Because you know who it is. Who is it?

AMANULLAH: Some child playing in the snow. A lost shepherd. A ghost. I don't know.

TARZI: How would he know?

SORAYA: Because this is a trap and he set it.

TARZI: He wouldn't do that. Why would he do that?

AMANULLAH: Look. Whoever it is, they're going. My masterplan must have failed.

TARZI: Answer me, Soraya.

AMANULLAH: They've gone. She was wrong, about everything. Tell him.

SORAYA: How can I know if I was wrong? How can you expect me to trust you?

TARZI: What have you done, Amanullah?

AMANULLAH: I have done nothing, for once. It was just words, Soraya. I said what I had to say to stay in power.

SORAYA: If that's true, then you were not really king anyway. So which are you, Amanullah, a puppet or a murderer?

AMANULLAH: I'm your husband.

SORAYA: You told them you would divorce me.

TARZI: Told them? The tribal chieftains? What else did he tell them?

AMANULLAH: Soraya, no –

SORAYA: They offered him a deal – he could remain as king if he would divorce me, exile my family, close all the schools for girls, abolish all reformist laws, restore Shariat law, restore the veil. My husband agreed. He gave away all our rights. And my father's life.

AMANULLAH: No, Tarzi –

SORAYA: All my family to be exiled except Mahmud Tarzi, who is to be tried. But perhaps a trial seemed too much trouble. This way is simpler. Let us escape and let an assassin follow us. Or drive us. That's why he's not scared, that's why he gave away his gun, that's why he's digging our graves, waiting for that man to take him safely back to Kabul and to bury us here, in this nowhere.

AMANULLAH: I wouldn't do that. I would never –

SORAYA: I was there, Amanullah, I heard you say it.

AMANULLAH: I negotiated, to buy us time, to form a plan. Tarzi, you know how it is, we say things. I would never betray you.

TARZI: Some said you had your father killed. I never believed them, before. 'Cut down with a bullet, like the beasts he was meant to be hunting.'

AMANULLAH: I did not kill my father.

TARZI: I've never seen you weep since the day you heard of his death. I have seen you lie, many times. I don't believe I ever have seen you weep, not really. But my heart weeps for you, my son. For all our dreams.

AMANULLAH: I did not kill my father. You know I didn't. It was the British.

SORAYA: It's always the British. Or the Soviets. Point your finger in 360 degrees and you still won't see who has brought us to this. I don't care if you killed your father. He was a selfish arrogant fool who changed nothing. I thought you were different. I believed in you, Amanullah Khan. I didn't care if you lied as long as it was to get what we wanted. That was worth lying for, worth your father dying for. But now I see all that matters is you, you hanging on to your precious life, your mighty power, your stupid motorcar. It wasn't the British in that room today, signing my father's death warrant, was it? It was you.

AMANULLAH: It was worthless. I knew it would be. The tribes have even less regard for pieces of paper than the Soviets. And so should you have. Forget what was said and see what is happening. We are here, together, alive, so far, and I will lay down my life before I let anyone harm you. I am not scared because I know I am going to die. I signed my own death warrant the day your father convinced me to become king. That is why I have tried to do as much as I can, however I can, before the next man comes along and does nothing so he can stay alive a little longer.

SORAYA: You always know what to say. I want to believe you. I want to, but...

AMANULLAH: I gave my gun to the driver because I need him alive or we are all lost and our country will be in chaos. That is all I am scared of. That and you losing your faith in me. I cannot do this without you. Both of you. You may think that I'm puppet or a murderer or a selfish arrogant fool, but I was a better king than my father and I will be a better king than any backwards, bloodthirsty warlord. And you will be better puppetmasters.

He goes to the boot of the car. SORAYA stiffens, grips TARZI, scared.

SORAYA: What is he doing?

TARZI: What are you doing, Amanullah?

AMANULLAH: I am trying.

He throws something to SORAYA and TARZI – gloves. AMANULLAH starts digging.

TARZI looks at him a long time. He picks up the gloves.

SORAYA: You believe him? You forgive him?

TARZI: We must try to get moving again.

SORAYA: How can we? The snow's too deep. We don't even have the keys. The driver is probably dead by now.

TARZI: Probably, yes. Probably we will all be dead before this thing is free.

The DRIVER starts to dig. She looks back over her shoulder, and then back at the men, digging.

Blackout.

SCENE 2

Lights up, a little. It's later – nightfall. AMANULLAH, SORAYA and TARZI finish digging.

AMANULLAH: I think we've done it.

SORAYA: I almost feel warm. Almost.

He offers his coat. After a pause, she takes it.

TARZI: It's a nice motorcar. I hadn't noticed before.

AMANULLAH: I'll get you one when I'm king again.

TARZI: Will you build me a road to drive it on?

AMANULLAH: Will you get me the money?

TARZI: Forget the money, just say yes. That's what you need to remember, now that we have got rid of our illusions. Now we need to remember what we dreamt, all those years ago.

AMANULLAH: I remember now. When I was a child, my father tried to teach me how to drive a motorcar. I kept stalling. It was my fault, but I blamed the road and asked him why he couldn't build a proper road? And not just in Kabul either. If he was a king, why couldn't he build a great road, from the south to the north, from the cities to the mountains, the desert to the snow, from the palace to the poorest dwelling?

TARZI: Ah yes, now I remember.

AMANULLAH: He smiled and said he would build it, as a gift to me. But he never did.

SORAYA: I remember when he died, you said that you would build the road then, as a monument to him.

AMANULLAH: When we get back, I will build it. Not for the dead. For the living. For the future. To show my people the way forward. To show them that this great country belongs to us all.

Pause.

SORAYA: The driver. I see him.

TARZI: Where?

SORAYA: There. Can't you see him?

TARZI: It's too dark. I can't see anything.

AMANULLAH: She's right. I see him. And I don't see any henchmen.

TARZI: He's a good man, I could tell.

AMANULLAH: A brave man.

TARZI: A hero. Maybe we should make him king.

SORAYA: Maybe he can't see us. We should call to him. What's his name?

AMANULLAH: I forgot to ask.

They call – 'hey, we're here, over here'. Then fall silent, excited, waiting. He arrives. AMANULLAH embraces him.

Welcome back my friend.

TARZI: We'd almost given you up.

AMANULLAH: No, we knew you'd come through.

SORAYA: Thank you. It can't have been easy.

DRIVER: Sorry for the delay, sir. The weather.

AMANULLAH: But did it get there? Did they reply?

DRIVER: Eventually.

He takes out a piece of paper and hands it to AMANULLAH, who reads it.

SORAYA: What does it say?

TARZI: Are they on their way?

Pause.

AMANULLAH: I don't understand. What did you tell them?

DRIVER: What you told me to, sir.

SORAYA: What does it say?

TARZI: Is it bad news?

AMANULLAH: It doesn't make sense. You must have told them something else.

DRIVER: No, sir. Sorry, sir.

AMANULLAH: Give me the gun.

The DRIVER gives him the gun. AMANULLAH turns it on The DRIVER, threatening.

What did you tell them?

SORAYA: What does it say?

AMANULLAH: You tell her what it says.

DRIVER: I don't know, sir. I wouldn't read it.

SORAYA: Let me look.

She takes the piece of paper and reads it aloud.

'Received news of your plans for exile STOP Charkhi mission aborted STOP'… Received news of your plans for exile?

TARZI: What news? What plans?

SORAYA: Who would have told them that?

AMANULLAH: He would. So that they'd abort the mission. So they wouldn't come.

TARZI: But then why would he come back here?

AMANULLAH: I don't know. I told you it made no sense.

SORAYA: He's come back to lead them here. Whoever he's working for. He's come back to kill us.

TARZI: But we could kill him.

AMANULLAH: We will, if he doesn't tell us the truth right now. Who are you? Who do you work for?

DRIVER: I am just the driver. I work for you, sir. And with respect, sir, I think it does make sense.

AMANULLAH: What do you mean?

DRIVER: The telegram, sir. It makes sense to me. I work for you. I take orders from you. Maybe I'm more used to hearing it. I don't think anyone's told them that you have plans for exile. I think they're telling you.

AMANULLAH: Telling me?

DRIVER: I might be mistaken, but it sounds like they're telling you what to do. Giving you your orders as it were. I might be wrong.

TARZI: No, you're right. He's right. It would make sense.

AMANULLAH: How would it? They need me back in power, why would they change their plans?

DRIVER: Maybe someone's giving them orders, sir.

AMANULLAH: The Soviets don't take orders from anyone.

TARZI: Unless…if the British told them – stay out of this. Don't get involved and neither will we. Let Amanullah fall and wait to see what happens.

AMANULLAH: They wouldn't.

SORAYA: Why not? Wouldn't it be expedient – to negotiate, to make a deal if it suited their objectives?

AMANULLAH: They hate the British.

SORAYA: They have no love for you. And even if they did, I'm still not sure it would make any difference.

AMANULLAH: No, I don't believe it. They need me.

SORAYA: You would think so, hope so, but when it comes down to it…

TARZI: Perhaps they think the next man may be less trouble. Or the next man. Or the next. What does it matter to them who is in power? If he is not really in power.

AMANULLAH: No. It does matter. It has to matter.

SORAYA: At least they are letting us live.

She looks back, with relief. TARZI takes her hand.

TARZI: We should go now, before they change their minds.

AMANULLAH: No. I can't leave. This is my country. My people.

TARZI: (*To DRIVER.*) Can you get us safely to the airfield?

AMANULLAH: No, we're not going. We're not going anywhere. This is my home. Kill me here. I order you. I order you.

He gives the gun back to The DRIVER.

DRIVER: As you wish, sir.

He aims and fires. TARZI knocks the gun from his hand. The shot fires into the snow.

AMANULLAH stands, stunned. TARZI picks up the gun.

TARZI: No more orders, Amanullah.

SORAYA goes to AMANULLAH, holds him.

SORAYA: I'm sorry, I believe you, I believe you now.

TARZI: (*To DRIVER.*) If you take us to the airfield, the motorcar is yours.

The DRIVER smiles, takes out the car keys and lets them in.

DRIVER: We should go before news spreads. Whilst people still think he's king.

AMANULLAH begins to weep, quietly.

AMANULLAH: No.

TARZI: Bring him with you, Soraya.

They go to the car. The DRIVER lets them in.

DRIVER: You will be safer not all travelling together.

AMANULLAH: No, we have to stay together.

TARZI: Drop me on the outskirts. I will make my own way from there.

AMANULLAH: No, Tarzi – we have to stay…

SORAYA: We will meet up again.

TARZI: Yes, when it's safe.

AMANULLAH: It will never be safe if we go.

SORAYA puts on her veil.

No, Soraya, don't, please, take it off.

SORAYA: We can go somewhere where I'll never have to wear it again.

AMANULLAH: We can make that place here.

TARZI: We will, when we come back.

SORAYA: We will come back, one day.

AMANULLAH: No, now. Now is the time. Now is the time. Now…

He breaks down, heartbroken.

TARZI: Do not cry, Amanullah. It's time to go. We can go somewhere warm, by the sea. It is good to wake up and see the sea. It makes you forget your dreams.

The DRIVER starts the engine, looks over his shoulder, and reverses.

Fade to darkness and silence.

PART TWO
COMMUNISM, THE MUJAHIDEEN AND
THE TALIBAN
1979-1996

BLACK TULIPS
by David Edgar

First production

The Tricycle Theatre, London, 18 April 2009

The following cast performed in the remount in July 2010 at the Tricycle Theatre prior to the USA tour:

Characters / Cast

A UNIT COMMANDER (a Major in command of battalion, earlier a Captain in charge of a company, mid-30s to mid-20s)   Daniel Betts

1ST DEPUTY (a captain, the Communist Party representative in a battalion)   Tom McKay

1ST REPRESENTATIVE OF THE AFGHAN GOVERNMENT (a middle-aged civilian)   Nabil Elouahabi

AN INTERPRETER (a female civilian, early 30s to early 20s)   Shereen Martineau

A RIFLEMAN (a young conscript)   Karl Davies

A CAPTAIN (middle-aged)   Vincent Ebrahim

AN ENSIGN (a sapper in his 30s)   Rick Warden

A MAJOR (late middle aged)   Michael Cochrane

2ND REPRESENTATIVE OF THE AFGHAN GOVERNMENT (a middle-aged civilian)   Raad Rawi

2ND DEPUTY (a young Lieutenant)   Danny Rahim

NAHID (a young civilian Afghan woman)   Cloudia Swann

MEENA (a young civilian Afghan woman)   Sheena Bhattessa

Note: There's a distinction between a rank (Captain, Major), a job (sapper) and an office (unit Commander).

Director   Nicolas Kent
Designers   Pamela Howard and Miriam Nabarro
Lighting   James Farncombe
Sound   Tom Lishman

Setting

The play is about an army over a period of time, and could involve doubling, except for the two characters who appear in the first and last scene.

The play is set in an auditorium, with a lectern, a line of chairs and a large screen, forming a backdrop. A change in the projection indicates a time shift (as does a change in scene number in the script) but otherwise the action should feel like a continuous military briefing. The five scenes are set in 1987, 1985, 1984, 1982 and 1981.

When a character is being translated, both his language and the translation are rendered in English.

SCENE ONE

An army political DEPUTY, a civilian government REPRESENTATIVE and a female INTERPRETER wait on the stage. The battalion COMMANDER, a Major, enters. He has a walking stick and a limp. The 1ST DEPUTY and the INTERPRETER stand smartly, the 1ST REPRESENTATIVE a little slower.

The COMMANDER gestures them to sit which they do.

COMMANDER: Good afternoon. So, do we want the good news or the bad news?

The COMMANDER nods to an offstage technician. A huge map of Afghanistan appears on the screen.

(*To the 1ST DEPUTY.*) Ah. Remind us of the good news.

The COMMANDER sits, the 1ST DEPUTY stands.

1ST DEPUTY: The good news is that you will be joining our brave troops in defending the achievements of the democratic government of Afghanistan.

COMMANDER: That's it. Please.

1ST DEPUTY: Afghanistan. A landlocked central asian country approximately the size of France.

COMMANDER: But, unlike France…

1ST DEPUTY:…consisting largely of impassable high mountain chains and baking desert. Most of the population lives in circumstances which have not changed since the middle ages. The country possesses a primitive highway network, with its roadways largely confined to urban areas. And although there are plants and factories producing some electricity, steel, cement and such, the overwelming majority of its people are involved in subsistence agriculture. The population consists of a jumble of around twenty different ethnicities speaking many different languages.

COMMANDER: So, just like home.

1ST DEPUTY: Its history being one of successive invasions and resistance, from the time of Alexander the Great. Since 1945, Afghanistan experiences civil unrest, plots and uprisings. In 1973, the army launches a *coup d'état*. The new regime launches persecutions and repressions. Two years later, Muslim extremists in the Panjshir valley begin an insurgency against the

government. Three years after that, opposition forces seized /
power –

COMMANDER: (*Stands.*) Thank you, I think we get the picture.

The 1ST DEPUTY sits.

In summary: you are being sent into an alien and hostile land, to
do battle with a resolute enemy in dangerous and inhospitable
terrain. In this vital work you will be suitably equipped and
supported by rockets and artillery, and from the air. Your
mission is to protect other countries – including ours – from
attack, and to aid the Afghan government's policy of national
reconciliation. You will be part of that reconstruction process,
building roads and schools and hospitals. But you will also work
as soldiers to protect the country from those who want to keep
large parts of it in conditions of primitive mediaeval barbarism.
We are privileged to have a representative of the government of
Afghanistan to address us.

The COMMANDER and 1ST DEPUTY sit. The 1ST
REPRESENTATIVE is speaking in Dari but rendered in English.

1ST REPRESENTATIVE: On behalf of the Democratic Republic of
Afghanistan, the working people of Afghanistan and the central
committee of the People's Democratic Party of Afghanistan, I /
welcome –

The INTERPRETER stops him, so she can translate.

INTERPRETER: On behalf of the government, people and
Communist Party of Afghanistan.

1ST REPRESENTATIVE: I welcome the continued fraternal assistance
provided by the Limited Contingent of the Soviet Armed Forces.

INTERPRETER: I am grateful for the continued help of the
LCOSAF.

1ST REPRESENTATIVE: Expressing our gratitude, in particular, for
its definitive contribution to our historic struggle against the
landlords, the counter-revolutionary stooges in their pay, and
their imperialist puppet-masters.

INTERPRETER: Thanking you for your military assistance against
the opposition and their American backers.

1ST REPRESENTATIVE: Long live the inviolable friendship of the
Afghan and Soviet peoples!

INTERPRETER: Long live the friendship between our nations.

1ST REPRESENTATIVE: Long live the central committee of the Communist Party of the Soviet Union, and its general secretary Comrade MS Gorbachov!

INTERPRETER: Praise to the communist party. Oh, and Mr Gorbachov.

1ST REPRESENTATIVE: Long live the heroic soldier-internationalists of the 40th army!

INTERPRETER: And to you.

The 1ST REPRESENTATIVE gestures that he's going to attempt his final statement in 'Russian'.

1ST REPRESENTATIVE: (*Heavy accent.*) And all hail to the Third Battalion of the 149th Motorized Rifle Regiment!

The INTERPRETER whispers to him.

So sorry. To the Third Battalion of the 148th Motorized Rifle Regiment, all hail!

COMMANDER: Thank you.

The INTERPRETER is about to lead the 1st REPRESENTATIVE out, as:

And now I believe there is a cultural / presentation –

A RIFLEMAN stands up in the audience.

RIFLEMAN: Comrade Major. In the spirit of openness, may I ask a question?

The COMMANDER glances quickly at the 1ST DEPUTY, who stands. The 1ST REPRESENTATIVE and the INTERPRETER wait.

COMMANDER: Yes, of course.

RIFLEMAN: I've had two elder brothers in the LCOSAF.

1ST DEPUTY: The Motherland is / grateful –

RIFLEMAN: One of them won the Order of the Red Star.

COMMANDER: We salute his courage.

RIFLEMAN: My question is about those who will protect us from the air.

1ST DEPUTY: Heroically.

COMMANDER: And vitally.

RIFLEMAN: And the fact that for all the talk of mastery of the skies, our helicopter gunships, our MiG-21s, and even our fixed-wingers are being shot out of the sky like pigeons by kids in baggy pants with US rocket launchers you can fire from your shoulder?

Pause.

1ST DEPUTY: Yes, despite their cynical denials, the imperialists / continue –

RIFLEMAN: So our boys in their IFVs are sitting ducks.

1ST DEPUTY: Comrade, I think it best if we continue / this –

RIFLEMAN: That if the resistance doesn't get you, then you'll die of / typhus or diptheria –

1ST DEPUTY: Comrade, I must / insist –

RIFLEMAN: That our suitable equipment isn't suitable. That we haven't learnt the lessons / of this war…

1ST DEPUTY: (*Calls, off.*) Sergeant!

COMMANDER: No, no. Let him speak.

1ST DEPUTY: Comrade Major…

COMMANDER: Please.

Slight pause.

'That we haven't learnt the lessons…'

RIFLEMAN: That we haven't learnt the lessons of this war because the people back home don't think it's important. That this whole fucking thing was doomed right from the start. Comrade Major.

He sits.

COMMANDER: Yes. Yes, of course. We've been here eight years. And you've some of you had brothers, cousins, maybe even uncles, done their two years, gone back to the world, and told their story. After all, when this thing started, some of you weren't even ten years old.

Pause.

And they'll tell you, sure, how things might have been different. If we'd had more troops. If we'd sealed the border with North-West Pakistan. If the Afghan government had gained more popular support, or if we'd had more support at home. If we'd cracked the drawbacks with the IFVs. If we'd retained our uncontested mastery of the air. Sometimes, yes, sure, it seems, however many battles we win on the ground, we just recruit more fighters for the other side.

Slight pause.

As you undertake your duties, all I ask you to recall is this. We were welcomed here. This country would be worse without our presence. When your tour is finished, when our tour is finished… We'll leave a better place than the one we found. I think we have to think…that, in that sense…our mission has succeeded.

A long pause.

1ST DEPUTY: Um, Major, I believe…

COMMANDER: You must understand, there was a time when things looked different.

A brisk CAPTAIN enters, as the COMMANDER goes out, followed by the 1ST DEPUTY. A Sapper ENSIGN enters and sits. The projection changes to the silhouettes of Soviet armour.

SCENE TWO

The CAPTAIN begins his presentation.

CAPTAIN: OK, my friends. People will tell you that there aren't enough of us. That the government has got too little backing in the countryside. That everything we do just seems to make the rebels stronger. And God knows there's still shortcomings with equipment on the ground. Say the cynics and the fainthearts and defeatists.

He looks round for something.

Talking of equipment…

The COMMANDER from the previous scene carries on a flip chart on an easel. He is now a CAPTAIN, two years younger, and without a limp.

Thank you, Comrade Captain.

The COMMANDER goes out, as:

So, when we arrived five years ago, were there deficiencies? Sure they're were. Basic principles of soldiering: always be higher than the enemy. However, there's a problem.

He draws a straight line across the paper.

The north German plain.

He draws another line.

The Manchurian plateau.

He draws a series of peaks.

The Hindu Kush. As is now accepted, the weaponry with which the Limited Contingent entered Afghanistan suffered from some minor oversights. Notably, that there was insufficient gun elevation on the Infantry Fighting Vehicles to be able to return fire from a mountain. Designed as they were for rolling unstoppably to Hanover. What did we do to confront these short-term snags? Well, in addition to undogmatic attitudes and socialist spontaneity by soldier-internationalists in the field, the new IFV. is noteworthy for the successful elimination of several temporary setbacks. And that's not to mention the addressing of further momentary shortfalls in the provision of the kit in which you face the enemy. The Soviet soldier is protected from all hazards, head to toe!

Above the mountain range, he draws a wild matrix of of arrows and moving lines.

But most crucially of all, we noted that a great way to gain vital elevation on the enemy is to fly the friendly skies. So what happens now? A spy satellite picks up a trace from Kandahar. In collaboration with our audacious special forces and our reconnaissance and fixed wing aircraft, our helicopter gunships are now able to locate and then destroy the insurgents, in the mountains, on the ground.

He tears the sheet off.

Don't let the gloom merchants tell you any different. Our mission is succeeding. The great surge ordered by our new dynamic leadership exceeds all expectations. We command the battleground because we command the air.

He goes out. The ENSIGN waits a moment, before standing, coming foward and putting his finger to his lips.

ENSIGN: Shhh.

He leaves the stage, returning pushing a trolley on which are three metal cylinders, what looks like a metal detector, and a pile of domestic objects, include a pen, a watch, a cigarette lighter, a tape recorder, some little metal butterfly-shaped objects and a thermos flask. As he wheels the trolley, he reiterates:

Shhh.

He whispers to the audience:

Where you lot from then? Anybody from Tashkent? Any Uzbeks, Tadjiks? Who's here from Turkmenistan?

Hardly any.

Understandable enough. Who wants to blow up Uncle Abdul? Or get blown up by Uncle Abdul. So, anyone from Vilnius? Tallinn? Leningrad? Anyone from Moscow?

Not many.

Anyone from Moscow and not contemplating sick leave? Anyone from any of our great cultural outward-looking progressive up-to-the-minute showcase Soviet metropolises?

Still not many.

Anybody from Dnipropetrovsk? Archangel? Lyubertsky? Tula?

Lots.

Ah. Welcome to the Workers' and Peasants' Army. Now, don't tell anyone I told you this. 'A mineclearer only makes two mistakes. The first is when he becomes a mineclearer'.

The cylinders.

Luigi. Tommy. Ivan. Luigi is an Italian TS-61. You can spot him by his fetching yellow hat. Tommy's a British MK-7. You are unlikely to see all of either of these dear guests unless you're me. And sometimes not even then.

Pause.

And yet. You never drive into the mountains. Or drive anywhere. Or leave base. Or return to base. Or cross the square to take a dump, without looking out for Tommy or Luigi. Luigi, anti-personnel. Tommy, anti-transport. Plus mines set off by radio, mines set off by mine clearance. Mines set on top of other mines, or set on top of bombs, or set to jump out of the ground. Mines you find with probes, with the whisper of a rustle in your earphones. Mines that are activated by the whisper of the rustle of your step. *Big* tip. A really great way to set off any of the above, wearing standard-issue footwear.

He walks, making a creaking noise. He waggles his trainer-clad feet.

Standard bandit-issue pirate Adidas. Or even Czech mountain boots. Hell, we gave them brotherly assistance. Payback time.

He goes to his pile of domestic objects.

And pens and watches, lighters, tape recorders. All found in bandit dugouts. Anyone fancying a brew?

He picks up the thermos, unscrews its base, revealing a big blob of black goo.

Fine piece of trophy kit. Sell this for a month's wages, down Kabul market on a Friday.

He scoops a bit of the goo on to his finger and holds it up.

Pakistani semtex. Expands and detonates with heat. The kind of heat you get when you fill your thermos up with tea. Something you don't want to find out through experience.

Turning to go back to the trolley, turning back:

Tip two. The standard-issue 16 kilo flackjacket will stop a bullet from a standard-stolen bandit-fired Kalashnikov. Unfortunately, it won't stop a bullet from a standard-vintage first world war British Enfield rifle. You tell me.

He goes to IVAN.

So, Ivan. A MON-50 directional shrapnel mine made in the USSR. Destroys any living thing in a 60 degree radius for a distance of up to 50 metres. Don't want to step on Ivan, either. Even if he's on our side.

So why all this advice? The goodness of my heart? Get you home to mummy in one piece? Bullshit. You step on Ivan, Tommy or Luigi, you're lost to the heroic struggle and it takes four men to lift what's left of you back down the mountain, so they can put you in a zinc box, load you up in a Black Tulip, and fly you back across the river. Hey, come on. Are you really worth all that attention?

He goes to the trolley and picks up the little shiny butterfly.

So these pretty shiny little things. What are these for? They are for scattering across the fields and meadows. Do they kill bandits? No. Do they kill kids? No. What they do is maim them. 'Cos you bury a dead kid, and head back to the struggle. Kid without a leg, or with half a face, needs looking after. We want the bandits looking after kids, not looking out for you.

He tosses the butterfly mine back on his trolley.

'Cos let me let you in on a little secret. Your average bandit doesn't engage in open combat all the time. In fact, he's happiest sneaking up on people from behind. So what do we do? Let me tell you. We deny him the behind. We destroy his cover. We burn his crops. We eliminate his means of life upon the land. That's what we're doing. That's our mission. And it's working.

Slight pause.

So, what else d'you want to know?

He winks at the audience, then wheels his trolley out. Enter an angry MAJOR. Projection change: a tree of Muslim organisations.

SCENE THREE

The angry MAJOR is followed on to the stage by the COMMANDER, now a Captain, three years younger than in scene one. He sits to wait his turn.

MAJOR: You'll want to know about the enemy. Oh, and it isn't who we thought it was four years ago. After all, four years ago, we didn't think this was a war.

He points at the projected organisational tree.

Jamiat-i-Islami. The Islamic Society. Ethnic Tadjiks, Turkmen and Uzbeks, and a smaller number of Pushtuns. Goal: the establishment of a fundamentalist Islamic state in Afghanistan. Hezb-e-Islami-Hekmatyr. The Islamic Party, Hekmatyr faction. Tadjiks and Pushtuns only, but same goal. Hezb-e-Islami-Khalis, also the Islamic Party, but the Khalis faction, split from the first one on the grounds it wasn't fundamentalist enough. Mahaz-e-Melli Islami: the National Islamic Front of Afghanistan. Ettihad-i-Islami: the Islamic Union for the Liberation of Afghanistan, dedicated naturally to achieving the reverse. Harakat-e-Inqilab-Islami: the Islamic Revolutionary movement, a similarly reactionary body founded eleven years ago in Pakistan. Jebh-e-Nejat-i-Melli Afghanistan: the Afghan National Liberation Front, also founded and resident in Pakistan. And you thought you were fighting the Americans.

Instead, you're going to be up against a ragbag jumble of squabbling blackarses whose only common aim is to take their country back into the stone age. Who conscript ten year olds to fire rockets and lay mines. Who gouge eyes and slit tongues. Who cut off the penises of your dead comrades and stuff them in their mouths. Whose favoured method of summary execution is to cut around a prisoner's belly, roll his skin up to his head and tie it in a bow. To which practices we are enjoined to be 'culturally sensitive'. While the Americans sit back in Washington and write the cheques.

He makes to go, turns back.

They refused to come to Moscow for our Olympics but expect us to trot over to Los Angeles for theirs.

He makes to go, turns back.

So what does your motherland require of you? She wants to see you standing up as an example to this benighted country. She doesn't want you smoking dope or shooting up or drinking antifreeze. She doesn't want you trading army property for candy, drugs or moonshine. She wants to see you in your standard uniform, not flaunting trophy kit or sneakers. She wants you standing proudly in the turret of your IFV, holding up your Kalashnikov, the best combat rifle in the world!

Praise to the unshakable friendship of the Afghan and Soviet People! Praise to the wisdom, diligence and unbending will of the Communist Party and its general secretary Comrade KU Chernenko!

He sits. The COMMANDER stands.

COMMANDER: I think the point the Major makes is this.

He counts the rows in the auditorium. Just over half.

One, two, three, four, five, six, seven, eight, nine, ten, eleven, twelve, thirteen, fourteen, fifteen, sixteen.

That's the ones of you who'll be incapacitated during your course of duty. That's right. Over half. What, over half of you will be wounded rendering assistance to the Afghan people? No, not quite.

Pause.

Viral Hepititis. Shigellosis, amebiosis, paratyphus, cholera and dysentery. All of them nasty, some of them deadly. But the good news is, they're all avoidable. So long as you take responsibility for yourself and those around you.

He looks up and down the rows.

Basic hygiene. No, you're not at the Hotel Ukraine. You won't be showering every day. But that's all the more reason to pay attention to these basic hints and tips.

Don't buy fresh fruit or vegetables.

Don't buy anything from native stalls or stores. Not every Afghan retailer is as committed to the defence of Afghan/Soviet friendship as you are.

MAJOR: (*To himself.*) Hm.

COMMANDER: Though of course that's not to say…

Slight pause.

And finally, don't drink from wells. In fact, don't drink from anything. Until you've added one of these.

He holds up a pill.

This is the most important thing you carry and it doesn't weigh anything at all. I personally couldn't care less if your sleeping bag is standard issue or courtesy of a dead mujahadeen. But whatever you do, don't leave these at base. You put this in the water.

He goes out. The MAJOR stands.

MAJOR: Or put another way: trust no-one. Western propaganda drips with vituperative slanders about Soviet brutality and rape. Our answer: to survive the desert and the mountain, we must become the wolves that we are fighting. Thus will our mission overcome all obstacles, and continue on the glorious path to victory.

He goes out. Change projection to pictures of happy Afghans involved in socialist construction projects with their Soviet allies.

SCENE FOUR

Enter a 2ND REPRESENTATIVE of the Afghan Government, with the INTERPRETER from the first scene. She is significantly younger.

2ND REPRESENTATIVE: My friends. You have just crossed the Amu Darya river to my country, the Democratic Republic of Afghanistan. You do so on a glorious mission.

INTERPRETER: You've crossed into Afghanistan to complete a noble task.

2ND REPRESENTATIVE: I am here to tell you a little bit about it.

INTERPRETER: I am here to brief you.

2ND REPRESENTATIVE: May I ask how many of you are Uzbeks, Tadjiks or Turkmen?

INTERPRETER: How many of you come from the Central Asian Republics?

Lots.

2ND REPRESENTATIVE: For you, then, Afghanistan won't be a surprise. For those from other parts, it may seems strange and maybe at first a little threatening.

INTERPRETER: For you, it will be familiar. For others it may be more of a challenge.

2ND REPRESENTATIVE: But you will come to terms with the climate and I hope you will come to love the people.

INTERPRETER: But you'll get used to it.

2ND REPRESENTATIVE: Afghans are hardy, spirited and have strong opinions. They have fervent religious views and it is important to respect that.

INTERPRETER: It is important to respect the Afghans' opinions and beliefs.

2ND REPRESENTATIVE: It is important to do nothing that might seem to defame a religious building.

INTERPRETER: You must show deference to the country's ancient culture.

2ND REPRESENTATIVE: You must respect the modesty of Afghan women.

INTERPRETER: You must respect the dignity of Afghan women.

2ND REPRESENTATIVE: Among the Afghans, hospitality is valued very highly.

INTERPRETER: We are very friendly people.

2ND REPRESENTATIVE: But I have a word of warning.

INTERPRETER: However, I have some sound advice.

2ND REPRESENTATIVE: The Afghan people are not hospitable to everyone.

Slight pause.

INTERPRETER: Even the friendly Afghans can display negative characteristics.

2ND REPRESENTATIVE: There is a harsh tradition of vendetta in the tribal lands.

INTERPRETER: There are backward elements among the peasantry.

2ND REPRESENTATIVE: As the saying goes, 'have you an enemy?' 'Of course, I have a cousin'.

INTERPRETER: He repeats a comic Afghan proverb.

2ND REPRESENTATIVE: But just as frequently, this thirst for bloody vengeance is directed at outsiders.

Pause.

INTERPRETER: On occasions…

2ND REPRESENTATIVE: The Afghan people have never accepted occupation by foreigners with guns. Historically, they have responded to all such attempts with extraordinary determination and brutality. As I believe was the opinion of the current General Secretary of the Communist Party, Comrade YV Andropov, when he was head of your KGB.

INTERPRETER: Um, he is saying that the counter / –revolutionary forces are…

2ND REPRESENTATIVE: Despite your efforts, it is likely that their will to fight will outlast yours.

Slight pause. The INTERPRETER has given up.

For all that you might protect yourselves behind the thickened glass of your combat vehicles, for all that you rely on shells and bombs and fire from the sky, for all that you might seek to strip the countryside, in order to destroy their will and means to fight…

INTERPRETER: (*Not knowing what to say.*) I, uh…

2ND REPRESENTATIVE: … I fear that for every rebel that you starve or maim, for every wife or sister who you kill or rape, you will create ten more. Are you all right?

INTERPRETER: I'm sorry, I… My sister…

Slight pause.

Uh, some soldiers in a village…

2ND REPRESENTATIVE: Yes, I know.

Shifting to accented 'Russian':

But naturally, all this is academic. Your mission is to plant trees, dig wells and build schools.

He goes out. The INTERPRETER doesn't know what to do, so sits. The projection changes into a map of the Soviet Union and its southern neighbours, huge and red.

SCENE FIVE

Enter a 2nd political DEPUTY, in this case a Lieutenant, and two more Afghan women: NAHID, MEENA. Enter the same COMMANDER. The INTERPRETER and the COMMANDER are six years younger than they were in the first scene. The COMMANDER is now a Captain, heading a company.

COMMANDER: Comrades, I have great news for you. You have the great honour of joining our heroic troops in the Limited Contingent of Soviet Armed Forces, rendering fraternal assistance to the friendly Afghan people and protecting the progressive gains of the Great April Afghan Revolution. Comrade Lieutenant.

He sits. The 2ND DEPUTY stands.

2ND DEPUTY: Comrades, Afghanistan. A country of rich contrasts, in which breathtaking mountain peaks rise majestically over mighty desert plains. The timeless traditions of village life vie for allegiance with thrusting, modern towns and cities, where developments in transport and communications rapidly accelerate. Although the majority of the population still live off the land, a young and energetic working class produces steel and electricity in thriving factories and plants. There is a rich and vibrant mixture of nationalities, speaking a wide diversity of tongues.

The country has a great tradition of resistance to imperialist aggression. Winning independence from the colonialists in 1919, Afghanistan was first recognised by the world's first workers' state, the Union of Soviet Socialist Republics. Following the Great April Revolution of 1978, steady progresss has been towards the achievement of a secular socialist society. True, there was a point at which that progress was threatened. Serious violations of socialist legality occured, which undermined the commitment of the masses to the revolutionary road. However, with the wise advice of the General Secretary of the Communist Party of the USSR, Comrade LI Brezhnev, these distortions were corrected. Certain unprincipled figures were removed from power, and the People's Democratic Party of Afghanistan resumed its forward march.

The COMMANDER stands. The 2ND DEPUTY sits.

COMMANDER: In summary: although, for many of you, Afghanistan is a geographic neighbour, you are being sent into what may seem at first to be a strange and even backward country. You do so in a noble cause. You have come not as an invader or an occupier, but to render international aid to that friendly neighbour, and to prevent possible hostile actions by the governments of other nearby countries of less benign intent. Always remember: You have been invited here.

So what are we fighting *for*? Please welcome our dear guests.

The 2ND DEPUTY nods to NAHID, who stands and reads from notes:

NAHID: My name is Nahid. I live in Helmand province. My family is very poor. Under the old system our farm was mortgaged and we had to give three quarters of our product to the landlord. Now our mortgage is cancelled and thanks to our government we will soon own our land outright.

COMMANDER: No wonder that the rich landlords are leading terroristic bands against the government.

The 2ND DEPUTY gestures NAHID to sit, and gestures MEENA to stand.

MEENA: (*Reads from notes.*) My name is Meena. I live in the Panjshir Valley. My mother was made to wear the burka. She married… She was married forcibly against her will, as part of a settlement between two tribes. Now our government has banned this…

She doesn't understand a word. The INTERPRETER checks it and prompts:

INTERPRETER: (*Checks and prompts.*) Inimical.

MEENA: In-imical feudal practice. Beg pardon, practices. And I may wear the clothes I like and marry who I want.

COMMANDER: No wonder reactionary tribesmen resist new legislation for equal rights. No wonder they attack schools and colleges and the women who learn and teach there.

The 2ND DEPUTY gestures MEENA to sit. The INTERPRETER stands. She has notes but speaks more confidently, increasingly off the cuff.

INTERPRETER: My name is Ramar. I live in Kabul. I see the women of our courageous Soviet ally, working alongside men as doctors, teachers, engineers and even helicopter pilots. To see this has inspired me to train too as a teacher. I work in a elementary school which was built by Soviet volunteers. I live now in a fine flat with my sister who's a doctor. We enjoy the many cultural achievements of our government and look forward to the completion of the Kabul tramline. My goal is to improve my Russian and contribute thereby to the friendship of our two great peoples. My sister hopes one day she will go to the countryside to promote the goals of health and literacy, to free young women in the villages from ignorance and bondage.

COMMANDER: Thank you.

The INTERPRETER sits.

So.

If anyone asks you why you're here, then tell them of these brave young women and their lives.

Slight pause.

And if they ask again, ask them a question. If our mission falters, what will be the consequence? What happens if we fail?

A moment.

All hail to the fifth company of the 148th Motorized Rifle Regiment! All hail to the heroic fourtieth army, and the Union of Soviet Socialist Republics!

He marches briskly out. The 2ND DEPUTY follows. The three WOMEN take a little longer.
End of play

WOOD FOR THE FIRE

by Lee Blessing

First production

The Tricycle Theatre, London, July 2010

Characters / Cast

(In order of appearance)

OWENS CIA Station Chief, Islamabad	Rick Warden
GENERAL AKHTAR Director, Pakistani Inter-Services Intelligence	Vincent Ebrahim
KAREN Deputy Station Chief	Cloudia Swann
ABDUL Afghan Commander	Danny Rahim

Director	Rachel Grunwald
Designer	Pamela Howard
Lighting	James Farncombe
Sound	Tom Lishman

Time and setting

Scene 1: ISI Headquarters, Rawalpindi, 1981

Scene 2: CIA Station Offices, Islamabad, 1982

Scene 3: A little way outside Peshawar, 1983

Scene 4: ISI Headquarters, Rawalpindi, 1985

Scene 5: A little way outside Peshawar, 1986

(1981. Inter-Services Intelligence Headquarters, Rawalpindi, Pakistan. GENERAL AKHTAR, Director of the ISI, and OWENS, CIA Station Chief for Islamabad, have tea in a garden. SOUNDS of lawn sprinklers in the distance.)

OWENS: I love your army bases. They're so clean. People mowing the lawns, washing the sidewalks, fresh paint everywhere . . . You should do this with the rest of Pakistan.

GENERAL AKHTAR: *(With a gentle laugh.)* We are trying. But we must be realistic. Our country is crowded, dusty; we have far to go. Here at Inter-Services Intelligence however, it's easier to make progress.

OWENS: Why is that?

GENERAL AKHTAR: Because our goal is always before us. Our bright, shining model.

OWENS: Your model?

GENERAL AKHTAR: You. The CIA. General Zia created us in your image. We in the ISI are trying to be like you—in a small way, of course.

OWENS: We're complimented.

GENERAL AKHTAR: You should be. The CIA is wonderful. The "antennae", so to speak, of American foreign policy. Without you, America would stumble in the dark.

OWENS: You think so?

GENERAL AKHTAR: Every nation needs antennae. You especially, of course, in the Cold War. But Pakistan as well. Around us is danger everywhere: On one side, the Soviet army in Afghanistan. On the other side, India—

OWENS: General Akhtar, this is all very edifying.

GENERAL AKHTAR: Thank you.

OWENS: But I came here today for a purpose. I need to see the camps up by the Afghan border where the mujahedin fighters are training.

GENERAL AKHTAR: Really?

OWENS: Really. I need to meet the commanders, shake their hands—that sort of thing.

GENERAL AKHTAR: I'm sure in due time—

OWENS: No, no. No more time. I've waited long enough. We're sending a lot of money and equipment to these people, and I haven't met them yet. That's got to change.

GENERAL AKHTAR: You should have called about this.

OWENS: I have called—for weeks. No one gives me a straight answer.

GENERAL AKHTAR: And so you have come to see me?

OWENS: Yes. Can we please get this ironed out?

GENERAL AKHTAR: You must understand, it is a very complex question.

OWENS: What's complex? I go up to the border, I look around, say hello to the fighters and come back.

GENERAL AKHTAR: The border area is very dangerous. The Soviets have operatives near there. If they were to kidnap you—

OWENS: I'm sure you can protect me.

GENERAL AKHTAR: A CIA station chief in a Soviet jail in Kabul—it would be disastrous!

OWENS: That isn't going to happen.

GENERAL AKHTAR: General Zia would need to authorize such a visit.

OWENS: You're kidding. You need the leader of your nation to approve a day trip?

GENERAL AKHTAR: General Zia and I go back a very long time.

OWENS: I'm sure you do.

GENERAL AKHTAR: He is my superior officer. Out of loyalty alone, I would consult him.

OWENS: Loyalty is a beautiful thing.

GENERAL AKHTAR: You know, some say I'm too loyal. Someone right here in Inter-Services Intelligence once suggested that if Zia said it will rain frogs, I'd be the first one outside with my frog net.

(OWENS gives an involuntary laugh.)

OWENS: Sorry. Hadn't heard that one.

GENERAL AKHTAR: It's because I'm loyal that Zia made me head of the ISI. We see things the same way.

OWENS: This is wonderful, but—

GENERAL AKHTAR: And we both want the same thing: a nation that is safe and secure on all sides.

Take India, for example.

OWENS: I'm really not here to–

GENERAL AKHTAR: Take India.

OWENS: All right.

GENERAL AKHTAR: We face an eternal threat from them.

OWENS: That's rather pessimistic.

GENERAL AKHTAR: It's realistic. We need new thoughts from you on India.

OWENS: I have no new thoughts on the subject of India.

GENERAL AKHTAR: What about the recent atrocities in Kashmir?

OWENS: Those were months ago, and they're disputed. General, we've been through all that.

GENERAL AKHTAR

We think you are far too cooperative with New Delhi.

OWENS: Of course you do. But India is our ally.

GENERAL AKHTAR: So are we. It makes no sense; you try to be a friend to both of us. But we are like a divorced couple–fighting over the children, throwing knives in the kitchen. All you ever say is, "Let's sit down to tea".

OWENS: If we could sit down–

GENERAL AKHTAR: You refuse to criticize the Indians. But they criticize you all the time. They say the most appalling things behind your back.

OWENS: I don't care! I–!

(Suddenly stopping himself, with a wry smile..)

We're talking about India.

GENERAL AKHTAR: Yes. It's addictive, isn't it? More tea?

OWENS: Thanks.

(As GENERAL AKHTAR pours.)

So. When can I get up there?

GENERAL AKHTAR: To Kashmir?

OWENS: The Afghan border.

GENERAL AKHTAR: Ah. You want to be in the middle of things.

OWENS: Yes, I do.

GENERAL AKHTAR: To "get your hands dirty".

OWENS: If possible, and without leaving fingerprints.

GENERAL AKHTAR: A clandestine operation.

OWENS: Exactly.

GENERAL AKHTAR: Like your work in Viet Nam.

OWENS: Pardon?

GENERAL AKHTAR: You were always in the field there. Your hands were very dirty. The stories have been wonderful, by the way.

OWENS: Thanks. We're off the subject.

GENERAL AKHTAR: You went many places–Laos, Cambodia. Secret missions. You at the forefront.

OWENS: Yes. So?

GENERAL AKHTAR: And did you win?

OWENS: There are many reasons for going into the field. It's not just about victory.

GENERAL AKHTAR: General Zia wishes to point out, with all due respect, that times have changed. Pakistan is not Viet Nam. There, the whole country was a battlefield. Here, things are different. We have a government.

(Gesturing at their surroundings.)

We have lawns, we have sidewalks. We have no civil war. We are in charge.

OWENS: No one disagrees–

GENERAL AKHTAR: And if we are to help you supply the mujahedin–

OWENS: "If"? I thought we were well past "if".

GENERAL AKHTAR: Then we must make the decisions.

OWENS: *(After a beat.)* General Akhtar, we both know what my mission is here. Killing Soviets. Tying down their troops, rubbing their noses in it, giving them–

GENERAL AKHTAR: Their own Viet Nam?

OWENS: In a word. But we can't do that if you won't work with us.

GENERAL AKHTAR: Perfectly reasonable. And how does that help us?

OWENS: Pardon?

GENERAL AKHTAR: You are in Rawalpindi, not Kabul. You ask us to help. But how will you help us?

OWENS: All sorts of ways. As Cold War allies—

GENERAL AKHTAR: No, no, no. How will you help us with India?

OWENS: There, we have to stay neutral.

GENERAL AKHTAR: You see the problem.

OWENS: What problem? India doesn't apply to this.

GENERAL AKHTAR: Mr. Owens—here, India applies to everything. How many nuclear devices do they have now? How many American fighter jets? I'm sure you're keeping track at Langley. And like Afghanistan, India is our neighbor forever. You will be here for awhile, the Russians will be here for awhile—perhaps a long while—but not forever. You see what I mean?

OWENS: You're saying that someday you'll need … how can I put it? … your kind of Afghanistan.

GENERAL AKHTAR: Precisely.

OWEN: So what does that mean, bottom line?

GENERAL AKHTAR: General Zia will help you supply the Afghan fighters, but only if you agree to a few of his personal requests.

OWENS: Requests?

GENERAL AKHTAR: Which are non-negotiable.

OWENS: Such as?

GENERAL AKHTAR: No American, CIA or other, crosses into Afghanistan. All payments, all shipments of weapons, come to us. Everything comes to us and through us. We receive it, we distribute.

OWENS: Some of our weapons are pretty sophisticated. We'll need to train people.

GENERAL AKHTAR: You can train our people. We train the mujahedin. General Zia respectfully requests that the CIA confine itself to being a conduit only.

OWENS: A conduit? He wants me sitting in Islamabad, writing checks and shipping mules and mortars and whatever else to … to you?

GENERAL AKHTAR: If you would be so kind.

OWENS: And you'll take it all, and–

GENERAL AKHTAR: See it gets into the right hands, yes. The best fighters. Strongest, most dedicated.

OWENS: People I don't know. People I've never met. A lot of money's changing hands here, General Akhtar. We need to know where it's going.

GENERAL AKHTAR: We shall make regular reports.

OWENS: Which I can verify how?

GENERAL AKHTAR: We will verify everything. Please understand, this is a delicate situation. As General Zia says, "the water in Afghanistan must boil at the right temperature." We at ISI know best what the temperature should be.

OWENS: Does Zia see the fire ever getting hotter? I mean, we are supposedly committed to a free and democratic Afghanistan at some point, are we not?

GENERAL AKHTAR: At some point. Exactly. Very nicely put. But at the moment, there is only enough money to purchase a constant state of rebellion there, nothing more. No victory–for now, at least. Simply another Viet Nam.

OWENS: So those are the conditions? I mean, the requests?

GENERAL AKHTAR: Yes.

OWENS: No.

GENERAL AKHTAR: Pardon me?

OWENS: These people are allies–just as much as you are. They're giving up their lives. I have to meet them; I have to shake their hands. I'm going whether you take me or not.

GENERAL AKHTAR: But–

OWENS: I have to be able to do my job, General.

GENERAL AKHTAR: General Zia would be very angry.

OWENS: I don't care.

GENERAL AKHTAR: Even if he agreed, you would have to go at night–for security. It would be dark; you wouldn't see Afghanistan.

OWENS: I would see the fighters, which is more than I'm seeing now.

GENERAL AKHTAR: I will talk with him. If he agrees–if–then we will set the time.

OWENS: Set it soon. If you don't, I will go on my own.

(Lifting his cup, toasting.)

To allies?

GENERAL AKHTAR: *(Reluctantly joining him in the toast.)* To allies.

(They sip their tea. Distant sound of an electric hedge-clipper. Lights shift to follow OWENS, who moves to the CIA Station offices in Islamabad. With him in the office is KAREN, the DEPUTY CHIEF.)

OWENS: Of course I'm angry! You think I shouldn't be angry?

KAREN: Well ...

OWENS: They blindfolded me! Drove me around for hours, in the middle of the night!

KAREN: Chief, it was a month ago.

OWENS: And that makes it better?! That I didn't find out 'til now? You don't take a CIA station chief and ... hoodwink him like that! They created a whole camp! Trotted out mujahedin fighters for me to meet. I watched them fire off a few rounds with those crappy rifles we're supplying.

KAREN: Which ones?

OWENS: The usual. Enfields, vintage crap. Single-shot, World War Two. Plus some AK-47's. That wasn't quite as embarrassing. Oh, and the grand finale: a couple rounds with an antiaircraft gun. They were so grateful, so friendly. We shook hands; I had tears in my eyes. General Akhtar had his arm around my shoulder. All the time I was being treated like a big, fucking stooge!

KAREN: How did you find out it was a phony camp?

OWENS: One of our contacts. Someone even the Paks don't know about. I can't believe it. I thought I had a relationship with Akhtar. He drove me in circles for half the night. When we stopped, we were less than twenty miles from town.

KAREN: What did it look like?

OWENS: It was night! It looked like nothing! Bunch of tents in the middle of … it could have been anywhere. But of course, they told me it was the border.

KAREN: You did meet some fighters.

OWENS: Fighters, not leaders. Who knows if they even knew what was going on? They spoke no English; everything was translated by the Paks. I thought they were muj commanders! I've never been lied to like this in my life.

KAREN: Well. That's … terrible behavior. I'm sorry you went through that.

OWENS: Thank you.

KAREN: What are you going to do?

OWENS: I'll tell you what I'm going to do. I'm going up there anyway. On my own.

KAREN: Really?

OWENS: Yes, really. Screw them. We're the CIA, damn it. You don't do this sort of thing. You just don't!

KAREN: I can understand why you're upset. But how will going up there on your own improve things?

OWENS: *(Looking at her with amazement.)* Are you kidding? Is that a serious question?

KAREN: I thought it was.

OWENS: I don't get this, Karen. You're supposed to be my Deputy. I could use a little support here.

KAREN: I support you. I just don't see—

OWENS: Can you honestly tell me you like working this way? Sitting in an office? Analyzing data? Looking at satellite photos we could be looking at in Washington, for God's—

KAREN: All that may be true. But. But.

OWENS: But what?

KAREN: Isn't that what we're supposed to be doing?

OWENS: We are giving huge amounts of money to people who won't even let us see where it goes.

KAREN: So what?

OWENS: What do you mean, "so what"?!

KAREN: If Langley has no problem–

OWENS: Langley's not here. Langley's bending over for a dictator who calls himself an ally.

KAREN: General Zia is an ally.

OWENS: Zia allowed his own Islamic extremists to burn down our embassy with our staff still in it! Not great ally behavior.

KAREN: That was years ago.

OWENS: Two years.

KAREN: I wish you could see the bright side of things.

OWENS: And what, pray tell, is that?

KAREN: The photos. Satellite photos are showing tons of destruction. Soviet tanks, troops.

It's costing the Russians a lot more in men and material than we're contributing.

OWENS: So it's cost effective?

KAREN: Apparently.

OWENS: And that makes you happy?

KAREN: It makes Langley happy, and that makes me happy.

OWENS: It doesn't bother you that we're asking people to die to further our goals– people we've never even tried to meet?

KAREN: They have their goals too. They're not just fighting for us.

OWENS: I know you're young.

KAREN: Not that young.

OWENS: I know you haven't been in a war before.

KAREN: We're not in a war now. They are.

OWENS: But when you form an alliance, you support it with a thing we like to call human contact.

KAREN: I don't know how you used to do things–

OWENS: Back in the Boer War, you mean?

KAREN: In Viet Nam.

OWENS: Oh, way back.

KAREN: But I was trained to find out what's required in a certain situation and then do it, whatever it is. In the case of this operation, it's funneling.

OWENS: Funneling?

KAREN: Funneling. Money comes from Congress, we turn it into weapons and supplies, we hand it to the Pakistanis: good things happen in Afghanistan. Funneling. There's really nothing more to it than that.

OWENS: You honestly think so?

KAREN: Headquarters thinks so. We should, too. They're not telling us to take any field trips to the border. I really think you should reconsider.

OWENS: You do, eh?

KAREN: I would reconsider.

OWENS: No matter how much you'd been humiliated?

KAREN: You shouldn't think of it as humiliation. Think of it more as a mid-career, I don't know ... correction.

OWENS: Correction?

KAREN: Adjustment. That's a nicer word. We do things new ways; everyone has to adjust.

And what a great time to make an adjustment. Has there ever been a better moment in the Cold War? I mean, here we are, buying antique guns from Turkey, from communist China for God's sake, to give to the mujahedin.

OWENS: To give to Pakistan to give to the mujahedin.

KAREN: To kill Russians. Russians are dying like crazy, without a single American soldier in harm's way. It's a dream situation.

OWENS: It is, eh?

KAREN: Seems that way to me.

OWENS: Then why am I not having more fun?

KAREN: I don't know. Maybe we should talk about that. Do you feel you owe the Afghans something? 'Cause I'm not sure they feel that way about you.

OWENS: I don't even know them! There's a whole spectrum of fighters out there, from old-line royalists to out-and-out Muslim radicals, and right now we have no ties to any of them. We're not building any bonds. We're not building trust.

KAREN: Isn't that cleaner?

OWENS: What are you talking about?

KAREN: We're involved in Afghanistan right now, but a few years ago it was Viet Nam. Tomorrow it'll be somewhere else. Our job is opposing the Soviets, wherever they go. We can't worry about what happens to the little nations we fight in along the way, and we can't worry about tomorrow's battles today. With any luck, we won't even be here for tomorrow's battles.

OWENS: I wish I liked you better, Karen.

KAREN: I do, too. There'd be more hope for you.

(A beat.)

So, are you going to screw this up? I have the feeling you're going to screw this up.

OWENS: I refuse to manage a war that I can't touch.

KAREN: So you're going up there?

OWENS: I'm going up there, and you're going to cover for me.

KAREN: It's not my job to blow the whistle. But you're making a mistake.

OWENS: Think whatever you like, but do not cross me. Or you will be headed out of here faster than you can say–

KAREN: Viet Nam?

OWENS: You're a hell of a Deputy, you know that?

KAREN: Thank you, sir. Put it in your next report.

(OWENS stares at her as lights dim. As OWENS and KAREN exit, SOUND of a motorcycle approaching in the distance. It grows louder until suddenly, very close, it shuts off. OWENS reenters, now in a nondescript overcoat and shivering with the cold. Lights barely rise. Night. From time to time, SOUND of dogs barking far in the distance.)

OWENS: *(To someone behind him, yet unseen.)* I'm sorry I have to stop, but it's cold on that back of that bike. I mean, really, really cold!

(ABDUL, a mujahedin commander, enters. He's not in traditional dress however. Instead, he wears the helmet and pressure suit of a Soviet fighter pilot. He pulls off his helmet, revealing a heavy beard, and smiles.)

ABDUL: We're almost there.

OWENS: *(Jumping up and down, swinging his arms to warm up.)* I don't care. We can start again in a minute.

ABDUL: Peshawar is dangerous. Especially at night.

OWENS: Tell me about it. I almost shit myself when I saw you.

(As ABDUL laughs.)

It's not funny. Thought I was being kidnapped by the KGB.

ABDUL: It's a perfectly good flight suit. The Soviet pilot didn't need it anymore. When war brings gifts, I must accept.

OWENS: Fine. But I drove a hundred miles from Islamabad to meet a mujahedin commander, not some sort of … Afghan from space. Never do that to me again.

ABDUL: *(Laughing, then looking around.)* Let's go. The house isn't far.

OWENS: Not yet. Not 'til I can feel my feet.

(OWENS moves in circles, stamping his feet.)

ABDUL: There will be something warm to eat. Not like the border. Not like where we fight. No fires at night up there. Everything we eat is cold. Sometimes we don't eat for days.

OWENS: Why not?

ABDUL: The Russians attack the roads. They bomb them shut—no supplies.

OWENS: I realize it's hard for you right now—

ABDUL: Hard? What do you know about it?

OWENS: I want to know more. Much more.

ABDUL: You want to know about the villages they blow up? The massacres? They try to find us, shoot us—sometimes they kill our families instead. If you are Afghan, they will kill you. They don't care.

OWENS: I understand.

ABDUL: Do you?

OWENS: I'm here, aren't I? Freezing. I want to see it, Abdul. I want to go up there myself, into Afghanistan. Is that possible? Would you take me?

ABDUL: Dressed like us, you mean?

OWENS: Yes.

ABDUL: So they will shoot at you, too.

OWENS: Maybe.

ABDUL: We can arrange it. It's safer at night.

OWENS: I'd like to stay a couple days. We couldn't tell your men who I am, though. That has to be secret.

ABDUL: What can I tell them?

OWENS: I don't know. You could say I'm a reporter. Canadian. Something like that.

ABDUL: *(With the trace of a smile.)* We'll see. What gifts have you brought me?

OWENS: Pardon? I don't understand.

ABDUL: What gifts? I don't see any guns. Do you have money?

OWENS: Not now.

ABDUL: No guns, no money? You want me to take you to Afghanistan, but you bring me nothing? Why should I trust you?

OWENS: I will bring money. And guns. This is a getting-to-know-you meeting. If we like each other, if we can do business, then I'll bring gifts. Next time. Plenty, believe me.

ABDUL: When?

OWENS: Soon.

ABDUL: You risk our lives to maybe bring something … soon?

OWENS: What's wrong with that?

ABDUL: *(Shaking his head, turning to leave.)* I'll take you back.

OWENS: What are you talking about?

ABDUL: You're worse than the ISI. At least they give us something.

OWENS: They do? How much? What do they give you?

ABDUL: Not enough. Rifles from another lifetime. A trickle of cash.

(His resentment building.)

I fought the Russians as soon as they invaded. I fought them in Kabul. The Pakistanis know how hard we fight. But do they give us as much as they give the others? No. For us, almost nothing.

OWENS: Why?

ABDUL: We're not religious enough. We don't insult America the minute your back is turned. The ISI choose who they help. They help Hekmatyar.

OWENS: He's a good fighter.

ABDUL: So are we. Hekmatyar will do what they want. That's all ISI cares about. When the war is over, he will do what they want.

OWENS: Whatever the Pakistani agenda may be, the problem right now is the Soviets, right?

ABDUL: You come here, you are just like them. You want everything from us. You bring nothing in return.

OWENS: That's what I want to talk about. We all have to work with the Pakistanis, that's … reality. But maybe you and I can work together, too. Just us, I mean.

ABDUL: Just us?

OWENS: A deal on the side. No middle men. See what we can get accomplished, yes? That's why I want to go up there. I want to see what you need.

ABDUL: *(Taking a longer look at him.)* Do you think we can win?

OWENS: What do you mean?

ABDUL: Do you think we can defeat them?

OWENS: The Russians? Well … ultimate outcomes are hard to predict. The Soviets have a huge investment.

ABDUL: So did the pilot who wore this suit. I ask you again: do you think we can win?

OWENS: I … I don't know.

ABDUL: *(Turning to leave.)* We're going back.

OWENS: Wait. Wait a minute! Listen to me. What I'm trying to say is, it's possible. But you have to be realistic. You're fighting one of the most powerful land armies in the–

ABDUL: We can win or we can't. Which is it?

OWENS: *(After a beat.)* You can win. I believe that. If I didn't … I wouldn't be up here.

ABDUL: Give us better guns.

OWENS: Like what? What do you mean?

ABDUL: Anti-tank guns.

OWENS: RPGs?

ABDUL: RPGs, heavy machine guns, all of it. C-4.

OWENS: Plastic explosives? We can do that.

ABDUL: Delay detonators.

OWENS: For time bombs? Yes. Yes, we can get those.

ABDUL: All better, too. More—much, much more. And better. Stingers.

OWENS: What?

ABDUL: Stinger missiles.

OWENS: Stingers?

ABDUL: To shoot down their helicopters.

OWENS: We don't give anyone stingers. That's … I'm sorry, that's off the table.

ABDUL: It's what we need.

OWENS: Maybe someday. Not now.

ABDUL: *(After a beat.)* Money, then. We need money for everything.

OWENS: For loyalty?

ABDUL: Loyalty is everything.

OWENS: I think I can do this. No, I mean … I will do it.

ABDUL: If you do, we will win.

OWENS: We need a couple things, too. Soviet weaponry, equipment. Anything you find on the battlefield—especially new stuff. We need to analyze it. Can you do that for us? Without involving the ISI?

(As ABDUL nods.)

Also, we need some eyes and ears on the black market, up on the border. I want to know if the rifles and ammo we've been supplying suddenly drop in price. If people are dumping those, then we've got a problem with the pipeline.

ABDUL: Very well.

(ABDUL offers his hand.)

OWENS: *(Shaking hands.)* I just want to say one thing. May I?

> *(As ABDUL nods.)*

I understand the difference between you and me.

ABDUL: And what is that?

OWENS: I know if you lose, I still have a home to go back to.

ABDUL: Yes.

OWENS: *(After a beat.)* Oh, and can I say one more thing?

> *(As ABDUL nods again.)*

I am fr-e-e-e-zing!!!

ABDUL: *(With a smile.)* Then why are we still here? There's tea where I'm staying.

OWENS: Is it warm?

> *(ABDUL laughs.)*

ABDUL: Warm enough. For now at least.

> *(The two exit as lights shift to ISI Headquarters in Rawalpindi once again. 1985. SOUND of sprinklers in the background. GENERAL AKHTAR and KAREN sit in the garden, going over requisition forms.)*

GENERAL AKHTAR: We'll have to finish early today. I have a meeting I can't shift.

KAREN: Most of these are the usual requests, right?

GENERAL AKHTAR: Oh, yes.

KAREN: *(Looking at GENERAL AKHTAR's form.)* Are those enough "E cell" detonators?

GENERAL AKHTAR: Can we get more?

KAREN: Absolutely. And more RPGs. Lots more of those.

GENERAL AKHTAR: Excellent?

KAREN: Also, electronic intercept equipment. We can give you that now.

GENERAL AKHTAR: You can?

KAREN: Yes, we can. The candy store is officially open.

> *(They both start writing things down.)*

GENERAL AKHTAR: Every year the money grows.

KAREN: This year it's doubling. Two hundred fifty million.

GENERAL AKHTAR: Amazing.

KAREN: Hard to know how to spend it all.

(Smiling.)

But we'll find a way, right?

GENERAL AKHTAR: *(Chuckling.)* Oh, yes. So much has changed. Yesterday General Zia yesterday shook his head and smiled. All this new momentum! He now believes the Afghans can win.

KAREN: So does a lot of Congress.

GENERAL AKHTAR: Time at last to throw more wood on the fire.

KAREN: Pardon?

GENERAL AKHTAR: It is something Mr. Owens used to say.

KAREN: Oh. Haven't thought of him in awhile.

GENERAL AKHTAR: I would ask for wood for the fire. He would say, "But whose fire? Who is boiling this water?" He would never simply trust me.

KAREN: *(Checking GENERAL AKHTAR's sheet.)* I will. You need more plastic explosives. Lots more.

GENERAL AKHTAR: This much?

KAREN: Yeah, go with that. Harder to make estimates now. A whole lot of folks are starting to feed the fire. Everyone and his brother's coming in.

GENERAL AKHTAR: The ISI and the CIA—working together. And real hope for victory! Who could have dreamed it?

KAREN: Russians on the run. Who could have dreamed that?

GENERAL AKHTAR: Indeed. Shall we continue? More wood for the fire?

KAREN: More wood for the fire.

GENERAL AKHTAR: More wood for the fire!

KAREN: *(Writing things down as she says them.)* Electronic detonators. Have you got those?

GENERAL AKHTAR: Wood for the fire!

KAREN: Sniper rifles?

GENERAL AKHTAR: Wood for the fire!

KAREN: Triple the number of mortars.

GENERAL AKHTAR: Wood for the fire!

KAREN: Triple everything.

GENERAL AKHTAR: Wood for the fire! Wood for the fire!

(Lights shift as GENERAL AKHTAR exits. KAREN remains at the table, which is now somewhere very different—Peshawar, 1986. ABDUL enters, now in more traditional dress for a mujahedin commander. KAREN, who doesn't rise, offers her hand to shake. ABDUL doesn't take it.)

KAREN: *(Smiling.)* Would you like some tea?

ABDUL: No, thank you.

KAREN: *(Shrugging.)* This is where you used to meet Mr. Owens, isn't it?

(As ABDUL nods.)

This city feels dangerous.

ABDUL: It is. Where is Mr. Owens?

KAREN: Different posting, different part of the world. He may even have gone home. I'm really not sure. Is there something you'd like me to tell him?

(As ABDUL shakes his head no.)

Well. Fine. I won't waste your time. Through the ISI we've been outfitting various mujahedin fighters—

ABDUL: Hekmatyar.

KAREN: Including Gulbuddin Hekmatyar, yes, with some new and better weapons.

ABDUL: Stingers.

KAREN: Yes, Stinger missiles, among other things. But not everyone has gotten them, and we hear this has caused a bit of friction among the … different fighting groups. I just want to assure you that it's not our purpose to starve you of weapons, and that we're doing our best to get the ISI to supply your faction as well.

ABDUL: That's all?

KAREN: That's all I have for now. Is there anything you'd like to share with me?

ABDUL: You will beg the ISI to give us weapons?

KAREN: It's not a matter of begging. We will request.

(A beat.)

We just don't want to see a lot of bad blood between the various factions. We realize there are many tribal, political, even religious differences–

ABDUL: Hekmatyar attacks us! He has killed my men.

KAREN: But we need you to bury those differences for now, as much as possible, and focus on the Russians. This is about the Russians, after all. This is … Please sit down. We really do need to talk this through.

ABDUL: *(Remaining standing.)* The Pakistanis lie to us–always. And you will beg from them? I am finished with them. And with you.

KAREN: Well … then … who, may I ask, would you have to turn to?

ABDUL: Hekmatyar.

KAREN: Excuse me?

ABDUL: If I make peace with him, I will have Stingers.

KAREN: You just said he killed–

ABDUL: He is Afghan! Who should I trust?

KAREN: If you'll just sit down–

ABDUL: No.

KAREN: You need to give us a chance.

ABDUL: I'm leaving. There's no one to trust here.

KAREN: *(Rising, calling after him as he exits.)* We're on your side! We're committed! There are more weapons every day! We'll find a way to get them to you! We'll–!

(But he's gone. She sighs, shakes her head, sits and stares. Finally she picks up her tea and sips. The SOUND of a muezzin calling the faithful to prayer builds from a very low level, rising and rising as lights slowly dim.)

THE END

MINISKIRTS OF KABUL

by David Greig

First production

The Tricycle Theatre, London, 18 April 2009

The following cast performed in the remount in July 2010 at the Tricycle Theatre prior to the USA tour:

Characters / Cast

| WRITER | Jemma Redgrave |
| NAJIBULLAH | Daniel Rabin |

Director	Indhu Rubasingham
Designer	Miriam Nabarro
Lighting	James Farncombe
Sound	Tom Lishman

Setting

The United Nations Compound, Kabul, 26 September 1996.

'Today even the scarf is being left at home and miniskirts, worn by pert schoolgirls, blossom on the streets of Kabul and on the Kabul University campus.'

Professor Louis Dupree – *A History of Afghanistan*, 1973.

He lifts weights.
In the distance, the sound of shelling.

She enters.
He stops

Don't mind me.

He continues to lift weights.
She watches.
He finishes.

Sit

No. Thank you.

Tea.

Thank you.

I'm sorry I have nothing stronger I can offer you.

That's fine.

I wasn't expecting a visitor today.

No.

Did you bring whisky?

Whisky?

Sometimes when people visit they bring whisky.

I'm sorry. If I'd thought. I didn't think. I didn't bring anything.

Sit

She sits.
He sits.

You look good.

Thank you.

Healthy.

I like to stay fit.

Do you run?

Running is not practical for me.

No.

I'm under house arrest.

Of course.

Besides, Kabul is not a good city for jogging.

More shells land in the distance.

Do you have a regime?

Weights, circuits – I have some equipment here in the house. The UN supplied me with some benches and so forth. I was a boxer. When I was the President I got fat. These last years I've got back into shape. I like to stay strong. You know what they call me?

I hear they call you Najib the Bull.

Najib the Ox.
I prefer Ox.

Why?

Because I am as strong as an ox.

It's strange to see you. I've seen videos of you, and photographs in newspapers. But being here with you. You're unexpected.

I'm more handsome in real life.

You are, as a matter of fact.

Are you from the UN?

No.

American?

I'm British.

Are you a diplomat?

No.

Normally I'm given details of any visits.

I didn't go through the official channels.

What channels did you go though?

This is not a normal visit.

I don't understand.

I'm imagining you.

It wasn't possible to arrange a meeting any other way.

Is it allowed?

It appears so.

I can't imagine the UN allowing people to just 'imagine' their way in to meet me.

You can.
I mean 'one' can.
One can imagine anything.

Can one imagine a bottle of whisky.

One can try.
She finds a bottle of whisky.
She gives it to him.

Johnny Walker – My favourite brand.

Is it?

You should know.

What do you want?

Only to talk.

We only have a short time. Is it all right if we begin?

As you wish.

Perhaps you could begin by describing where we are?

You know where we are.

Yes but pretend I don't know. Paint me a picture.

We are in the reception soom of the guest house in the United Nations compound. You can see all this with your own eyes.

I want to see it with your eyes.

It's a small guest house. The furniture is made of cane. The walls are white. It's perfectly acceptable accommodation. It's clean. I'm well looked after. In the yard there are trees. The sun is shining. There is a pool. There was a pool. The pool is empty now. I never used the pool anyway. There is a verandah.
Do you want me to say more.

If you want.

This is not my house. These are not my choices. I am a guest.

How long have you been here?

Four years.

Alone?

My brother is here. Sometimes I have official visitors. Diplomats. UN people. Not many. Nobody likes to acknowledge that I'm still here. I'm an embarrassment.

My life is very very boring I can assure you. I wake up. I exercise. I listen to the radio, I'm learning English so I listen to the BBC world service. I watch the satellite television channels from India. I'm translating a book so I work on that. I try to spend my time fruitfully.

Which book?

The Great Game by Peter Hopkirk.
Have you read it?

I'm sorry no.
What's it about?

It's a history of foreign involvement in Afghanistan in the nineteenth century. The British. The Russians. The wars. It's interesting. We Afghans always make the same mistake.

What mistake?

We always –

A massive explosion nearby.

Holy shit! Fuck! Jesus Christ.

He laughs.

Jesus.

What?

Nothing.

What's wrong.

You seem so calm.

The ground shook.

You've never been under fire before have you?

No.

Don't worry about the bombs you can hear. If you heard the bomb it hasn't killed you. The bombs to be afraid of are the ones you don't hear.

Who's firing the bombs?

The Taliban. Peasants. They're fighting to drive Massoud and his people out of Kabul.

They're getting closer.

It looks that way.

Does that scare you?

They're not interested in me. They want the city. The city is decadent and corrupt but me in particular – no. They won't hit the UN compound deliberately.

Deliberately.

I told you, they're peasants. Their aim is not great.

Do you think the city will fall to the Taliban?

Do you?

Do you?

Yes.
I think they will win.

Am I right?

Yes.

Imagine we had cake.

Just then, when the rocket fell, you laughed at me.

I apologise.

Did you find it funny?

A little bit.

Why?

You were afraid – you jumped.

Why was that funny.

It makes me laugh that's all. There's no meaning to it.

133

I'm just interested because –

I laughed because you made a funny face. Like when a person jumps out of their skin.

When a person jumps out of their skin.

There is no meaning to it.
None.

Look – why are you here? What do you want with me?

I want to find out about you.

Read a book.

I have read books but the books leave me with questions.

What sort of questions?

I want to understand you.

I am perfectly comprehensible.

Not to me.

You want everything to be easy? You want me to be like you?

No, it's more complicated than that.

My country has been imagined enough. My country is the creation of foreign imaginings. The border between Pakistan and Afghanistan is an imaginary line – Pakistan is a dreamed up country – Pakistan – which – by the way – is paying for those Taliban peasants to right now throw rockets at my city – Every blood conflict in the world today has its origins in the imagination of British surveyors. You come here imagining. You expect me to co-operate?

I'm sorry.

Imagining warriors and tribesmen, imagining oriental sultans, imagining veiled women. Imagining your way into my lives to… what? Own me?

I'm just saying that I have read all the books I could find and I have talked to people but I want to understand the world from your point of view. So that involves thinking about you. Mohammed Najibullah. Imagining what it was like to be you.

Was?

Is.
I meant 'is.'

A shell lands nearby.
Neither he nor she flinches.

You British – your empire goes on.
Up here.
In your head.

I think the British Empire was a bad thing.

Do you?

I do.

Not in your heart of hearts.

Now you're imagining me.

The sun's rising.
What time is it?

The clock has stopped.

Maybe that's why it's so quiet.

Where were you born?

Here. In Kabul. My father was a trader. We moved around from place to place. Kabul. Peshawar. Kandahar. I was very curious about the world. I read every book I could find. I listened to the radio. I read about engineers who made bridges, architects who built towers and dams. I heard about crops made to grow fatser by scientists. The Russians even sent a man into space. Everywhere I looked I saw a wonderful future. I wanted the future to come to Afghanistan.

That's a very optimistic view.

I am an optimist!
I am an optimist yes.

When did you become interested in politics?

In 1965 I joined the People's Democratic Party of Afghanistan I joined as soon as it was formed. I was there at the very beginning.

Did you like it?

What do you mean?

Did you like being a member of that political party?

Of course I liked it. I was a young man on the right side of
history and...there were girls in the party – modern girls who
talked and argued. We smoked and argued over coffee. We were
young. The world was ours to inherit. Of course I liked it.

You became an assistant to the party leader.

I did what I was asked.

You went to University to study medicine.

Yes.

Why did you choose medicine?

I wanted to become a doctor.

What attracted you to that career?

I wanted to save lives.

It took you ten years to graduate.

Yes.

Why did it take you so long?

I kept going to prison.

Why?

I was involved in too many political activities – writing articles
– agitating.

Did you get involved in fights?

Look – I'm not a tribal man. My father was a trader. I was born
in Kabul and here we don't have a gang behind us of cousins
you know and – I don't come from a family with land. If I
wanted the future I had to bring it into being myself. All of us –
we had to fight to defend the future – because the conservatives,
the mullahs – they wanted to keep Afghanistan in the past – So
yes – I got into fights.

Did you kill anybody?

Once.

Once?

I killed another student during an argument.

What were you arguing about?

I don't remember.

You killed him and you don't remember?

I don't remember what the argument was about.

With your bare hands?

Of course with my bare hands.

Why did you kill him?

To prove the point.

You never did become a doctor.

No.

Do you ever regret that?

How many lives can I save as a doctor? Tens, hundreds maybe because you cure some disease but people starve because they don't own land. They become sick because they're poor. Women die because they have no rights. I wanted to solve these problems.

Another explosion.
She flinches.
Even he is nervous now.

Fucking hell.

They're getting closer.

Are you sure they weren't aiming for the compound that time?

Certain.

You said their aim was bad.

I advise you to move your chair just a little away from the window.
That's better.

The sound of two jet fighters screaming over head.

Can you imagine a gun?

No.
Why?

I'm only curious.

The sound of bombs falling.

Were you an activist at university?

Everybody was an activist at university.

What do you mean?

Masood was at the university studying engineering. Hekmatyar was at the university. Rachid Dostum. Every communist leader, every Mujaheddin leader every warlord were all at Kabul university in 1973. There were only eight thousand students. Everybody knew everybody. Masood and the conservatives stood for tribe and custom and king, the modernists stood for development and change. And then there were the islamists, Hekmatyar and his party. Kabul University in 1973 was a powerful place. We all knew we had reached a crossroads in time. History could go one way or it could go another.

Surely history can only move in one direction.

Not in Afghanistan.
Afghanistan has a complicated relationship with time.

Were the Taliban at Kabul University?

No.

After university you were out of favour with the party for a while.

In the communist party you're nobody unless you've been out of favour for a while.

You're making a joke.

There were two factions. One faction believed the revolution must come now – immediately. The other that the revolution would come in time.

What did you believe?

That it would come in time.

Then the Russians came.

The country was in trouble.

The party was in trouble and so the Russians invaded.

The Russians didn't invade.

The Russians arrived.

They were invited.
They were invited by a sovereign democratic government.
To help maintain security against an insurgent group of islamist militias.

I read that the Russians said you were very efficient as head of the secret service. That's why the Russians supported you to be President.

I did the job well.

Did you torture people?

Yes.

But you're a doctor.

Surgery sometimes involves cutting.

Cutting people?

Cutting out cancers. Allowing the body to heal.

You sound proud of your work.

My work revealed me to be efficient. This was useful for me.

Why?

I wanted power.

You wanted power? Even then?

Of course.
You're very squeamish about power.
You British.
You want education
You want women to work.
You want modernisation.
You want roads.
To achieve these things you need power.
Power is good.

And you employed violence to gain and hold on to power.

Yes.

I'm curious about the specific ways you did that.

I made people afraid and I killed people.

How many people did you kill?

Me personally?

Yes.

With my own hands or by my order?

With your own hands.

Not many. A few.

A few.

I don't remember.

How many by your order?

A few thousand.

When you say these things I feel – sick.

Do you have any idea who I was dealing with? Do you have any idea who these bastards are? What these bastards were capable of? These bastards who wanted to keep Afghanistan in the dark ages? I was defending my people.

In order to have reasonable people in power – reasonable people must be prepared to be unreasonable in the pursuit of that power.

I've read that under communism there were miniskirts on the streets of Kabul.

Miniskirts?

Short skirts.

Where did you read this?

In newspapers and articles. I've seen it written lots of times. 'Under the communists women wore miniskirts on the streets of Kabul.' Is that true?

Women had freedom under my regime. There was no regulation about how women or men should dress. I encouraged modern clothes for men and women. In the civil service men and women wore smart clothes.

In Kabul in the 1980s did you see girls wearing miniskirts on the streets?

Are you asking about prostitutes?

I don't know. Did prostitutes wear miniskirts?

Prostitutes wore burqas.

What!

Prostitutes in Kabul wear clothing that covers their face so that they can't be identified. A woman would not want her face to be seen if she was doing that kind of work.

Are you joking?

Have you come all this way – imagined yourself all this way – imagined yourself sitting with me in a city under siege – to ask me about women's fashion?

I'm interested in how it felt to be a woman in Kabul in the nineteen eighties.

It felt better than now.

Better than being bombed.

Is this what people talk about when they talk about Afghanistan? They talk about fashion?

They talk about women.

We imported western clothes from Russia and also from Czechoslovakia. These clothes were very popular with women who worked in Kabul. Many women worked as civil servants in the ministries. The clothes were smart and practical. You can imagine.

A woman's old fashioned soviet skirt.

When we were young, at university we used to have parties in people's houses. We couldn't afford to go to night clubs or travel abroad and behave the way that the children of landowners did. So instead we would meet in houses and listen to music. Boys and girls would mix together and talk. We were pioneers. We were trying to invent a new way of being Afghan. We were trying to invent a new society.

Women would wear skirts like this in the eighties?

At work, yes.

Do you like women?

Too much.

What do you mean?

Nothing.

Are you flirting with me?

Of course.

What clothes did you wear when you were torturing people?

I mostly wore dark suits.

Was there any particular reason you wore dark suits?

I wore dark suits because they looked good.

Gunfire.

They've reached the outskirts of the city.
Masood must be retreating.

Are you scared?

Can you imagine anything?

I can try.

Can you imagine the Spice Girls?

What?

Do you know them?

Of course I know them.

I love the Spice Girls.
Lets imagine the Spice Girls.
Let's imagine them playing a concert here for us.

You want me to make the Spice Girls appear in the UN guest house in Kabul under Taliban shell fire.

Why not?

It's a tall order.

What's the point of an imagination if you don't use it!

One day. When I'm president again. I will invite them to Kabul. I will have the Spice Girls play in the football stadium. Imagine that.

Maybe we can make them appear on television.

The Spice Girls appear on television.

They sing Wannabe.

Real would have been more fun.

Yes.

We don't have long.

No.

When the Russians left, everyone thought your government would fall but in fact you held out for four years.

People underestimated me. In fact it was me who asked the Russians to leave. The Russians had become the problem. As long as the Russians were in the country then America would continue to fund the rebels. I thought that if the Russians left there was a chance for me to negotiate with the moderate conservatives and to isolate the Islamists.

Would you have worked with Ahmed Shah Masood?

Of course I would have worked with him.

Would you have worked with the islamists?

No.

Why not them?

How many times do I have to tell you? – you can't talk to these people. They don't belong here. They come from Egypt. They came from Pakistan. They're funded by Saudi Arabia and the US. Nobody wants them here.

Masood talked to them.

And look what is happening to him.

For four years you hung on to power.

Yes.

How did you manage that?

I am good at it.

What does being good at holding on to power in Afghanistan involve?

This is a tribal country. The moment one tribe stands out as being stronger than the others, the others will combine to bring that family down. Sometimes a weak position is better than a strong one.

I know how to manage weakness.

You were weak without the Russians.

When communism collapsed there was no more money. It was very difficult to keep going.

What did you do?

I approached the Americans.

What happened?

Gorbachev proposed a transitional unity government to President Bush at a summit in Malta. President Bush rejected the plan.

He thought you were the problem.

He thought communism was the problem.

But you are communist.

I am Najibullah.

The Americans rejected your offer.

Yes.

Do you think America made a mistake?

Don't you?
Look outside.
Look at this mess.

You had no money.
Your plan was rejected.
Why didn't you leave?

I still hoped.

Even then.

I told you, I am an optimist.

What was your downfall?

I was betrayed.

By whom.

Tanai, a General of mine, Tanai switched sides. Suddenly the air force belonged to the other side. I had no chance. They picked me up at the airport as I was trying to leave. The UN gave me sanctuary.

You left it to the last minute. You could have left Kabul at any time.

What do you mean?

You knew your government was on the brink of collapse. You knew you couldn't hold out any longer. Russia or India would surely have given you asylum. Why didn't you leave before the last minute.

I couldn't believe the world would be so stupid as to let the Kabul fall to the mujaheddin.

You made a mistake.

Did I?
Let me show you something.

He leaves the room.
She looks out the window.
Gunfire comes closer.
She moves away from the window again.
The lights flicker on and off.

Here, I've found it.

What?

The *New York Time*'s from June 14th 1989.
'President Najibullah today rejected demands for the removal of his Soviet backed Government as a first step toward a political settlement of the war in Afghanistan. He declared that such a move would propel the country toward becoming "another Lebanon," in which no single political group would have the authority to hold Afghanistan together.'

A bang.
The lights go out.
Silence.

The generator will come on in a moment.

Silence.
Gunfire.

Silence.

Imagine a torch.

He reads by torchlight.

'"For the United States," he asked, "which is more appropriate: a nonaligned Afghanistan – free, independent, demilitarized and professing democracy – or a fanatic, extremist and fundamentalist regime?" Alluding to Iran, he added: "Hasn't the United States already tasted the bitterness of fundamentalism? Is it anxious to taste another bitter pepper?"'

'Mr. Najibullah also denied suggestions that as a former head of the Afghan secret police, he is unfit to take part in peace talks. He said the suggestions were particularly inappropriate coming from the United States because President Bush formerly directed the Central Intelligence Agency. "If working as the head of such an organization is a basis for people not voting for you, then how did it happen that in a civilized country like the United States, the people voted for Mr. Bush?" Mr. Najibullah asked rhetorically. "Mr. Bush should support me because he is my colleague."'

Why you are still here?

What do you mean?

Why aren't you in exile somewhere? You've had four years here. Surely some country would take you. You could have spent the last four years in Moscow or Cairo or Madrid…maybe you could have worked for some NGO or…

Don't you understand? This is not a great game for me. This is my country. I don't want freedom on the streets of Madrid. I want freedom on the streets of Kabul. I don't want dams on the rivers of Egypt. I want dams and power stations here – in these valleys. I want roads across the deserts here. In Afghanistan. For you this is imaginary. For me it is real.

Do you regret anything?

Yes.

What?

That I did not kill Tanai.

Fighting and shouts outside.

Bangs very close.

Can you imagine a way out of here?

For you?

For you.

This is a moment of change.
Every moment of change is an opportunity.

Do you think this is an opportunity?

Maybe.

How could that be?

There are only two people capable of running this country.
Masood and Me.
Maybe the people will come back to me.

If there was an election, would you win?

Why would we have an election?

Don't you want democracy rather than violence?

You talk about democracy as though there is no violence within
it. Democracy contains violence. Democracy is a demonstration
of the potential violent power of the majority.

A vote is surely better than a war.

In Afghanistan people have no fear of war. What Afghans fear is
the majority. To govern in Afghanistan one must be capable of
negotiating between many different possible sources of violence
and one must be capable of violence oneself. Democracy is not
a possibility for us. It is not desirable for us. It may never be
possible for us.

You're angry.

Of course I'm angry.

What if there is a way out?

What?

Maybe there is a possibility.

Tell me.

I can imagine something like this: You're the best politician.
Masood is the best commander. Both of you are charismatic

147

men. You were at university together. Both of you have seen your governments fail. Both of you asked for and didn't receive American support. I can imagine Masood coming to you. You've been in contact with him all this time. Perhaps he feels responsible for you. Imagine he comes and offers to take you out of Kabul. Take you North with him. Form an alliance.

You can imagine that.

I can.
Would you like me to imagine that?

No.
There is an opportunity.
I have to be here to take it.
This is my city.
I'll hold on.

The sun rises.
Gunfire is very close now.

They're coming.
I can hear their jeeps.
I'll talk to them.
I'll go out and talk to them.
What clothes should I wear to meet them?
What do you think?

What do you think?

I imagine something like this.

Afghan clothes.
He takes off his suit and shirt.
He dresses in afghan clothes, an afghan waistcoat.

What happens next?

You want to know.

I do.

This morning. September 27th 1996 Kabul falls to the Taliban. The UN do not send a helicopter to rescue you. Some reports say that in the last hours before dawn your old enemy Ahmed Shah Masood comes to the UN compound and offers to take you to safety in the north. You refuse. Armed men break into the compound just before dawn. Some reports say these men include the former communist General Tanai but most reports

say they are Taliban footsoldiers. The Taliban general had lost
a father and a brother to your secret service who had pushed
them out of a helicopter. Imagine what it's like to be pushed out
of a helicopter. The Taliban capture you. They beat you. They
castrate you. They tie your dying body to a jeep and drive round
the compound pulling you behind them in the dirt. Finally they
take you to a busy road junction where they hang you from a
concrete lamp post. They put money in your pocket and stuff
cigarettes in your mouth as a symbol of your decadence.
I don't know what you did at the end.
No one wrote it down.
I imagine you fought.
You spent four years lifting weights. You were a boxer. They
called you the ox.
I imagine you fought.

The End

THE LION OF KABUL

by Colin Teevan

First production

The Tricycle Theatre, London, 18 April 2009

The following cast performed in the remount in July 2010 at the Tricycle Theatre prior to the USA tour:

Characters / Cast

RABIA	Shereen Martineau
ISMAEL	Raad Rawi
KHAN	Nabil Elouahabi
HERATI	Vincent Ebrahim
PRISONER	Daniel Rabin
PRISONER	Danny Rahim
GUARD	Daniel Betts
GUARD	Rick Warden

Director	Indhu Rubasingham
Designer	Miriam Nabarro
Lighting	James Farncombe
Sound	Tom Lishman

for
Denise Preston

Afghanistan. August 1998. Night.

Night-time animal noises, distant, peaceful.

This is interrupted by the hum of an old generator chugging into life. Then an old, buzzing electric floodlight is turned on to reveal run-down, crumbling walls, rusty fences that abut a dirt walkway. It resembles a crumbling prison. At the front of the stage, another crumbling wall waist high.

Voices approach from off.

RABIA: What did he mean, the guard?

ISMAEL: Nothing.

RABIA: What did he say about the Minister? I could make out that much.

Enter RABIA, a woman in her late thirties, briskly. She is of Pakistani / Indian origin but born and raised in Britain. She wears a scarf loosely over her head. She is professional and efficient as one would expect a director of operations of a UN agency to be. She stops and waits.

Enter ISMAEL, an Afghan man in his late thirties, early forties. He is dressed and bearded in accordance with Taliban rules, but he is not a Taleb, he is RABIA's translator and assistant.

ISMAEL: He said nothing, Rabia Sahib. He said go in, wait there. He's too afraid to say anything.

RABIA: And are you afraid, Ismael?

ISMAEL does not reply.

(*Shivering.*) But why here? At night? (*Looks around her.*) I feel like I've landed on the moon.

ISMAEL: Like the man in the moon?

RABIA: More like the men who went to the moon. Standing on a completely alien world. Isolated. Alone.

ISMAEL: No man has been to the moon.

RABIA looks at ISMAEL to see if he's joking. He's not.

RABIA: Yes they have, Ismael. Several.

ISMAEL looks to RABIA to see if she's joking. She isn't.

ISMAEL: I don't believe.

RABIA: Americans. 1969. Thirty years ago. Didn't you know?

ISMAEL: It's not possible.

RABIA: It is possible. It was possible. It's been possible for some time. Up there, looking down on us.

ISMAEL shakes his head and looks down.

ISMAEL: We should not look at the moon. It's too beautiful, it distracts us from Allah.

RABIA: It might be too beautiful, but Americans have walked upon it. Why would I lie about a thing like that?

ISMAEL shrugs.

That's not an answer. Don't you believe me?

ISMAEL: If you say so, Rabia Sahib.

RABIA: It's not that I say so, Ismael, it's that it happened.

ISMAEL: You have seen the world outside, Rabia Sahib.

RABIA: Like a man on the moon, I've seen the world outside. Some day I'll take you, Ismael, I'll show you the world outside.

ISMAEL shrugs. Perhaps he wants this but he dare not hope.

RABIA looks around once more, peering into the darkness beyond the floodlights. She peers into the darkness of the auditorium.

Is this where he said?

ISMAEL nods.

RABIA peers over the wall at the front of the stage, and looks down. There is a sizeable drop that she discovers on the other side of the wall.

Why here, of all places?

ISMAEL shrugs. Now that they have reached the rendezvous, he is palpably less responsive.

RABIA does not notice a change in ISMAEL initially. She has arrived with great energy and purpose, focused on what she must do, but at present she has nothing at which to direct this energy. The small talk has run dry.

Pause.

What time did he say?

ISMAEL: After Maghrib.

RABIA: That's not a time. We could be here all night.

ISMAEL does not reply.

Is it because of the bombing in Khost? Is that why they went missing? Revenge?

ISMAEL: (*Shrugs.*) Because of the American bombing, because of Bin Laden Sahib, because of the war. Because, God willed it.

RABIA: God wills an awful lot on this country.

ISMAEL shrugs, not looking at her.

You've gone into Afghan mode. You're not looking at me. You must sense the enemy at hand.

(*Beat.*) You do think it's safe, don't you?

ISMAEL: (*Not looking at her.*) For you it is safe.

RABIA: Yes. It's a relative question, I suppose, when you live on the moon.

ISMAEL darts a look at her. She looks at ISMAEL.

How much longer can we stay in Kabul? I do hope they're okay. Do you think they're okay? (*Upset and irritated.*) Why isn't the Minister here yet?

ISMAEL shrugs, never looking at her. Pause. RABIA gives up trying to engage ISMAEL in her outrage and frustration. She looks over wall towards auditorium.

They're awake. Look at them. Poor bastards!

ISMAEL flinches. Is the obscenity calculated to bring him back to Western mode? He does not respond.

(*Looking out to audience.*) How long have they been there?

ISMAEL: All the time.

RABIA: (*Pointing.*) Him?

ISMAEL: The longest, since before.

RABIA: Before the Russians?

ISMAEL nods.

Miracle he's still here. Fate must have willed that it be so. What's wrong with his eye? Is he missing an eye? He is, isn't he? And his leg? He's limping.

ISMAEL: (*Shrugs.*) Grenade.

RABIA: Poor bastard! All that time. To think what he's seen with that one eye.

ISMAEL: He's eaten, all that time. More than can be said for most.

Beat.

RABIA: Yes.

Pause. RABIA, annoyed with herself, cannot contain her frustration. Any pretence of humour is gone.

Why the zoo of all places? I've been to the Ministry every day this week. Every day they turn me away. Do they have no respect for the Agency? We're United Nations for God's sake. Don't they care? How can they expect us to recognise them? (*Pause.*) Does the Minister not know who I am? Who I represent…?

RABIA breaks off. She must compose herself. RABIA looks at ISMAEL. He will not look at her.

Ismael? Ismael? They're your colleagues, Gul and Faisal, don't you…aren't you worried? Worried that they're hurt, or dead? Angry? Angry that all we're trying to do is help and they treat us like this? Abduct our workers? Tell us nothing?

ISMAEL shrugs, uncomfortably.

Don't tell me that God willed it. Something has happened to them. You can look at me, Ismael, there's no one about, apart from them – (*Gestures towards auditorium.*) – and they're not subject to Shari'ah, yet. I hope. Look at me, Ismael? You look at me when we're in the office.

Pause. ISMAEL looks at her, he shifts uncomfortably.

ISMAEL: That is there, Rabia Sahib.

RABIA: Don't you care about them? Which side are you on, Ismael?

ISMAEL looks at her. 'Is it about sides?' He would ask if he dared, but at that moment he becomes aware that someone is coming. He averts his gaze.

(*As much to herself.*) It smells of rotting meat here.

Enter KHAN, a Mullah. He is surprisingly young for such, no more than thirty. He is dressed as a Taliban. He has an eye-patch over one eye. He is accompanied by HERATI, a judge. A man in his sixties and one who seems throughout to resemble an animal trapped in the headlights. All four are aware that KHAN's driver and guards stand at a distance, though perhaps RABIA is less aware of this than the others. KHAN speaks calmly, quietly and charmingly. It should slowly become clear that he is addressing RABIA through ISMAEL, though he finds it easiest to look towards the auditorium.

KHAN: You must excuse me for keeping representative of United
    Nations Agency waiting, but you must understand, it was
    Maghrib.

RABIA: Minister – ?

KHAN: My duty to Allah comes before all other duties.

RABIA wants to respond, but bites her tongue and instead:

RABIA: You're not the Minister. I asked to see the Minister.

KHAN looking out and continuing to address himself to ISMAEL.

KHAN: My name is Khan, I am Mullah, scholar of Islam. I represent
    Ministry in this affair. This is Herati Sahib, he is qaazi. Halta
    wadarezha Herati [*Stand over there, Herati.*]

RABIA looks to ISMAEL for clarification.

ISMAEL: (*Looking down.*) A judge, Director Sahib –

RABIA: A judge – ?

KHAN: I trust Director Khanum's met Marjan, our lion? He's been
    here /

RABIA: Since before the Russians, I know, Khan Sahib, but I did
    not –

KHAN: Through war against infidel Russian, and after, through
    time of Mujahideen, when Muslim brother fought with Muslim
    brother –

RABIA: Is this why you asked me here? A history lesson through the
    eyes of a lion?

KHAN: Has Director Khanum been told how our lion lost his eye?

RABIA: Khanum, Ismael?

ISMAEL: (*Looking down.*) Woman.

RABIA: No. Yes. The Director Sahib wants to know where her aid
    workers Gul Mohammed and Faisal Qadiri are. / I want to
    know –

KHAN: A mujahid, holy warrior, came to zoo during time of
    Mujahideen. Many times he had seen Marjan's keeper, Akbar,
    down there in the pit with him. And Akbar would go right up to
    Marjan with his food, stroke him, pet him, play with him. The
    Mujahid thought: 'This lion is no savage beast. This lion is like
    house cat. If unarmed keeper –'

RABIA: I did not come here, Khan Sahib, Herati Sahib to –

KHAN bristles but continues.

KHAN: The Mujahid thought: 'I will demonstrate how brave I am to all these people watching' /

RABIA: (*Appealing for help.*) Ismael – ?

ISMAEL looks down. KHAN does not break his speech.

KHAN: 'I will show them that Allah is on my side and side of my warlord. I will defeat this lion.' And Mujahid jumped over wall and into pit to fight Marjan. But Marjan, did not behave like a pussycat at this little invasion. He roared and pounced on Mujahid and savaged him. He tore off his leg and ate it as Mujahid lay bleeding to death on the floor of this very pit. What Mujahid did not understand about lion is that this is his territory. And his keeper, who kept him alive through all fighting and food shortages of Russians and Civil War, often going without food himself so lion might survive, his keeper Akbar was like brother. But foreigner, who wanted to prove to rest of world how brave and strong he was, was invading his and his brother's territory and would be dealt with mercilessly. It was just action. The justice of Allah. Sharia'ah. You do not need movies or pictures or music or books to tell you about the world, they are lies, you only have to look at nature. Is that not right, Herati Sahib? Dagha seh nadee, Herati? [*Is that not right, Herati?*]

HERATI flinches and nods barely perceptibly, though he has no idea what he is agreeing to. RABIA has been impatiently awaiting an opening:

RABIA: You said you were going to explain / how he lost his –

KHAN: But Mujahid's brother, another bad Muslim, he did not understand justice of Allah. Mujahid had been in the wrong, he had received just punishment. But brother wanted revenge. Revenge when one is in wrong is not justice. He returned here, and like coward, threw grenade at Marjan. And Marjan lost eye. Like I and many of my brothers have lost eyes, as result of unjust action by bad Muslims /

RABIA: In the land of the blind, the one-eyed man –

KHAN: This is purpose of Taliban, to end injustice. We fought and we defeated Muslims who had gone wrong, who terrorised their communities, robbed from them, committed crimes against women and children and poor /

RABIA: I have not come here / to listen to – ?

KHAN: We treated them not with mercy, but with justice. We are just, like lion. Aren't we Herati Sahib?

HERATI shifts uncomfortably. KHAN does not care if he agrees.

Brother, what is your name?

RABIA: Brother?

ISMAEL: Ismael.

KHAN: And you are good Muslim, Ismael?

ISMAEL nods.

RABIA: Excuse me, I am Rabia Haq, I am Director of Operations, Ismael is just –

KHAN: You work for Director of Operations, Ismael?

ISMAEL nods.

RABIA: This is – !

KHAN: And since we understand Director of Operations is herself Muslim –

RABIA: My origins are not –

KHAN: (*Never breaking his speech.*) And since Director of Operations is not accompanied by male relative –

RABIA: Have you brought me here to humiliate me – ?

KHAN: If Director wishes us to help her in matter of two missing aid workers…

RABIA stops where she is, waiting to see which way this will develop.

Might you please inform her to direct her comments /

RABIA: Khan Sahib, whatever your position –

KHAN: Through you.

RABIA: Through him? He is my subordinate, my translator, my assistant. And we don't need a translator since you speak excellent English. You did not learn that in a madrassa. You learnt that somewhere where they have no difficulties in addressing a woman directly –

KHAN: My origins are equally no business of Director of Operations.

RABIA: I demand to know what has happened to my to field workers Gul Mohammed and Faisal Qadiri! I demand justice! I demand –

KHAN: Ismael, it is your duty to inform Director of Operations to respect my culture.

RABIA: I will not stand for this. Ismael.

RABIA goes to leave a second time.

KHAN: (*Raising his voice so the departing RABIA might hear.*) Ismael, United Nations have been kind enough to have charter translated into Pashto. From this we understand that United Nations has commitment to respecting local culture. This is local culture.

Pause. RABIA, furious, is torn between leaving and her duty to stay. She knows she must stay. KHAN looking front continues to address ISMAEL.

Director must respect Shari'ah as we respect fact that Agency has lost two employees.

RABIA: They are colleagues.

KHAN shrugs.

And what do you mean lost?

Silence.

(*More insistent.*) What do you mean lost, Mullah Khan?

RABIA looks from KHAN. She realises that she will not receive an answer from KHAN. Instead:

OK, ask him, Ismael: what does the Mullah mean lost?

ISMAEL is confused. He dare not address KHAN.

KHAN: It is sufficient that Director of Operations address her remarks through you, Ismael, as one might chairman of meeting. I am not stupid, I hear Director of Operations perfectly well. And I understand her.

RABIA: O you understand me, do you?

KHAN: And I wish to help her.

RABIA: Well let the chair, and the judge, note that we did not lose our colleagues, Gul and Faisal. On Sunday last they were distributing sacks of rice on the Food for Widows Scheme. On Monday morning the Agency lorry was found, the men and the rice were gone. They are good men. They have wives and families to feed. They did not run away. They were not lost. They were abducted, or worse –

KHAN: When I said lost, I used it as metaphor, to save Director
Khanum's feelings. Afghan workers Director Khanum refers to
are dead.

*Pause. RABIA is shocked. KHAN is unflinching. ISMAEL attempts to
hide his emotions. RABIA finally controls herself.*

RABIA: And you invited me to the zoo to tell me this? Is that to
save my feelings too? I knew they were dead, I knew when the
lorry was found. Damn it. Damn it. I hoped it wouldn't be so. I
prayed –

KHAN: Director prayed?

RABIA: Why shouldn't I pray?

KHAN: It is simply that Director dresses like bad Muslim.

RABIA: It is none of your business what kind of Muslim I am. Or
whether I am. Why? Why were they murdered? Ismael ask him!
For the rice?

KHAN shrugs.

KHAN: Perhaps they behaved improperly to one of the women.

RABIA: They wouldn't. We trained them –

KHAN: Perhaps their training with foreigners is what led them to
behave improperly.

RABIA: How? You have no proof. They were murdered and you call
it justice.

KHAN: Director of Operations assumes we are responsible. We are
on side of justice. We are trying to help her.

RABIA: By slandering them when they cannot defend themselves?

KHAN: I said perhaps. Perhaps they behaved improperly. Perhaps
that is not case. I do not know. We are not responsible.

RABIA: Who is then? How do you know what happened to them?
Did you find their bodies? You must know where the bodies
are, to be sure, to have proof they are dead? You must return
their bodies. So their families might bury them. It is important
to people here / they believe the soul of the dead will only go to
paradise if it's buried –

KHAN: Is Director of Operations Khanum telling me what is
important to people of my country? To their faith? Muslim
woman who has gone wrong?

RABIA: How dare you judge me. I am not yours to judge –

KHAN: Her father and her husband should be ashamed /

RABIA: Ashamed. My father is proud –

KHAN: Of her. Why has she come here /

RABIA: He arrived in Britain forty years ago with nothing –

KHAN: With her faysha clothes and her kaffar ways?

RABIA: Ismael, what is he saying? / Ismael?

KHAN: What does it matter if they or she are buried? /

RABIA: The murder of our aid workers, the treatment of our charities / jeopardise –

KHAN: They shall all burn in hell.

RABIA: What did you say –?

KHAN: What does it matter if non-believers are buried or not? The whore, the infidel shall burn in hell.

RABIA: And that is why I have renounced my religion.

RABIA does not know what to do with her fury. Through an extreme act of will, she calms herself. She can no longer look at KHAN.

You are a Mullah, Khan Sahib, is that not so?

KHAN: Though my origins are not important, yes, I studied at Madrassa.

RABIA: But your English…?

Pause.

KHAN: I trained with police in Mumbai. But my origins, like those of Director Khanum's are not important.

RABIA: A policeman? This is a complex international matter. Gul and Faisal might have been Afghan citizens, but they worked for a UN agency.

KHAN: Faisal and Gul were Afghans / they are our jurisdiction.

RABIA: Ask him, ask him do Gul and Faisal not have rights as individuals?

KHAN: No. Gul and Faisal only have rights as members of community. What is individual? Individual is leaf in wind. The community is tree and can withstand storm.

RABIA: Doesn't he understand, Ismael? The UN, the NGOs are on the brink of pulling out.

KHAN: If that is what God wills.

RABIA: What about your people? They will starve.

KHAN does not reply.

He said he wanted to help me, Ismael. Could you ask him where their bodies are then? Their families have a right to bury them. We believe they were good people. We know they were good people. We wish to show them honour in death. Their bodies –

KHAN: I'm afraid their bodies cannot be returned.

RABIA: Could you ask Khan Sahib why not?

ISMAEL looks to KHAN. KHAN is still, then shrugs and gestures towards the auditorium. When there is no response to her request, RABIA looks up. She sees where KHAN has gestured. She is at first confused then slowly the implication of the gesture dawns on her. She puts her hand to her mouth. She is speechless, initially.

KHAN: We are not responsible –

RABIA: The lion – ?

KHAN: This is not our justice.

RABIA: The lion – ?

KHAN: The Taliban does not approve /

RABIA: How can you / ?

KHAN: Of citizens taking law into own hands /

RABIA: Stand there and calmly say – ?

KHAN: The kind of action Allah has willed us to save Afghanistan from –

RABIA: God no! They were people. Not meat. / Meat for animals!

KHAN: We do not approve, I said. Before Taliban, there was chaos. When Russians left, the world forgot Afghanistan. While warlords of Mujahideen set about seizing power for themselves. They killed anyone who got in their way. You could not move about this country. Every hundred metres along the road, checkpoint. Each one, if you couldn't pay what they demand, you were raped, or robbed or killed. But, while those bad Muslims might have forgotten their God, their God had not forgotten them. He gave us new Amir-ul Momineen, a commander of the faithful, to lead us from these dark times.

RABIA: And is feeding aid-workers, men who distribute food to the hungry, is feeding them to the lions the justice of Allah? Ismael, I am asking him, through you.

KHAN: No, no it is not justice. Is it justice, Herati Sahib? Adaalat? [*Justice.*]

HERATI is terrified. He does not understand English. He nods vigorously, then shakes his head vigorously.

We do not believe in citizens taking law into own hands.

Pause.

RABIA: This is an outrage. Beyond an outrage. This jeopardises the whole UN presence here. We cannot be party to...we cannot endanger... I demand justice, Ismael, tell him we demand justice.

KHAN: But we did not commit this act.

RABIA: But you are in control.

KHAN: Director recognises Taliban as legitimate government?

RABIA: Are you trying to use these men's deaths as a bargaining tool?

KHAN: Is United Nations asking Taliban as government of country?

RABIA: This Director of Operations of a United Nations agency is asking you, the representative of the Ministry of Justice, for your help, in tracking down the men who did this.

KHAN: Does Director Khanum, as a representative of UN, recognise Taliban as legitimate government of Afghanistan?

RABIA: If you pursue justice in this matter – If the world knows that outrages such as this do not go unpunished. Tell the Minister that. Tell the Leader of the Faithful that if he is seen to be just in this matter /

KHAN: Mullah Omar is always just, Ismael.

ISMAEL winces at having this remark attributed to him.

It is people of the West who have no principles, who are godless, who are unjust.

RABIA: We respect human rights, we respect freedom.

KHAN: Is it not our human right to reject your freedom? That is one human right you do not recognise. You will not recognise us until we look like you and act like you and are slaves to your economic system. We don't want to be like you. We don't want to watch your television, films. We don't want your freedom.

Pause. RABIA has decided she does not care for another lecture. She turns to go.

But we are just. And we shall give you justice because we are consistent. We do not change what we said yesterday because of new circumstances today, justice of Allah does not alter, nor do we bargain with justice of Allah.

RABIA: So you will find the people who did this?

KHAN: They have been found.

RABIA: Who are they? Why did they do this?

KHAN: They are brothers. Poor men. They said the aid-workers Gul and Faisal offered one man's wife sack of rice.

RABIA: And they killed them for that?

KHAN: They said she told them she was not widow, but she was poor. They said to take bag of rice anyway.

RABIA: But surely that's an act –

KHAN: Her husband says they demand sexual favours in return.

RABIA: Never. They wouldn't. / They were both married –

KHAN: As Director of Operations Khanum said herself, they had been trained by you /

RABIA: So they are guilty simply by/ association –

KHAN: Trained by people who allow freedom to women. This leads to adultery and destruction of Islam.

RABIA: Had they any proof?

KHAN: He is her husband, that is what he asserts.

RABIA: And her?

KHAN: But it is wrong. They should not have killed them –

RABIA: What about the wife – ?

KHAN: If they had complaint –

RABIA: She could tell you the truth –

KHAN: They should have taken their complaint to Shari'ah court.

RABIA: They should have let you kill them!

KHAN: They should have let us dispense justice, that is what they have done wrong.

RABIA: Murdering is what they have done wrong.

KHAN shrugs.

What about the wife, Ismael?

KHAN: She is not your business.

RABIA: So she is dead?

KHAN: She is not important.

RABIA: The men, then, what have you done with these men? Are they in prison?

KHAN does not reply.

You have not killed them?

KHAN: They are not dead.

KHAN: I have brought them here, to you.

RABIA: To me?

KHAN: I said we wish to help Director Khanum and Agency.

RABIA: Thank you, Mullah Khan.

KHAN: So she might help us.

KHAN signals off. Two armed Taliban GUARDS bring in two PRISONERS, severely beaten. They are clearly terrified and being brought into the presence of a foreign woman confuses them further.

RABIA: What have you done to them?

Neither the GUARDS nor the PRISONERS look at RABIA. KHAN does not not respond.

Khan Sahib? Ismael?

KHAN does not reply. ISMAEL no longer acknowledges her. KHAN signals to the GUARDS to leave the PRISONERS between himself and RABIA.

KHAN: These men have been questioned and tried and found guilty by own admission of taking justice into own hands and therefore disrespecting justice of Allah as laid down by Shari'ah. (*Beat.*) We wish to hand them over to Director of Operations. Is that not your judgement Herati Sahib?

RABIA: Why?

KHAN: So you might punish them.

KHAN shrugs.

RABIA: But we are a food distribution agency.

KHAN: If you feel ill-equipped to dispense justice, you may set them free.

RABIA: But they murdered my colleagues.

KHAN: I have offered them to you to punish.

RABIA: We can't. We can't. You said yourself we must respect the laws and customs of a country.

KHAN smiles.

KHAN: So that is Director of Operations Khanum's decision. They must be punished according to the justice of our country.

RABIA: (*Unsure.*) That is the position as stated in the UN charter.

RABIA is unsure where this is leading.

KHAN: So Herati Sahib, they are acknowledging our justice. What is your judgement? (*To HERATI.*) Tarsi bayad khpal deh qazawat faisala tungah wukee, Herati [*What is the judgement you must give, Herati?*]

Pause.

HERATI: (*A broken voice, in Pashto.*) Qanoon wayee chi... [*The law determines...*]

RABIA: What did he say, Ismael?

KHAN: Qaazi, pazoora khabari waka. Kaardee waka. [*Speak up, Qaazi. Do your job.*]

HERATI: (*Reciting.*) Chi qanoon ye pa khpoloo la su akhesty wo aw da shariyeh mahkama ta beehteraami kareda, woh bayad dagha khalak hum, deh Gul aw Faisal pashaan hedaamsi. [*The law determines that for the taking of justice into their own hands and for disrespecting the Sharia'ah Court, these men be put to death in the same manner they caused the death of the two men Gul and Faisal.*]

RABIA: What did he say, Ismael? Tell me...?

KHAN: Nafar aamaada ka. [*Prepare the men.*]

The men are brought to the wall at the front of the stage. RABIA begins to understand HERATI's judgement.

RABIA: No. No, I didn't ask for that, you cannot say I did.

KHAN: Ismael –

RABIA: No.

KHAN: Ismael!

ISMAEL: Mullah Khan Sahib?

KHAN: As foreign woman, Director of Operations may not witness execution.

RABIA: Don't you worry, I'm going. I'm going and with me shall go our agency and all the other UN agencies and NGOS.

KHAN: If that is will of God that you shall leave, *Inshallah.*

RABIA: How can you expect us to stay when our workers are treated like this? When you try to manipulate us?

For the first time KHAN forgets his own protocol and turns and looks at RABIA.

KHAN: We do not manipulate you. We offer you same hospitality we offer any guest, you, our brother Osama. You will not make us change today what we said yesterday. You will not make liars of us. We will not lose honour.

KHAN recomposes himself. He resumes not looking at her.

RABIA: What about your people?

KHAN: Allah will feed people. It was the foreigners' choice to come, if foreigners want to go, that is their decision. They have forgotten us before. They will forget us again.

RABIA: I shall go then. They are awaiting my report in Geneva.

RABIA turns to go but ISMAEL does not follow.

Ismael, we are leaving.

ISMAEL confused, terrified, moves to go.

KHAN: Brother Ismael, are you woman's slave?

RABIA: He's my employee.

KHAN: Brother Ismael is citizen of this country.

RABIA: Ismael, come with me. You cannot be party to this.

ISMAEL: (*Never looking at her or KHAN.*) But the Agency is leaving, the Director Khanum said. You are like that man on the moon. You arrive in our strange world, isolated, alone, but then you leave. I am of the moon. I am not of your world.

Pause. ISMAEL does not, cannot move.

RABIA: Ismael, which side are you on?

ISMAEL: I am on the side of those who must live here after you have gone.

Pause. RABIA leaves. No one looks at her as she does so.

KHAN: (*In Pashto.*) Nafar aamaada ka. [*Prepare the men.*]

Lights fade as the guards prepare to feed the prisoners to the lions.

PART THREE
ENDURING FREEDOM
1996-2010

HONEY

by Ben Ockrent

———————————

First production

The Tricycle Theatre, London, 19 April 2009

The following cast performed in the remount in July 2010 at the Tricycle Theatre prior to the USA tour:

Characters / Cast

MASOOD KHALILI	Vincent Ebrahim
ROBIN RAPHEL (Assistant US Secretary of State for South Asia)	Jemma Redgrave
GARY SCHROEN (CIA Operative)	Michael Cochrane
AHMAD SHAH MASSOUD (Defence Minister in the Rabbani Afghan Government)	Daniel Rabin
ATTENDANT	Nabil Elouahabi
REPORTER	Danny Rahim
CAMERAMAN	Raad Rawi

Director   Nicolas Kent
Designer   Pamela Howard
Lighting   James Farncombe
Sound   Tom Lishman

Setting

The play is set in:

1996, Islamabad US Embassy;

Commander Massoud's Office, Kabul;

2001, Sept 8th in Northern Afghanistan Commander Massoud's bedroom;

Sept 9th, another room in the same house.

SCENE ONE

KHALILI (late forties, in a suit) stands alone at the front of the stage. He addresses the audience.

KHALILI: When I was a child my father said I read poetry like a drum: I made a big noise but I was hollow inside. As I grew up I learnt to understand. You can say all you like but it means nothing if you don't believe it. Deep down, (*Gesturing to his heart.*) in here, mean every word you say. Indeed, I believe Mr Schroen meant what he said that night. That in his heart he believed it was possible, all those promises. So why did things turn out the way they did? (*Shrugging.*) Only Allah can say. All I know is when we spoke that night, I heard no drum. Not from any of us there that night.

He turns to watch the following scene.

SCENE TWO

The Islamabad CIA station. August 1996. A dingy, characterless office. An old desk. Some chairs.

RAPHEL (late forties, smartly dressed, no-nonsense) sits at the desk. It's not her own desk but she's sat at it all the same. SCHROEN (early fifties, tatty old suit, passionate) leans on the desk expectantly.

RAPHEL: I get on a plane. I fly all the way to Islamabad and for this? That's it? For an in?

SCHROEN: It's more than just an in.

RAPHEL: But as far as Massoud's concerned.

SCHROEN: It's just an in.

RAPHEL: And you think he'll buy that.

SCHROEN: I don't think he'll have any choice. If we can engage him here, now, with this…

RAPHEL: What, Mr Schroen, you see a future?

SCHROEN: We'll have a relationship. That's something that can service us both.

RAPHEL: What kind of a relationship?

SCHROEN: What d'you mean?

RAPHEL: As far as Massoud's concerned. I mean that's what he'll ask, isn't it? Once we've got them all back. Once we're in.

SCHROEN: Listen, this is wrapped up in a… We'll deal with later… later. That's what I'll say.

RAPHEL: The Lion of Panjshir. Someone with a name like that. That's not someone you wanna dictate terms to. Not in his own…well, not in Panjshir.

SCHROEN: Not anywhere.

RAPHEL: Then you appreciate the way he's gonna feel about this? About us? Mr Schroen, we left him. From his point of view it's more or less that simple. Now five years down the line we wanna jump back into bed? That's unusual. You understand what I'm saying? He's not used to compromise. Not anymore. Not Massoud.

SCHROEN: Assistant Secretary, if he doesn't buy this I'm gonna have to go back with more or the whole thing's lost. I don't have anything more. We need to get them back. I'll make him understand.

RAPHEL: You'll 'make' him?

SCHROEN: With respect, m'am, I grew up in East St Louis. My dad was a union electrician.

RAPHEL: Mr Schroen, what's your point?

SCHROEN: I'm not one of your Ivy-Leaguers out here looking to flesh out his resumé. I wanna do this right. For him as much as ourselves. He looks into my eyes and he'll read that.

RAPHEL: He better. Because this won't exactly light him up. Not in itself. Not Massoud.

SCHROEN: He's not unrealistic. He understands my position here.

RAPHEL: We're talking about military supplies, medical aid, political support, finances, international recognition of the threat of the Taliban. This is what he needs. That's what he'll say.

SCHROEN: And the only way he's gonna get them is by giving us this in. That's the whole point. That's what I'll say. He helps us here and we show Washington he's with us. He gets that stuff. Later.

RAPHEL: And we get?

SCHROEN: What d'you mean?

RAPHEL: I need clarity here. If I'm gonna sell this in DC I need to know exactly what this 'relationship' means. We recover them all, then what? What about later?

SCHROEN: Listen, I have no men on the ground. No operatives. None. He's the Afghan Minister for Defence. We set up this relationship with Massoud and he can help us. Assistant Secretary, he's not Hekmatyr. And he's sure as hell not the Taliban. With this thing up and running we could change the whole landscape out there. Who knows – maybe even take out bin Laden. God knows Clinton's running out of time. (*A beat.*) Or would you rather we had another Pearl Harbour on our hands?

She stares at him.

A noisy aeroplane engine begins to roar as it picks up pace, hurtling down a runway for take-off. RAPHEL exits. SCHROEN picks up a small shoulder bag, smartens himself up and exits.

SCENE THREE

KHALILI stands alone again at the front of the stage.

KHALILI: I was Ambassador to India at the time. Schroen contacted me in New Delhi, looking for an introduction to Commander. I called Commander and it was agreed I would escort Schroen to Kabul myself. We had spoken before but this was the first time we meet face to face and when I see him out there on the tarmac…well, let's be honest, I thought he'd sent his dentist. I thought there'd been some mistake. No security officers, no communication equipment, no luggage… My first reaction was indeed concern. Concern that the man was a lunatic. That this whole meeting was something he'd planned himself. Indeed, maybe even in defiance of headquarters. But even so I was still hopeful. In the five years since our defeat of the Soviets, my country had collapsed. Entirely. And so for the Americans to return… This man could change everything. I believed that. Indeed, if it was change that he desired.

SCENE FOUR

Commander AHMAD SHAH MASSOUD's office, Kabul. September 1996. A table and some chairs. Surrounding the chairs are tall piles of books.

MASSOUD (mid-forties, in a white Afghan robe and a round, soft, wool Panjshiri cap) enters. He is tall but not physically imposing, quiet, formal, intense. SCHROEN enters to one side.

As the aeroplane engines crescendo quickly – as if descending for landing – and fade out, KHALILI turns into the scene.

SCHROEN: (*Clumsily.*) Chetour hasti, sahat shoma khub ast zenda bashi manda nabashi salamat bashi jour bashi.

MASSOUD: Excellent. This is very good. Please… (*Gesturing to a chair.*) Willkommen.

SCHROEN: Willkommen?

MASSOUD: This was the Austrian Embassy before the invasion. Willkommen. It's German.

SCHROEN: I know where it's from.

MASSOUD: So Willkommen.

KHALILI and MASSOUD both wait.

SCHROEN: (*A beat.*) Dankershun.

MASSOUD: Excellent!

They all sit.

I trust you had a safe flight?

SCHROEN: We made it. I guess that's about all that can be expected.

KHALILI: We flew Ariana.

MASSOUD: Ah. Inshallah Airlines. Not the prettiest bird in the sky, perhaps, but she's never crashed yet.

SCHROEN: First time for everything, right?

MASSOUD: (*Sardonic.*) Well you're here.

A MALE ATTENDANT enters with three teas and begins to distribute them.

Tea. Served with honey, ginger, lemon. The very best for my guest.

SCHROEN is served his cup.

SCHROEN: (*To the ATTENDANT.*) Thank you.

MASSOUD and KHALILI wait for him to drink. SCHROEN takes the hint. He sips the tea.

Delicious.

MASSOUD: You see? Didn't I tell you?

SCHROEN: Yes you did.

MASSOUD: Yes I did.

MASSOUD beams at KHALILI. And opens his arms to SCHROEN – the floor is his.

So…

SCHROEN stirs his tea as he waits for the ATTENDANT to leave. Finally they are alone again…

SCHROEN: Commander, three years ago a twenty-eight year-old man from Quetta, Mir Amal Kasi, pulled his car into the CIA headquarters in Virginia. He climbed out with an AK-47 assault rifle and shot five men as they waited at the gate. The next day Kasi flew to Pakistan and disappeared.

MASSOUD: I know about Kasi.

SCHROEN: One month later a twenty-four year-old man from Kuwait, Ramzi Yousef, detonated a bomb in the B-2 level of an underground garage at the World Trade Centre. It killed six people in the cafeteria above and injured some one thousand more in the floors beyond that. You know about Yousef?

MASSOUD: Of course.

SCHROEN: It's the view of the American administration that they represent a new breed of radical Islamic terrorism. They are not defined by any particular terrorist group, they do not belong to any one particular nationality. What they do share is a common enemy: the United States.

MASSOUD: I'd say this is accurate.

SCHROEN: Commander, left unchecked, we believe Afghanistan is set to become a centre for global terrorism. Yousef trained here. It's where we believe Kasi is now. That's something we'd like to address. The United States is coming back. Our attention is very firmly focussed over here. In Afghanistan. In a stable, safe Afghanistan. And with you central to that.

SCHROEN hesitates for a beat.

MASSOUD: But…

SCHROEN: But we have to find an in. Somewhere to start that focus.

KHALILI: An 'in'?

SCHROEN: A starting point. Just something to get the ball rolling.

MASSOUD: What did you have in mind?

SCHROEN: Commander, we'd like our Stinger missiles back.

MASSOUD glances at KHALILI.

We kept detailed records of the serial numbers. We've got a pretty good idea of how many we distributed. How many got used. We think it's about time we took back the ones that didn't.

MASSOUD: The missiles you distributed yourself.

SCHROEN: The Stingers served you very well. Without them there's no reason to doubt those Soviet helicopters would still be circling the skies above us today. (*As lightly as possible.*) Only there's a few Stingers left over and we're just a little…concerned that they might find their way into the hands of hostile forces. Or governments. Or…terrorists.

MASSOUD: That they might now get used against you.

SCHROEN: That's the situation.

KHALILI: It's quite a situation.

SCHROEN: Yes it is.

MASSOUD: And just so we're all reading from the same book…how many is quite?

SCHROEN pulls out a pad and starts to write.

Please, we can speak freely here.

Reluctantly, SCHROEN puts away the pad.

SCHROEN: (*Uncomfortably.*) Two thousand five hundred missiles were originally distributed. We built them. But as you may remember, they were distributed for us by the Pakistani secret service. By the ISI.

MASSOUD: Do you want to know how many of those Pakistan chose to send to me?

SCHROEN: Very much. That would be useful.

MASSOUD: Eight. And only at the end of the fight. Of your two thousand five hundred missiles the ISI sent me eight.

SCHROEN tries to press on.

SCHROEN: Okay. And where would those be now? Your eight?

MASSOUD: In my possession.

SCHROEN: All of them?

MASSOUD: Despite the high esteem you have for them, we managed.

SCHROEN: Good. Good for you. And we'd obviously be prepared to buy all eight. And that's not all.

MASSOUD: Let me guess...you want my help with the rest.

SCHROEN: Very much.

MASSOUD drinks his tea.

MASSOUD: Of these two thousand five hundred, how many remain active?

SCHROEN: We believe... (*Reluctantly.*) Around six hundred.

MASSOUD and KHALILI glance at one another – this is worse than he'd expected.

As Minister for Defence no-one's better placed to help us here than you. We'd like you to speak to your sub-commanders, other Afghan fighters you know, see if they'll be willing to sell theirs too. You would gather them all yourself. And when you've collected enough to justify it, we'll arrange for a C-130 to fly out and pick them up.

SCHROEN sits forwards – here comes the sweetener...

Beyond what we pay you for your own, you will be in charge of re-purchasing the rest. You can dictate your own deals there, that's at your own discretion, we don't care. We just want them back.

It doesn't quite have the impact he was hoping for.

Commander, with respect, we're talking about a great deal of money here. This could make a big difference to your situation.

KHALILI: Mr Schroen, who has these six hundred Stingers? Where are they?

SCHROEN: Well... I don't know. Initially the Afghan rebels they were distributed to and now...whoever else they may have sold them on to. Many...the majority are still here in the South. Some are in Iran. Some as far afield as Africa.

MASSOUD: And to who is it that these people have loyalty?

SCHROEN: Some to you, to the Afghanistan government.

MASSOUD: And the others?

SCHROEN: (*A beat.*) Are with the Taliban.

MASSOUD: How many missiles do the Taliban have?

SCHROEN: We believe Mullah Omar has collected fifty-three so far.

MASSOUD: And for these, for these fifty-three missiles you put in his hands, how much would you pay him to get them back?

SCHROEN: Somewhere between five to eight million dollars.

MASSOUD takes a moment to absorb this figure.

And that's not…we appreciate your position there. We'd be recovering those ourselves. We don't expect you to negotiate with your enemies over this. We're sensitive to that.

KHALILI: You are serious?

SCHROEN: (*A beat.*) Excuse me?

KHALILI: You are asking for us to be a part of something that will put millions of dollars into the hands of our enemies?

SCHROEN: That's not…that's reducing it somewhat…

MASSOUD: You know Mullah Omar is helping the terrorists you seek to destroy.

SCHROEN: At this stage we have no evidence of any connection between terrorism and the Taliban.

MASSOUD: And of course you don't. Not when your glasses are the Pakistanis.

SCHROEN: Commander, please. Try to see this from my point of view.

MASSOUD: You seek to arm the Taliban and you ask me to see this from your point of view?

SCHROEN: Not arm, Commander. Disarm.

MASSOUD: And what do you think they'll spend your five million dollars on? They ban everything else.

SCHROEN: Gentlemen, we're not leaving them armed.

MASSOUD: Then take the missiles by force.

SCHROEN: We can't do that.

MASSOUD: Why not?

SCHROEN: Because we are not the military. And, anyway, the US military have no authority here. Please don't underestimate what I'm offering. This is something. It's an in. It's a start.

MASSOUD: Of?

SCHROEN: A relationship. Of a future, working together. This can show the Pentagon and the White House and Capitol Hill that you are someone we can work with. This establishes you as our contact here. It gives us a direct channel of co-operation. Trust me it's worth it. As far as you're concerned five million dollars in the hands of the Taliban is worth this relationship with the USA.

MASSOUD: What kind of relationship?

SCHROEN: What kind?

MASSOUD: You buy back every Stinger in the land. Then what? What happens for us?

The ATTENDANT enters again with a tray of pastries and cakes. He leaves them on the table and re-fills everyone's cups with tea. SCHROEN waits again. This time the fuss with which the ATTENDANT goes about his job annoys SCHROEN. Finally, he leaves. SCHROEN stirs his tea, taking a moment to re-focus.

SCHROEN: Commander, what do you know about Osama bin Laden?

MASSOUD: Only that he is the most ambitious of a great many similar sheiks.

SCHROEN: You know he writes poems? Just sent one to our Secretary of Defense.

KHALILI and MASSOUD wait to find out where this is leading.

'O William, tomorrow you will be informed
As to which young man will face your swaggering brother
A youngster enters the midst of battle smiling, and
Retreats with his spearhead stained with blood'

MASSOUD: Very dramatic. He is at least consistent.

SCHROEN: Gentlemen, bin Laden signed it off 'from the Peaks of the Hindu Kush, Afghanistan.'

MASSOUD shifts.

It had been Ramzi Yousef's intention to blow a hole so big in the World Trade Centre he'd send both the towers toppling down on each other. The only reason he failed was because he ran out of cash. Bin Laden has over two hundred and fifty million dollars at his disposal. I can't emphasise enough the threat this man represents.

MASSOUD: We know this.

SCHROEN: Then what's to discuss? First the Stingers, then bin Laden. Help us and there's things we can provide you with.

KHALILI: You keep saying this, Mr Schroen, but you don't say what. What is it you can give us?

SCHROEN: (*Evasively.*) Well…initially… I suppose secure communications gear. For your intelligence aides.

MASSOUD looks unimpressed.

And that would be yours to keep.

MASSOUD: Communications gear?

SCHROEN: Initially. Just to begin with.

MASSOUD: And then?

SCHROEN: And then…we would form policy based on the progress of your government here and its cooperation with us back in DC. But the key thing for you…what you need to focus on here is that it's your contribution with the Stingers… That's how we get recognition in Washington. That's how this whole thing starts.

MASSOUD thinks for a beat. He collects the tray of pastries and cakes and holds it out to SCHROEN.

MASSOUD: Goshfeel. Traditional Afghan pastry. Very popular. But these here are the best. I have them made for me especially. Better than anywhere else. Try one.

SCHROEN: Thank you, I'm not hungry.

MASSOUD: Have one.

SCHROEN: I'm fine.

MASSOUD: Have a cake.

SCHROEN studies MASSOUD briefly – the tray still extended – this is some sort of challenge – he's not backing down. SCHROEN's on MASSOUD's territory, he can't refuse him here. If this is some sort of a power-struggle, SCHROEN can't afford to embarrass MASSOUD. Reluctantly, he helps himself to a cake.

Eat it.

SCHROEN takes a bite. MASSOUD doesn't seem satisfied.

(*Gesturing.*) Please.

SCHROEN takes another bite. MASSOUD and KHALILI watch. It makes SCHROEN self-conscious. He begins to make a mess, which he struggles to clean up. MASSOUD lets the moment drag, apparently relishing SCHROEN's self-consciousness. The cakes are serving their purpose: SCHROEN's lost his momentum and self-confidence. Finally SCHROEN finishes the cake. He sits there in his crumbs. MASSOUD has succeeded in re-affirming his status here. Eventually...

Now tell me, Mr Schroen. Have you actually seen the Taliban?

SCHROEN: Not in the flesh, sir, no.

MASSOUD: Shall I describe them to you?

SCHROEN: Go ahead.

MASSOUD: Even though they describe themselves as students, they carry more rockets than they have enemies to shell. They fix and fly Soviet fighter aircraft, even though it is a mystery where they learn how to fly. They are paid for by wealthy sheiks, Pakistan and now you...

SCHROEN: Pakistan don't fund them. We deal with Pakistan. Pakistan is our ally.

MASSOUD: With respect, Benazir Bhutto is authorizing it herself.

SCHROEN: Well...with respect, what Bhutto's foreign minister and ISI chief are both telling us contradicts that. Bhutto backs the Geneva Accords not the Taliban.

MASSOUD: As you say. This is what they tell you. What Pakistan's ISI say and do are different things.

SCHROEN: Alright, listen we're not naïve. She's engaged with the Taliban. She's not denying that. But the aid they've provided has been minimal, non-lethal.

KHALILI: She said this to who? Robin Raphel?

SCHROEN: (*A beat.*) Perhaps.

KHALILI: Mr Schroen, Raphel will believe anything Bhutto tells her.

SCHROEN: Raphel is the Assistant Secretary for South Asia. She knows her own mind.

KHALILI: Raphel sees Afghanistan as a wild place threatening the stability of Pakistan.

SCHROEN: Raphel wants to bring peace to this region.

MASSOUD: Via whatever means told to her by Pakistan.

SCHROEN: (*Snapping.*) Via whatever means possible! Look, she met with the Taliban. She thinks they are becoming a legitimate presence here. I am offering you a way in. A means to engage. Come in on this with us.

MASSOUD: 'Us'? What 'us'? For five years there has been no 'us'!

SCHROEN shuffles. He didn't want to take the conversation in this direction. He helps himself to another cake – almost aggressively. But as MASSOUD kicks off, SCHROEN realises how ridiculous it would be to eat right now – and just sits there with it.

Since the Soviets left, Pakistan…yes Pakistan and its Arab Islamist allies field thousands of paramilitary and military forces in Afghanistan to help Taliban. We have been given to hands of fanatics, extremsits, terrorists, mercenaries, drug mafias, professional murderers. Help us send them away, Mr Schroen. Help us now!

SCHROEN: Commander, just who do you think I am?!

MASSOUD: I think you are a representative of the United States of America!

SCHROEN: And who is that, sir?! The Pentagon? The White House? Capitol Hill? I'm sorry but they're not listening. None of them. Right now, I'm just about the only one who is.

MASSOUD: (*Desperate.*) Then you go home and you make them listen.

SCHROEN: And still you over-estimate me.

MASSOUD: It is my estimation you want to help!

SCHROEN: I do, Commander. But I am not America!

Remembering the cake in his hand, SCHROEN chucks it down onto the tray. The ATTENDANT enters again.

MASSOUD: (*To the ATTENDANT, without looking over.*) Leave us!

The ATTENDANT exits. Short pause. MASSOUD glances at KHALILI. He's about to do something unusual.

(*Gentle, defeated.*) Mr Schroen, I have fought many hard battles in my life. I'm not sure I know how else to live now than at war. I am not proud to be like this but I am proud of what we have survived. And now, for first time, I am worried. If you do not help us…right this minute, today… Kabul will fall. You understand what I'm telling you, Mr Schroen? You understand?

MASSOUD glances at KHALILI again, almost as if looking for some evidence of approval. KHALILI doesn't know how to offer it. Such a thing has never been asked of him by MASSOUD.

SCHROEN licks his fingers.

SCHROEN: (*Finally laying down his cards.*) Commander, you have been honest with me, so I will be honest with you. Back home, back in the United States of America we are entering an economic boom of historic proportions. Since the defeat of Communism there has been a breathtaking increase in global interdependence. Satellites, air travel, the world wide web… these things have collapsed time and space and America has reaped their rewards. For Clinton, terrorist attacks are a painful example of the fact that we live in an interdependent world that is not yet an integrated global community. He believes terrorism and…fundamentalism are inevitable, intricately connected to the sources of global progress and ultimately doomed. Osama bin Laden, the Taliban…for Clinton they are a challenge to be managed, not solved. In his view your war against them is a war that cannot be won. He's not…he won't be behind this. I can't offer you the help you need. Not yet. I'm sorry.

SCHOREN gives MASSOUD a moment to let this sink in. Then gently…

MASSOUD: Then why are you here?

SCHROEN: Because I disagree with my President. Clinton will not remain in office forever and who knows, with that change might come a shift in perspective. Until then we hold on.

MASSOUD glances at KHALILI.

It's really very simple, Commander. I dunno how to say it any more clearly. We can help you. But you've gotta help us first.

MASSOUD stares down at the tray of cakes. Finally resolved, defeated, he looks back up at SCHROEN.

MASSOUD: We have an old saying in Afghanistan: 'Your mouth cannot be sweet when you talk about honey; you must have honey in your mouth.'

SCHROEN: (*A beat.*) Meaning?

MASSOUD: We've talked enough. I'll sell you my Stingers. Now you find me my honey.

They stare at each other briefly. The sound of the aeroplane engine slowly builds again. MASSOUD and SCHROEN exit in different directions.

SCENE FIVE

KHALILI heads to the front of the stage.

KHALILI: The Taliban continued their campaign north. And, indeed, within six days of this meeting we lost Kabul. Commander delivered what he promised Mr Schroen. And chasing his honey-pot, he clung on to the belief that this new relationship with our Amercian dentist would lead to bigger political support. Five more years passed since that meeting and we found ourselves pushed back as far as the mountains of Farkhar. Still fighting the Taliban. Still alone. Commander continued to believe in what Schroen promised. Always. Even then. But despite my efforts, no help came. By now it was 2001. Clinton had been gone for months and still we saw no change. I was back in New Delhi when Commander rang. He said 'if you're standing, run. If you're sitting, stand and run. Come like the wind.' It was a Tuesday. We have a tradition in my family never to travel on this day. So I tell him: 'Later...later I come'. But of course I travelled. I flew. And in reward for my bravery? (*He hesitates.*) Well I suppose Commander saved my life. And with my passport of all things. With a small book, no less, Commander saved my life.

SCENE SIX

KHALILI turns back into the scene. A bed and a bedside table have replaced the desk. A mattress lies on the floor beside them. The chairs remain. A book and a passport sit on the bedside table. There's the hum of an air conditioner unit and a generator somewhere in the background.

MASSOUD sits on the bed, reading. KHALILI joins him. After reading for a short while, KHALILI glances up at MASSOUD. He tries to turn back to his book, but he can't concentrate. Eventually…

KHALILI: Commander…was there any reason in particular you wanted me for?

MASSOUD thinks for a beat…and suddenly snaps into action, jumping up.

MASSOUD: Of course, Khalili Saab! Look!

KHALILI looks. He doesn't know what he's supposed to see. He looks back to MASSOUD.

I have an air-conditioner now. Russian! The best money can buy! You see?!

KHALILI stares at MASSOUD like he's a mad man.

KHALILI: An air-conditioner?! You fly me here…on a Tuesday…for an air-conditioner?

MASSOUD: What do you think?

KHALILI: I think it's noisy. I think it's of very little importance!

MASSOUD: Then what about my watch? Is this not the best watch you ever saw?

KHALILI: It's the same watch you've worn your whole life. I've seen this watch a thousand times before.

MASSOUD glances about the room. He spots the book on the bedside table and picks it up.

MASSOUD: Aha! Then what about my Hafiz? Now I know you have never seen such a beautiful book as this.

KHALILI considers it briefly.

KHALILI: This… (*Conceding.*) This I do like.

MASSOUD: (*Beaming.*) You see?! Now come. (*Holding out the book.*) Let's make a fall.

KHALILI takes the book.

You asked me why I called you here. Let's put the question to Hafiz. I'll ask him. You open the book and answer.

KHALILI: Very well.

MASSOUD closes his eyes tight, thinking hard about his question.

Ready?

MASSOUD: Ready.

KHALILI holds the book vertically between both palms in front of his face. He lowers his forehead forward on to it and makes a silent prayer. He then flips open the book at a random page. Gliding a finger down through a poem, his smile drops. He hesitates. Tired of waiting, MASSOUD opens his eyes.

Well? What does he say?

KHALILI: (*Reading.*) 'Tonight, plant the seed of love in your heart,
Root out the tree of hostility and hate.
Oh, you two
Who are sitting here together;
So many moons will pass,
So many suns will come and go,
Value Tonight. Value it.
You will not have this night again.'

KHALILI can't look up from the book. MASSOUD shifts. Eventually…

MASSOUD: Well this one's easy. Come, Khalili Saab. Look at that moon. Look at those stars! It means we will never see another night like this again. That's all.

KHALILI: You're telling me I came all this way to look at the moon?

MASSOUD: Is the moon not enough?

KHALILI: Commander, they're not coming. The West. They won't help you.

MASSOUD: With our enemies growing in such numbers, I disagree.

KHALILI: But they don't believe the numbers.

MASSOUD: Then you must make them believe.

KHALILI: Make them? You say there's two thousand in al-quaeda now…

MASSOUD: More! Twenty thousand!

KHALILI: But they don't see it. Commander, they don't care.

MASSOUD: Then they will be made to care. We share the same enemies, Afghanistan and the West. Our problems are theirs. They know that.

KHALILI: They've known it for five years!

MASSOUD: (*Losing his temper.*) Then it's surely just a matter of time!

MASSOUD calms down. He stretches out his hand.

Khalili Saab, look at this hand.

KHALILI hesitates.

Look at it.

KHALILI looks.

Can you see the lines in my palm?

KHALILI: (*A beat.*) Yes.

MASSOUD: Can you see the whites of my nails?

KHALILI: Yes, Commander.

MASSOUD: It is as clear to me as this that they will come. (*Gathering momentum.*) And when they have helped us rid our country of this darkness, you and I will put our clothes in a bag hung across our backs, and we will walk. We will walk from village to village, from Mosque to Mosque, school to school…until we have told every Afghan alive of our vision for this country. It is a vision that leads a people. Not a gun. Not a book. That vision is ours, Khalili Saab. Yours and mine. Afghanistan has not lifted the white flag to the Taliban yet.

MASSOUD beams at KHALILI. It's infectious. KHALILI can't help but nod in agreement.

Good. (*Relieved.*) Good. (*Short pause.*) Now before we go to bed. Please. Read me just one more poem.

KHALILI opens up Hafiz once more.

Not Hafiz. Something else. You decide.

KHALILI thinks briefly, before putting away the book.

KHALILI: 'So many friendships
That time destroyed,
Scattered across oceans.
So many causes
That time held back,
All but one:

At the dawn of the universe
There was a candle of love.
And every evening it glows
Stronger
And Stronger.'

MASSOUD: Who wrote this?

KHALILI: (*A beat.*) My father.

MASSOUD: Then we truly have nothing to fear.

MASSOUD exits.

SCENE SEVEN

Night slowly shifts into day…

KHALILI: I went to bed. It had more covers on it than I'd seen on Commander's. I woke up. I had a coffee and grapes by my side. I asked the boy where it had come from and he told me Commander had sent it to me himself. Commander once said: 'If everything in life is straw and hay and there is just one seed that is love: take it.' Here we were in the middle of nowhere – al-quaeda at our door. Killing, getting killed. No money. No Kabul. And Commander sends me coffee to my bed. He doesn't even drink coffee. But even in a time and place such as this, his concern was not for himself. (*A beat.*) We can take the seed, all of us. But who among us will take the time to plant it?

SCENE EIGHT

A table. Some chairs.

MASSOUD enters. He's energetic, inspired. KHALILI snaps back into the scene, simultaneous with MASSOUD's entrance.

MASSOUD: Khalili Saab, there's two Arab reporters I've kept waiting for far too long. Let's do the interview – you can translate. Then we'll go to the Oxus River. You know they say it was one of the four rivers of the Garden of Eden!?

KHALILI: Then forget the reporters. Let's go now.

MASSOUD: Later. I've already bid them in.

MASSOUD notices KHALILI's passport on the bedside table. He picks it up.

And keep this in your pocket. You're not in your embassy now.

KHALILI takes it and struggles very briefly to wedge it into this shirt pocket.

Here.

MASSOUD takes the passport and forces it into the pocket.

You see? (*Patting his own heart.*) Safe and sound.

KHALILI grins, happy to have been fussed-over by his friend.

A REPORTER and a CAMERA MAN (carrying a large camera and a tripod) enter. They are both thickly-set, focused, nervous.

Good. (*To the CAMERA MAN.*) You can set that up there.

The CAMERA MAN does as he's bid, silently assembling his tripod at chest height. He moves the table from in front of the Commander with such ease, MASSOUD and KHALILI are surprised.

KHALILI: (*Aside to MASSOUD.*) What is he, a photographer or a wrestler?! I've seen soldiers with less muscle. (*To the REPORTER.*) What paper did you say you were from?

REPORTER: We do not represent any paper. We belong to an Islamic Centre based in Europe.

KHALILI: Where in Europe?

REPORTER: Paris, London… We have many centres. All over.

KHALILI glances at MASSOUD. This doesn't feel right.

MASSOUD: (*To the REPORTER.*) What will your questions be about?

REPORTER: Sheik Osama bin Laden.

MASSOUD: (*A beat.*) What about him?

REPORTER: Why you are against him, why you said he was un-Islamic, why you said he kills Muslims. That sort of thing.

MASSOUD and KHALILI glance at each other.

KHALILI: (*Aside, to MASSOUD.*) You don't have to do this.

MASSOUD: But I do, Khalili Saab. Of course I do.

KHALILI: Why?

MASSOUD: Because we need the world's ears. How else are we going to make them listen?

He pats the chair next to him – the other side of himself from the REPORTER.

Come.

KHALILI sits. MASSOUD looks into KHALILI's eyes, smiles and squeezes his arm. He turns back to the REPORTER.

I'm ready.

The CAMERA MAN backs away.

REPORTER: (*Fast.*) Bismillah e errahman e erraheem!

A deep, shuddering, thud of an explosion, simultaneous with blackout.

Out of the noise of the explosion emerge the sounds of the aeroplane engines again. This time the engines continue crescendoing...into the projection of the two aeroplanes flying into the World Trade Centre.

THE NIGHT IS DARKEST BEFORE THE DAWN

by Abi Morgan

First production

The Tricycle Theatre, London, 19 April 2009

The following cast performed in the remount in July 2010 at the Tricycle Theatre prior to the USA tour:

Characters / Cast

MINOO (early 50s Afghan)	Cloudia Swann
HUMA (late 20-30s Afghan)	Shereen Martineau
ALEX (late 30s/early 40s American)	Daniel Betts
OMAID (early 30s Afghan)	Daniel Rabin
BEHRUKH (mid-teens Afghan)	Sheena Bhattessa
COMMANDHANELMAR (late 40's Afghan)	Nabil Elouahabi
TRIBESMAN	Raad Rawi
TRIBESMAN	Vincent Ebrahim
TRIBESMAN	Danny Rahim

Director	Indhu Rubasingham
Designer	Miriam Nabarro
Lighting	James Farncombe
Sound	Tom Lishman

Setting

The play is set in a rural smallholding, south of Kandahar. It is April 2002.

Dusk –

A bombed out building –

MINOO (early 50s) sits making bread by a fire. She is dressed in the familiar blue burkah of the Taliban era.

HUMA (late 20s / early 30s) stands waiting, in modern dress, her hair covered, a soft briefcase in her hand.

ALEX (late 30s / early 40s) sits, in shirt and slacks, drinking a small glass of tea. He is wearing a flak jacket.

Beyond endless chalky fields speckled with poppies.

HUMA: It's good.

ALEX: Oh yeah its fine as long you tuck that sugar cube –

HUMA: …under the tongue.

ALEX: Right.

HUMA: Yes.

ALEX: …right under the tongue.

> *MINOO nods, reaching for a kettle of tea going to pour ALEX more.*
>
> No. I'm good.

HUMA: He's had enough thank you.

> *MINOO ignores HUMA, pouring more tea, resuming making bread.*

ALEX: Oh, OK… OK…

> *ALEX shrugs, drinks.*
>
> Thanks… Great…
>
> *ALEX drinks.*
>
> I don't know how much more of this stuff I can drink. Couldn't we just go out there to talk to them?

HUMA: They'll be back soon. They're coming back?

> *MINOO shrugs –*

ALEX: What did she say?

HUMA: It is nearly sunset.

> *ALEX nods, looking out.*

ALEX: We've been here two hours.

HUMA: Ten more minutes OK?

ALEX: You said that yesterday.

ALEX shrugs, silently looking about him. MINOO reaches for the kettle goes to pour more tea.

No. Thank you.

MINOO hesitates, shrugs, and hangs the teapot back on the fire.

Tashakkur.

HUMA: I am surprised she even gave you tea.

ALEX hesitates mid-sip, raising his glass to MINOO, clearly embarrassed.

I guess it's because you're American.

Distant rumble of a truck –

Let me talk.

ALEX instinctively stands, HUMA gently moving in front of him.

ALEX: Won't it be better –

HUMA: No… I know the family.

ALEX: You need to make it clear.

HUMA: Yes.

ALEX: Only nine. Nine is not… It's not a class yet.

HUMA: I know what to say.

OMAID (late 30s) a tall dark man, swathed in robes and headdress enters surrounded by his tribesmen. Many have guns slung across backs, and rifles in hand. BEHRUKH (15 years) a few yards behind follows, carrying a hoe.

Aasalaamu Aleikum.

OMAID hesitates, considering, his tribesman close by.

OMAID: Who's the American?

OMAID joins his tribesman washing by a tap, the ritual before pray, washing hands, feet, nose, ears, mouth.

ALEX: Alex Braiton.

ALEX holds out his hand, ready to greet OMAID.

Al-Salaam.

OMAID does not look up from washing.

OMAID: I don't talk to journalists.

HUMA: He's not a journalist.

ALEX: Can you tell him – ?

HUMA: He works for an international charity.

OMAID: You run with the Americans now?

Silence.

HUMA: They want to put funding into our school.

ALEX: We've been waiting over two hours. Two hours.

OMAID looks at ALEX blankly, enjoying not understanding.

Yeah, you keep smiling at me.

ALEX shakes his head wearily.

Really, there's no place I'd rather be. We have been here two hours waiting for you.

HUMA: Please.

ALEX shrugs, concedes.

Behrukh, is that you?

BEHRUKH hesitates, hangs back, tentative.

You've grown.

HUMA wants to touch BEHRUKH, raising her hands to touch her, hesitating on seeing BEHRUKH's resistance.

We miss you. We've all missed you.

A TRIBESMAN tuts, BEHRUKH hurries to fetch a towel for the TRIBESMEN, then falls into line, laying out plates, preparing food with MINOO.

We have opened the school again.

Silence.

I have nine girls already who have agreed to return.

OMAID hesitates, smiles, amused.

OMAID: Nine? (*Beat.*) You do not have a school. You have a university.

OMAID considers ALEX, washing his face and hands; snorting water through his nostrils, hitting the dust on the ground.

ALEX: Are we OK? Is everything OK?

ALEX looks nervously at a passing TRIBESMAN, a gun still slung across his back.

Huma?

HUMA: We're fine.

ALEX: What is he saying?

HUMA: I'm telling him about the school.

ALEX: *Charity*? We are giving *money*. You have daughters?

HUMA: Please.

ALEX: Sir? Are you hearing me?

OMAID looks to ALEX, unwavering.

Forgive me if my temper is a little frayed, Sir, but it is the fourth time we have been here this week. Every time you say you will meet us and every time… It takes us over an hour each way… And my ass right now is kindasore. Those craters in the road, it doesn't make for a pleasant ride. So the least you can do now, Sir, now we are here –

OMAID smiles.

There's that smile again.

ALEX shakes his head, laughs, exasperated, reaching for a small pair of binoculars in his bag.

OMAID: So brave today, sister, with your American.

HUMA: He's not my American.

ALEX looks up, from his binoculars, considering.

ALEX: Are those poppies in that field?

HUMA hesitates, nods.

OMAID: I heard they killed your husband.

HUMA holds his look unwavering.

I go to watch the football.

HUMA: All the way to Kabul? I didn't know you liked it so much.

OMAID shrugs, moving on, avoiding HUMA's gaze.

I want Behrukh.

HUMA holds the forms and pen out to OMAID, to look at.

I have brought the forms for her to register. I can fill them in with you now. (*Silence.*) I am not leaving unless you give her to me.

OMAID stands, looking at her. He starts to laugh.

HUMA searches in her bag, taking out a pencil sharpener.

HUMA: Behrukh?

She places it on the ground in front of her.

Behrukh, do you know what this is?

BEHRUKH hesitates, looks to OMAID, almost fearful.

You remember?

BEHRUKH hesitates, nods.

Can you still write your name?

MINOO tuts, holding a bucket to BEHRUKH. BEHRUKH looks to OMAID, he nods. BEHRUKH makes to tend distant livestock, rattling the bucket of meal.

His organisation is interested in funding the school. They are willing to supply all the writing materials, books, stationery. Fifteen scholarships.

OMAID: No.

HUMA: Give her to me for one year.

OMAID's gaze follows ALEX, taking in the distant poppy field.

OMAID: You bring an American here?

HUMA: Brother –

OMAID: After everything, you return and you bring him.

HUMA: He is here to help us, Omaid.

OMAID: Us?

OMAID laughs.

ALEX: What does he say?

ALEX looks to HUMA for understanding.

OMAID: That is very nice. That is very funny. You are very funny Huma.

HUMA packs up her papers, pencils and sharpener into her bag.

ALEX: Are we going?

ALEX looks to OMAID, weary.

That's a pity. I'm sorry. Can you tell him… I am sorry.

ALEX peers out across the fields, squinting his eyes, the sun casting its fading light, revealing the sway of green poppy plants.

I thought it was just wheat. That they'd assigned wheat to these fields.

HUMA: He's asking why you are not growing wheat.

OMAID looks to ALEX, attempting to be understood.

OMAID: 5000 dollars...one field.

OMAID smiles, close to ALEX now.

Opium. (*Beat.*) For the non-believers.

BEHRUKH returns, tipping up her bucket, draining the last of the meal on the ground for the chickens, slapping the bottom of the bucket.

Where is the mullah to tell me not?

ALEX: They'll come and destroy them. The military will destroy all of it. Huma?

HUMA: He wants to know if you realise the military will destroy your fields.

OMAID: Tell him build me a dam and maybe I will grow something other than poppies.

OMAID pushes an elderly TRIBESMAN towards ALEX.

Tell him to take one of these other idiots if he wants to waste his money educating us.

ALEX looks to HUMA, searching for understanding.

Tell him they may have rid us of the Taliban but they must offer us more than their bombs and packets of onion seeds.

HUMA: He's angry. We're wasting our time here.

OMAID: We don't have flak jackets –

OMAID points to ALEX chest. ALEX looks down, half understanding.

...to protect us.

ALEX: This?... I promised my wife. My wife? She said she'd shoot me if I didn't wear it.

ALEX hesitates, sees OMAID is unamused.

OMAID makes to go, tutting to BEHRUKH to follow.

HUMA: 'He who has a slave-girl and teaches her good manners and improves her education will be rewarded twice.'

OMAID: And when the Taliban return? What good will your education do then? They will not be so merciful a second time Huma. Your husband learnt that.

HUMA: And you?

OMAID laughs, joining his TRIBESMEN as they kneel to pray, in a line, facing the setting sun.

ALEX: What the...? What...am I doing here? Really I should have... Gone to Mali...built toilets for elementary in Zambia...I mean we comes to these places...we drink tea...we offer them free education and they just laugh at us.

HUMA: (*Beat.*) You see the man on the right.

HUMA nods to a TRIBESMAN kneeling to pray next to OMAID.

That is his chief tribesman. On left is a cousin of his brother. They work for him but if he not grow opium they will cut his throat. They closed the markets so they sell it across the border. They cross through the mountains if they can. On mules or trucks –

The steady ritual of praying, the men bow back and forth.

The short one? He carries it. He has sister married to border guard. He was in my husband's class. A good boy. The fat one? He is father-in-law of Kandahar Chief of Police. Worse happens? Americans come and destroy the fields. Poppy always comes back, even if there is no water. Bombs ripping the earth... Poppy always comes back. Our blessing and our curse. What thrives here, also kills us.

ALEX: You know Omaid well?

HUMA nods.

HUMA: I married his brother. He was killed by the Taliban.

ALEX: Oh... OK... Right...

HUMA: (*Beat.*) They didn't tell you that in the office?

ALEX shakes his head.

Now I know you are being polite.

BEHRUKH passes, sorting through a pile of old sacking.

Behrukh?

Silence.

So quiet? You were always chatter chatter chatter. When you were five you did not sit still before your mouth would run away.

Silence.

We have classrooms. And a computer. Maybe one day you could be a teacher too.

BEHRUKH finishes up sorting bags, going to wash. HUMA, hesitates, joins her. Together they wash.

Hidi. And Muna. Gzifa was the first to come. Her mother brought her to the school herself.

OMAID: (*Calling over.*) Behrukh.

BEHRUKH reaches for a towel, dries her face, hands, moving on.

BEHRUKH: Our mother is dead.

HUMA: Yes.

BEHRUKH can barely look at ALEX, standing across the yard.

But we are free –

BEHRUKH: I still carry water every day.

MINOO and BEHRUKH join the others, kneeling to pray. HUMA looking on. HUMA looks back, a row of guns resting up against the wall. HUMA makes to go. ALEX stops her.

ALEX: You have nine girls. You need fifteen.

HUMA: He won't.

ALEX: Six more girls, Huma. Let him pray and after –

HUMA: After?

ALEX: Let's hope we eat.

ALEX resumes watching through his binoculars. HUMA considers waiting –

Prayers over, OMAID and his TRIBESMEN return, ready to eat. OMAID considers ALEX standing close by, shrugging to him to join us.

OMAID: You? (*Pointing to ALEX.*) New York?

MINOO, BEHRUKH, hurry to get things ready, hovering close by, passing food. ALEX and HUMA join them making to eat.

HUMA: He's asking where you're from?

ALEX: Amherst, just north-east of Buffalo. It is officially America's safest town. Some days we don't even lock our front doors.

OMAID smiles, quietly ridiculing ALEX.

There's that smile again.

OMAID: New York.

OMAID mimes a plane with his hand, absently.

Boom. Boom.

OMAID laughs, shovelling more food into his mouth.

ALEX: Motherfucker.

ALEX puts down his plate.

Look I know your wife and two sons were killed by American bombs. Huma?

ALEX looks to HUMA to translate. HUMA hesitates.

HUMA: He's saying –

ALEX pushes on.

ALEX: I know they were driving back from Kandahar market. Kandahar. I know your wife was pregnant with your fifth child. I am sincerely sorry for your loss.

HUMA: He's saying –

ALEX: Many many innocent lives have been and will be lost in this war but I truly believe that it should not stop you from sending your daughters to school. We need six more girls to qualify for our charity's funding. It would be one classroom. All girls. You sent them six years ago.

HUMA: I have the old papers that Ara used to register. But it is important that if you want them to re-register –

HUMA searches the papers, pulling a thick file out of her briefcase, handing it to OMAID.

OMAID: It was Ara who signed them... Ara wanted her to go to school.

HUMA: Yes.

OMAID: Because you and Farrin talked to her.

HUMA: It was of her own free will Omaid.

OMAID: Was it? 'She must go to school,' she said. I saw other men beat their wives. But she is strong...was strong... 'Take them then,' I said. 'While you can.' '94 the Taliban arrived. Ara cried all night. I said 'Why are you crying? Now she can stay home and cook. Now she can learn from you. At least our boys can still go to school.' So OK...they go to the Madrassa. They pray. They grow beards. We all look like old men. But still at least my boys had an education.

But Farrin says 'So what happens to Behrukh?' I say 'Brother don't make trouble for yourself.' He promised me.

HUMA: Your brother wanted to see his niece educated.

OMAID stands as if to strike HUMA. HUMA screams. ALEX goes to protect her. OMAID steps back.

OMAID: My brother is dead.

Distant rumble of trucks –

You just arrive. Suddenly you are back with your American. You say 'Come on, learn again.' (*Beat.*) We have learnt enough for one lifetime.

HUMA: You used to listen to your brother. She is a bright girl. I taught her how to sharpen a pencil. I taught her to write her name. Can she write her name still?

OMAID: My sons are gone. Now Behrukh must stay and help with the land.

OMAID makes to go. HUMA desperately searches in her bag.

HUMA: Behrukh –

HUMA places a pencil, sharpener and piece of paper down in front of BEHRUKH.

Show me. Show me if you can still write your name.

BEHRUKH hesitates, takes the pencil. OMAID makes to go.

This girl was a storyteller.

BEHRUKH struggles to write, but slowly writes her name until –

I use to ask her to stand in front of the class and read to everyone what she had written. Now she cannot even write her name. It is not enough. Not for one lifetime. Omaid please –

BEHRUKH shakes her head, clearly already forgotten. HUMA holds up the half written name.

OMAID: You think the Taliban has gone far? They are only a few kilometres away. Hiding across a border or in the mountains. They do not go away.

OMAID, close to HUMA now, almost gentle.

I saw what they did to my brother. You did not, Sister. Farrin was a big man, a strong man. His body was built for the land but always he was head in a book. If he had stayed here, stayed on the land. (*Beat.*) They tied his arms to one truck, his legs to another. They disembowelled him. They made the people watch and then the footballers come on. Kicking the ball, his guts still on the ground. The Taliban with the guns, shouting at them 'Play on…Play on' And 'Keep your head up… Keep watching. Don't look down… Watch the game.' (*Tapping the side of his head.*) I will be watching that game all my life.

Distant laughter –

She is all I have left.

HUMA: Then teach her. Educate her as you did your sons. Or are you too scared?

OMAID: I was not the one who was too scared, Huma. You were.

HUMA hesitates, shaken. OMAID shakes his head, moves away.

ALEX: What did he say?

OMAID walks across the yard, to greet an arriving truck.

HUMA: It doesn't matter.

The rise of smoke, a cluster of TRIBESMEN still lost in their card game, an opium pipe passed amongst them.

ALEX: Who are they?

OMAID in conversation with arriving mujahideen, with weapons sunk on the back of distant truck. ELMAR (40s) sits in a truck, a gun slung across his back, clearly the head of the group.

HUMA: (*Shrugs.*) Commandhan. Everyone knows him. He works with the military. They are needed to keep the Taliban at bay.

MINOO, sunk against the wall, plucks a chicken, the blood smearing her blue burkah as ELMAR passes, a gun slung across his back, head swathed in the turban of the mujahideen.

ELMAR: It is our teacher.

HUMA instinctively straightens, facing ELMAR, quietly imposing yet HUMA maintains her stance.

Good day, Sir.

OMAID nods to BEHRUKH to make tea.

ALEX: Aasalaamu Aleikum.

ELMAR: Wa-AleikumAassalaam.

HUMA nods, avoiding ELMAR's gaze.

The road is up. (*To ALEX.*) One of your mines.

ELMAR smiles at ALEX.

No cars will be getting out tonight.

HUMA: This is –

HUMA goes to introduce ALEX to ELMAR.

ALEX: Alex Braiton. I'm from –

ELMAR smiles.

ELMAR: I know who he is.

HUMA: He's giving funding to our school. (*To ALEX.*) I'm telling him you why you come.

ELMAR: I hear of this.

HUMA: I have nine girls. I came to ask if Behrukh would like to join our class.

ELMAR: So you have come to educate us?

HUMA goes to translate. ELMAR waves him away.

No need. No need. I speak your English very well. So you have come –

ALEX: ...to facilitate the re-establishment of the schools.

ELMAR: She is a good teacher?

ELMAR points to HUMA, laughs to himself.

ALEX: That's what I hear.

ELMAR: You have a lot of woman teachers?

ALEX: A handful. We'd like to see more.

OMAID hovers.

ELMAR: You OK?

OMAID: Yes. All fine.

ELMAR: You have worms in your ass?

The TRIBESMEN smile.

OMAID: You wish to eat, Commandhan.

ELMAR: No.

ELMAR looks to ALEX.

American. I like your films.

ELMAR smiles, gaze lingering on HUMA.

Gladiator?

ALEX: You know *Gladiator*? Yeah. Yeah. Russell Crowe. That's a great movie.

ELMAR: And *Titanic*. You know *Titanic*?

ALEX: Uh huh.

ELMAR: It is very very moving. I like this film.

ALEX: You and the rest of the world... Me not so much but... It's a favourite of my wife's.

ELMAR: They teach you much about life.

ALEX: I guess.

ELMAR takes a cup of tea, considering HUMA.

ELMAR: You have got fat.

HUMA: A little.

ELMAR: Who is going to run this school?

HUMA: I will.

ELMAR: Farrin was a very good teacher.

ALEX: Teacher? Right. Farrin? Do we have him on our books?

HUMA: No. Not anymore.

ELMAR: He married a local girl. We were not sure about her but he insisted he wanted an intelligent wife. You understand?

OMAID: Commandhan, do you wish to look around the farm now?

ELMAR tuts, silencing OMAID.

ELMAR: Farrin says 'I am going to build school'. Build?

ALEX: Right. Yeah... I think I understand.

ELMAR: Good school. Everyone come and he teach them how to read and right. With Huma. (*Pointing at HUMA.*) Wife?

ALEX nods, turning to look at HUMA, slowly understanding.

Then Taliban come. Taliban close down. We say 'Farrin, please...' But Farrin has intelligent wife. 'Ssh,' she says. 'You shall teach at night.'

OMAID: Commandham please.

ELMAR: 'No one will know.' Farrin loved his wife. Why not? She is a beautiful woman. Is she not a beautiful woman?

ALEX hesitates, nods.

ALEX: Beautiful? Yes. Yes she is.

ELMAR: Like Kate Winslet.

ALEX: Kate Winslet. Right. Back on course, films again.

ELMAR: And love… He loved her.

HUMA looks down, tears pricking her face.

For a bright man he was very stupid. Taliban come. They take him to Kabul. But not his wife.

ELMAR looks to HUMA.

Why did he die and you survive? Because you are beautiful? Now I think you grow a little fat. Huma, you know what they say? They say you survived because you were not stupid.

ALEX: Huma?

OMAID: She just came to ask about the school.

ELMAR: And you will not disappoint her.

OMAID: I need Behrukh to work the land.

BEHRUKH passes, ELMAR reaches out, pats her head.

ELMAR: We must look to our daughters now, Omaid. They are the intelligent ones.

ELMAR puts an arm around ALEX, gently leading him towards the TRIBESMEN, joining them as the opium pipe is passed around.

Education is important now. We must all be intelligent to survive.

ALEX: OK… Huma are you OK?

HUMA nods, unable to look at him.

ELMAR: There has been too much dying, too much blood in these hills. We have been fighting for too long. First the Russians, than the Taliban. So many martyrs, so many mujahideen fallen in this land. We must make their sacrifice worth it. We should talk. I would like to give money to this school.

OMAID looks on. HUMA, head hung, visibly shaken. OMAID makes to follow, HUMA looks up.

HUMA: Is it true? Do they say that? Brother…

OMAID hesitates.

OMAID: They say the night they came for Farrin, you hid and would not open the door. They say you were the one that taught at night but every day you got more scared. They say the girls would come to you and find Farrin teaching them. They say you were too sick with fear. They say you looked to him to take your class. (*Beat.*) A man alone with ten little girls, what were you thinking of?

They say in court you said 'I did not know. He would not tell me. My husband was a mystery to me.' But they say it was you that found paper. You smuggled pencils and sharpeners under your dress. Is that true? Is that true?

HUMA hesitates, nods her head.

BEHRUKH: Abba, no. No.

OMAID pushes HUMA away, broken.

OMAID: You break my heart, Sister.

HUMA suddenly sinks to the ground, weeping bitterly.

BEHRUKH: Don't cry. Don't cry Aunty.

OMAID looks on, before moving away.

HUMA: I am sorry I could not fight for you. I am sorry I did not come and find you. I am sorry I did not bring my books here and teach you in the dark of night so you could spell your name. I was not as brave… I was not as brave –

BEHRUKH runs and gets water, a cloth, coming back, helping HUMA to bed. Dabbing her face with a cloth BEHRUKH washes her, gently dries her face and hands.

HUMA: You are a good girl. You were always such a good kind clever girl.

Far off, distant laughter, ALEX sits with ELMAR and others, smoking from the opium pipe. BEHRUKH lays out a bed roll encouraging HUMA to sleep.

You will be brighter and quicker and cleverer than any of us. (*Beat.*) And maybe braver.

OMAID looks back, now sat with ALEX and ELMAR. He waves the opium pipe away. He looks back. HUMA sleeps, BEHRUKH close by.

ALEX: Holy mother of God.

ALEX clutches his head, the opium smoke hitting him.

OMAID: You like?

ALEX: Huh?

OMAID laughs to himself, licking a Rizla paper, lighting his cigarette. ALEX looks at him, clearly not understanding.

OMAID: I do not like but my men…they like… Every day is party now.

ALEX stands, steadies himself, walking over to the tap to drink. He gulps, stands, wipes his mouth, looks up.

My wife is buried beyond that tree. (*Points.*) My eldest son Dehqan. It means farmer… (*Points.*) My youngest. Atash. Fire. He would shout at the tanks, running after them throwing rocks. All the little kids. 'No, no, I'd say. They have come to set us free.'

OMAID gestures, to the ELMAR, sitting with the TRIBESMEN smoking.

Commandhan?

OMAID shrugs gives up. ALEX, resigned, smiles, washing his face, half listening yet not understanding OMAID as he talks to himself.

He is better than some. He takes what he makes from the land and puts it back into this community. Maybe he will even give you money for your school. But what happens after?

OMAID attempts to try and speak again, in broken English to ALEX.

They will come back.

ALEX: I'm sorry I don't understand.

OMAID shakes his head, heading off to take a piss.

I'm not built for this country.

ALEX reels a little as he tries to stand. ELMAR laughs.

ELMAR: But we are built for you. You like the pipe?

ALEX: Wow…yeah… It's…quite something…

ELMAR: That's what they all say. We are built for America. Why else do you come and help us?

ALEX: Excuse me.

ELMAR: Taliban go. America come. Why else are you here?

ALEX: No, I don't think…no really.

ELMAR: Poppy is our future. Poppy survives, even if we don't. Stronger than we are. You have to learn from it. Bend, grow, war, peace. You have to be like the poppy.

ALEX: I don't think so.

ELMAR laughs. ALEX gestures towards the fields.

They'll rip all your fields up you know.

ELMAR laughs, waving him away.

Not me... But someone will... So...(*Almost to self.*) gather your poppies while you can.

Around them the tribesman sleep. MINOO nudges a fire into life as BEHRUKH picks firewood.

ELMAR: You father?

ALEX: Huh? Oh right... Father? Yes.

ALEX nods, holding up three fingers.

Boy. Two girls. Three...Three... I haven't seen them in...five months...

ELMAR: I'm father. Five girls.

ALEX: That's a lot of wedding cake.

ELMAR: You teach my girls. You make them clever. When Taliban comes back, if Taliban comes back, they know something at least. I give you money for school. Money from poppies.

ELMAR smiles, sinking down to rest.

ALEX: What am I doing here?

ALEX touches his chest, realizes he's not wearing his flak jacket. He looks around, searching, stopping on seeing MINOO wearing it. He hesitates, shrugs, resigned. ALEX looks to the bombed out building. OMAID passes, half listening.

I take my kids to school every day. I don't even think about it. My eldest. She wants to be famous. I'm ashamed of that. I say 'You can be anything you want to be. A doctor? A lawyer?' 'I just want to be on the TV dad.' She'll change her mind. I'll change her mind. I say 'Don't you know how lucky you are? You have the world. You are waking up every day and you have the world.' She laughs.

OMAID looks at him bemused, clearly not understanding a word.

That's why I'm here.

OMAID shakes his head, smiles.

OMAID: I don't know what you're saying.

HUMA wakes with a start, disoriented. ALEX reaches for his cellphone.

ALEX: Do you ever get a signal here?

ALEX moving away, trying to find a signal with his phone.

ELMAR: Can't sleep teacher?

HUMA hesitates, nods to ELMAR sitting with OMAID.

I am going to send my girls. And you will do the same. You can have one of my own men. He will help you in the fields.

'Proclaim! And your Lord is the Most Bountiful Who taught the pen, Who taught man that which he knew not…'

It will not bring our sons back but…

You have a class, teacher. So teach them.

ELMAR scoops up the rough sacks of raw opium, nodding to his TRIBESMEN to help, heading back towards his truck. OMAID goes to help him, clocking BEHRUKH sitting by herself with a pencil and paper.

OMAID: So she says you are a storyteller?

OMAID considers, waiting for BEHRUKH's response; BEHRUKH stands, hesitant yet unwavering.

BEHRUKH: Yes Abba.

OMAID: As a little girl, you use to sit with your brothers whispering. They would sit listening, what were you telling them?

BEHRUKH: Just stories I heard at school.

OMAID considers, lifting up the sacks.

OMAID: We sleep –

BEHRUKH: And after I use tell them story of the farmer and the silver. (*Beat.*) Once there was a poor farmer who worked all his life very hard and lived carefully. But every year he would have no money. After a lifetime he said to himself, if I am to have anything in this world, I will have to trust in the most merciful Allah, Peace be unto him, that it will appear to me. So he prayed and he prayed but nothing. Then one day he was returning home when a thorn tore his robes. He was very angry so he dug up the bramble at the roots and destroyed it when underneath he saw an earthenware jar. He opened it and inside was more silver than he had ever seen in his life. But he said 'No, I wished for riches upon my own hearth, instead I have found this here. This is not what I asked for.' And he buried the jar of silver where he found it and went home to his wife. His wife was very angry and told a neighbour 'Go back and find that jar and I will share the silver with you.' So the neighbour returned and found the jar. But when he opened it it was filled with poisonous snakes. Thinking that the man and his wife had played a trick on him, he grew very angry. So he took the jar and climbed onto the roof of the man's house and threw it down in chimney while they were asleep. But when the man woke, it was not snakes he found, but a thousand silver coins scattered in his hearth. 'Finally' the man said, 'I can accept these riches.'

OMAID hesitates, looking to HUMA.

She came to our house, Abba. After everything, she came back. Please, Abba –

OMAID: One week. You go for one week and then... We will see.

BEHRUKH smiles her thanks, falling into unrolling her bedroll. BEHRUKH looks on, HUMA close by.

At night, Ara comes to me, she is calling and I am running but I can never get to her in time. (*Beat.*) I always wondered why you were never blessed with children. He punishes us in different ways.

OMAID makes to go, picking up the sacks, taking them over to ELMAR waiting.

HUMA: Did he ask for me when they – ?

OMAID: No.

HUMA nods. OMAID moves away to load the last of the sacks on the truck.

HUMA: Tomorrow you will write that story down, yes?

BEHRUKH nods, HUMA bends down and picks up the pencil and the sharpener, holding it out to BEHRUKH.

Push it in.

BEHRUKH hesitantly takes the sharpener, pushing the pencil inside.

Now turn. A little more pressure.

A long thread of pencil sharpening falling from the sharpener.

Steady. Steady.

ALEX on his cellphone, hesitates, watching BEHRUKH and HUMA.

The hum of cicadas –
The night hangs heavy –
The End

ON THE SIDE OF THE ANGELS
by Richard Bean

First production

The Tricycle Theatre, London, 19 April 2009

The following cast performed in the remount in July 2010 at the Tricycle Theatre prior to the USA tour:

Characters / Cast

FIONA (middle aged English woman)	Cloudia Swann
JACKIE (middle aged English woman)	Jemma Redgrave
JONATHAN (30s English)	Daniel Betts
GRAHAM (30s English)	Tom McKay
JALALUDDIN (Afghani worker)	Nabil Elouahabi
DAWOOD (middle aged Afghan male)	Daniel Rabin
TRIBESMAN (Afghan male young)	Raad Rabi
TRIBESMAN (Afghan male young)	Danny Rahim

Director	Indhu Rubasingham
Designer	Miriam Nabarro
Lighting	James Farncombe
Sound	Tom Lishman

Setting

Scene 1 An NGO Head Office in Croydon.

Scene 2 Somewhere north east of Herat.

Scene 3 The NGO Office in Kabul.

Scene 4 The NGO office in Croydon.

Dialogue in italics denotes that the speaker is speaking in Pashto.

SCENE 1

Head office of DIRECT ACTION WORLD POVERTY in Croydon. JACKIE, the Country Director, Afghanistan; FIONA, International Projects Manager; JONATHAN, Funding Manager.

FIONA: Kandahar. Awareness Raising of Post Natal Health issues for Women in – (rural)

JACKIE: – No.

FIONA: Herat. Micro Finance Initiatives and Women's – (entrepreneurial)

JACKIE: – No.

FIONA: Kabul. Conference and Event production skills training for…women –

JACKIE: No.

FIONA: This is a proper training programme for technicians. OK, it's for women.

JONATHAN: It's not Germaine Greer performing the *Vagina Monologues.*

JACKIE: Shut your eyes. Shut your eyes!

JONATHAN: For chrissakes! Alright! I've shut my eyes.

JACKIE: On the back of your eyelids paint your vision of a modern liberal democratic society. OK? What does it look like?

FIONA: It looks a bit like West Hampstead.

JACKIE: Jonathan?

JONATHAN: Crouch End.

JACKIE: Now, tell me, how many goats can you see?

FIONA: On the Finchley Road?

JACKIE: How many people are farming?

JONATHAN: I can't 'sell' farming.

JACKIE: Twenty four NGO workers have been murdered this year.

JONATHAN: You know how this business works.

JACKIE: Yes. Out of work actors hang around tube stations mugging career women for direct debits so that I can be sent off to fight a war against the Taliban on the ideological battleground of women's rights. I'm not a soldier. I don't want anything to do with Women's Rights, human rights, children's rights; rights are individualistic concepts and the one thing that Afghanistan doesn't have, and has never had, is any individuals.

JONATHAN: Oh come on!

JACKIE: All Afghans belong to a family, then a tribe, and then Islam. It's not my job to change that.

JONATHAN: Get real Jackie. Banks are going bust. People are cancelling their subscription to *Elle Decoration*. They're deciding they no longer LoveFilm. We're on that same list. We're a luxury.

JACKIE: I'm not stupid. I know that if you can show a photo of a young Afghan girl on her first day at school looking 'happily bewildered' –

JONATHAN: – I might be able to maintain funding at something like the 2006 levels, but farming, I mean, seriously and this is serious –

JACKIE: My job is to reduce poverty and improve their diet.

Gets her project proposals out.

So I have here my proposals. Mainly really boring farming projects, and some…

FIONA: Is the school in Kandahar one of those projects?

JACKIE: Yes.

FIONA: Most NGOs have withdrawn from Taliban controlled areas.

JONATHAN: We cannot be seen to be getting into bed with the Taliban. I mean the money would dry up, our donors –

JACKIE: The Taliban kill women in football stadiums, hey nobody's perfect.

FIONA: Icelandic Action Alliance, quite rightly in my opinion, abandoned that school because of Taliban interference.

JACKIE: Yes, and I rescued it and kept it open.

JONATHAN: Without girls!

JACKIE: If you close that school the boys will be sent to a madrassa in Pakistan where the syllabus is Monday, all day hatred; Tuesday, automatic weapons; Wednesday, how to park a 747 in a stationery cupboard.

FIONA: OK. (*Beat.*) We'll continue to fund that school, on one condition, it's kept an absolute secret. No Direct Action logos, paperwork, anything.

JONATHAN: If it gets out that the Taliban are our collegues, we're fucked.

FIONA: Tell me about farming.

JONATHAN: Pitch.

JACKIE: Large animal artificial insemination training;

JONATHAN: Sexy.

JACKIE: Fodder crop storage technology; diversification from rain fed cereal crops. He's fallen asleep!

JONATHAN: This is just going to be *the* dullest newsletter.

JACKIE: Land rights brokering. Ah! I said the word 'rights' and he got a hard on!

JONATHAN: OK, if you need me I'll be –

FIONA: – Sit down Jonathan.

JACKIE: Refugees that fled the fighting return to find that their fields have been taken over by a family that stayed. Who owns the land is a problem that can be solved either by brokering or in the traditional Afghan way. A bullet.

FIONA: I like it. Jonathan?

JONATHAN: OK, I'm hard apparently!

JACKIE: My Afghan worker, Jalaluddin is OK on all matters agricultural, but for this we need someone with UNHCR experience. But don't send me a woman. If I employ a woman, I have to employ a male relative so she can go outdoors. For example, if you send me Lily Allen, everywhere she goes, she has to be accompanied by Keith Allen.

FIONA: OK, we'll consider that. What's this one?

JACKIE: That's a requisition for an exercise bike. It's not safe to jog, now, and my bum is beginning to look big even in a burkha.

JONATHAN: Personal items –

FIONA: – Jonathan! You can have an exercise bike.

End of scene.

SCENE TWO

Afghanistan. The shade of an orchard. A table with tea. JACKIE, wearing a hijab; GRAHAM TRANTER. GRAHAM is a thirty year old wearing a keffiyeh; JALALUDDIN.

GRAHAM: I found that what worked in like er… Somalia was if you like get both parties to like stand on the disputed land yeah, no guns OK, that's like key, yeah, what I mean is, it's crucial this yeah, what I'm saying is, hold the meeting on the disputed land –

JACKIE: – Hold the meeting actually on the disputed land. Very good.

GRAHAM: What happens is then, the aggressor, is like disempowered, yeah, by a sense of negative honour yeah.

JACKIE: Shame.

GRAHAM: Shame and negative honour are like microscopically different concepts but –

JACKIE: – I really don't care. We have one hundred starving people here who have been robbed of their land by this thug. We have to do the right things to get them their land back.

GRAHAM: Cool. This negative honour thing works, cos they know they've taken the land, and if you like hold the meeting on the land then the negative honour thing like fucks them in the head. Understand?

JACKIE: Yes. You should do the American lecture circuit. OK, you lead.

GRAHAM: Cool.

A young Afghan, a bit western. JALALUDDIN approaches, and sits alongside JACKIE, as a colleague would.

JALALUDDIN: Dawood said he'll join us in a minute.

JACKIE: What's he doing?

GRAHAM: At this time of the day he'll be praying. Yeah?

JALALUDDIN: He is watching TV. His favourite programme. *Tulsi.*

GRAHAM: What is *Tulsi*?

JACKIE: It's a Bollywood soap. The most popular show in Afghanistan.

JALALUDDIN: Those Indian girls, they're so beautiful, always with their, what do you call it?

JACKIE: Belly buttons.

JALALUDDIN: Oh yes. That Tulsi. Mmm.

JACKIE: Why does every poppy-growing warlord in Afghanistan have three satellite dishes?

JALALUDDIN: Number one all Afghan stations, number two Indian Bollywood soap operas, number three ooooh, ha ha, ohhhh no. Can't say.

GRAHAM: *Sex Diamond*. Western porn.

JACKIE: Missionaries tried to bring Pacific Islanders to Christ. Most of them were eaten. Their only legacy was flu. Our flu will be porn.

JALALUDDIN: You know, one thing, I regret, make me sad, that my poor father died before he knew the pleasures available on the internet.

JACKIE: Jalaluddin, I don't want you looking at porn in the office OK.

GRAHAM: If Dawood drinks tea with us, we should be OK, yeah. If you drink tea with an Afghan you're his brother for life.

JACKIE: Bollocks. What's the name for that kind of scarf?

GRAHAM: It's a keffiyeh. It was useful in Somalia. It's iconic isn't it, of er…something.

JACKIE: Where did you get that one?

GRAHAM: Top Shop.

JALALUDDIN: My friend, please, take it off.

GRAHAM: Why?

JALALUDDIN: It is red and white. So it is Hamas. Hamas is Muslim brotherhood. Sunni Muslim, Taliban, and Dawood hate Taliban, he will kill you. With a knife.

GRAHAM takes the keffiyeh off.

GRAHAM: My mum bought me my first keffiyeh, when I was five, to go to Greenham Common.

JACKIE: You were at Greenham Common?

GRAHAM: Is that a problem?

JACKIE: No, just that I asked Head Office not to send me any women.

(*Beat.*) How is your mother?

GRAHAM: Hell, I dunno. She's got Alzheimers.

JALALUDDIN: My friend, you do your job, your brothers will look after your mother.

GRAHAM: I don't have any brothers, or sisters. She's in a home. I email.

JACKIE: She can't be that old, you're only thirty.

GRAHAM: She was fifty two when she had me. She wasn't married, I don't have a dad, she got this gay guy to like do the business –

JALALUDDIN: Wait. Your father is homosexual? And your mother is a lesbian?

GRAHAM: Yeah.

JALALUDDIN: Ah, we Afghans, we are so backward.

They stand. Enter DAWOOD. He has GUN 1 and GUN 2 with him. Tea is on a tray.

JACKIE: Salaam.

DAWOOD: Salaam.

JALALUDDIN: *These are my employers, Graham Tranter, and Mrs Jacqueline Adams, of Direct Action World Poverty. I will translate for them.*

DAWOOD: *Is she married?*

JALALUDDIN: *Yes. We do not care that you grow the poppy. We are here because we have one hundred of the Rohullah starving, and they tell us that you fired at them.*

DAWOOD: *How many of the Rohullah did you kill?*

GUN 2: *We haven't killed any of them.*

DAWOOD: *See, nothing. Now drink.*

They all drink tea. DAWOOD is undressing JACKIE with his eyes. During the next JALALUDDIN leads and it is presumed that JACKIE and GRAHAM do not speak the language.

JALALUDDIN: *The village shura met last night. I was expecting that you might be there.*

DAWOOD: *If I drink tea with the shura, then I am bound by the decisions of the shura. If I don't go to the shura, I am free man. Yes, I am free, it is good, I am enduring freedom. The shura can go fuck themselves many times over.*

JALALUDDIN: *The shura told me that the Rohullah families have farmed the land from the river to the trees for many generations.*

DAWOOD: *The Rohullah ran away like bees. I fought the Taliban. My brother was killed in the field by the river.*

JALALUDDIN: (*To JACKIE and GRAHAM.*) He fought the Taliban, and lost a brother. He is saying that the Rohullah ran away and brought shame on the Aimaq.

JACKIE: Is he going to plant the poppy by the river?

JALALUDDIN: *Will you plant the poppy in those fields?*

DAWOOD: *Is she the boss?*

JALALUDDIN: *No, no, no.*

DAWOOD: *Why should I trust you? You will talk to the Americans.*

JALALUDDIN: *I am an Afghan, we are drinking tea.*

DAWOOD: *I have constructed an irrigation channel. It's the water I need.*

JALALUDDIN: (*To JACKIE.*) He's drawing water from the river for the poppy.

GRAHAM: Tell him that we respect the Aimaq for their proud tradition of violence.

JACKIE: For their proud traditions.

GRAHAM: Ask him if there is a deal that can be done where the Rohullah get the fields and he retains access to the water.

JALALUDDIN: (*To DAWOOD.*) *What if the Rohullah get their fields back and you continue to draw water from the river?*

DAWOOD: *No, I want a MEHR for the death of my brother.*

JACKIE: What's this MEHR?

JALALUDDIN: (*To JACKIE.*) It means bride price.

DAWOOD: *One of their women looks like Tulsi.*

JALALUDDIN: *Tulsi? Ha, ha. Really. Nice.*

DAWOOD: *Yes. Very beautiful.*

JALALUDDIN: (*To JACKIE.*) He says the Rohullah have a girl he likes. She looks like Tulsi. Very sexy. Those Indian women, with those short saris, and dancing, and really wooaa, yes, very good.

JACKIE: He will take a wife as payment?

JALALUDDIN: The water, yes, and then a wife.

GRAHAM: Yeah, well tell him we're not gonna allow that –

JACKIE: – Graham, it's alright. Tomorrow broker a meeting between the Rohullah and Dawood. Take the decision from that meeting and get it confirmed at the shura. Make him go to the shura. Stay on for the week if you have to, do what it takes. If we don't get a deal, we've got a hundred starving Afghans, and possibly violence. Anything so we have a deal, the only deal I won't tolerate is Dawood forcing the Rohullah to grow the poppy. OK?

JALALUDDIN: OK. No problem.

JACKIE: Graham and I are going to head back to Kabul. Come on. Let's go. Tell him that we are going back to Kabul.

DAWOOD: *Is she going?*

JALALUDDIN: *Yes.*

DAWOOD: *Is she American?*

JALALUDDIN: *No, she's from Kettering. England. Where they make Weetabix.*

DAWOOD: *Ah. Weetabix. Good. Goodbye.*

End of scene.

SCENE THREE

Morning. The office in Kabul. JACKIE on the exercise bike. Enter GRAHAM, hung-over, delicate.

JACKIE: Ah, it's the Pope, with a hangover.

GRAHAM: Don't shout man.

JACKIE: You didn't drive did you?

GRAHAM: I left the motorbike in the embassy compound after the party. The bad news is I left the keys in it. Be alright. No-one can get in the compound.

JACKIE: I guess only at a fancy dress party would one see the Pope snogging Margaret Thatcher.

GRAHAM: I had to go for it man.

JACKIE: That's the third poor gullible child you've bedded in three months. Maybe we should change our name to Direct Adult Action World Poverty.

Enter JALALUDDIN.

GRAHAM: Salaam.

JALALUDDIN: Salaam.

JACKIE: Hi.

JALALUDDIN puts the Toyota keys on a hook.

We might have to leave the debrief until Graham's sobered up.

GRAHAM: No, I'll be fine.

JACKIE: OK. Fire.

During the next GRAHAM sits with his laptop taking notes. JACKIE takes notes on paper.

JALALUDDIN: I spend all week. Not easy. I bring Dawood and the Rohullah together on the disputed land like Graham say, and they drink tea. I think Dawood really felt a wave of negative honour, oh yes, very obvious. So we have a deal. The Rohullah will maintain the irrigation channel.

JACKIE: Good, so Dawood gets his water.

GRAHAM: For his poppy fields.

JACKIE: It's not my job to eliminate the poppy from Afghanistan.

GRAHAM: We could tell ISAF.

JACKIE: We are not part of the military intervention in this country. If we start to act as it's eyes and ears, we might as well start wearing green berets.

GRAHAM: OK. Cool. So water, what else?

JALALUDDIN: They took three girls.

GRAHAM: Oh fucking hell man. What do you mean?

JALALUDDIN: One for Dawood, one for his nephew, and one for his cousin. Dawood took the girl who looks like Tulsi. Yes.

GRAHAM: How old are the girls?

JALALUDDIN: Oh I don't know.

GRAHAM: Guess. I wanna know.

JALALUDDIN: Eleven, maybe the other one eleven, twelve, and Tulsi is maybe ten, I can't be sure.

GRAHAM: Oh fucking hell man!

JACKIE: You said last week, 'one of their women looks like the woman in Tulsi'.

JALALUDDIN: This girl does look a bit like Tulsi.

GRAHAM: She's ten years old.

JALALUDDIN: I am sorry, but you said very clearly, do a deal, the only thing you don't want is for the Rohullah to grow the poppy.

GRAHAM: I'm going back out there, I've –

JACKIE: Sit down Graham! When you say they took the girls, do you mean they kidnapped them or –

JALALUDDIN: – no, no, no! This is all proper. The shura have agreed it all. They are betrothed to be married.

GRAHAM: Christ man! We gotta do something!

JACKIE: At what age do Aimaq girls usually marry?

JALALUDDIN: Thirteen, fourteen.

GRAHAM: One of them's a fucking ten year old!

JACKIE: At what age will an Aimaq girl be betrothed?

JALALUDDIN: Five, six.

GRAHAM: There were some PRT guys at the party last night, we could go up there, I dunno, the PRT teams have armed back-up, north-east of Herat that would be Americans, we could go in there, and get those girls back.

JACKIE: No.

GRAHAM: Oh fucking hell! What about the Red Cross? The Red Crescent, they could go in on humanitarian grounds. Who is the regional organiser for the Red Crescent?

JACKIE: Dawood.

GRAHAM: Fuck!

JACKIE: Yes, fuck. Our job was to try and get the Rohullah land back. We've done that. That is one hell of an achievement in a country where nothing is written down, and the bad guys are in charge. This is a girl betrothed, perfectly normal, to an older man –

GRAHAM: – a porn addict.

JACKIE: You don't know that. The marriage is guaranteeing a future for her family. Think of it as the fairy tale where the woodcutter's daughter marries the prince.

GRAHAM: Call me old fashioned but unlike you, I think sex with ten year olds is wrong.

JACKIE: What did you say?

GRAHAM: I said that unlike you, yeah, I think sex with ten year olds is wrong.

JACKIE: Graham, I think you have mistaken my pragmatism for some kind of moral vacuum. Before I leave my apartment to come to work, I put my values in the fridge so to speak. I have not gone native. I am not Kurtz.

JALALUDDIN: What have I done wrong?

GRAHAM stands and looks as if he is preparing to leave.

JACKIE: Graham! Listen! You know perfectly well that there's no such thing as right and wrong in our business, there's only culture. It's our job to impose our values. You've put your mother in an old people's home.

GRAHAM: What's my fucking mother got to do with anything?

JACKIE: Have you seen anyone homeless in Afghanistan, any old people abandoned? You judge them, let them judge you. You think they treat women badly, they would not even believe that a human being could sink so low, could be so vile as to abandon their own mother, ill as she is, alone as she is, in local authority facility, and leave the country.

GRAHAM: You said that, like deliberately, to hurt me.

JACKIE: I'm trying to save your life. Jalaluddin, give me the Toyota keys. Graham, you're grounded. I'm telling you, don't even think about it. I've got the keys.

GRAHAM puts on a coat and leaves. JALALUDDIN stands.

Graham!

JALALUDDIN: I'm so sorry, I've really done a cock up, but you did say –

JACKIE: – be quiet! You've done nothing wrong.

JALALUDDIN: If Graham goes up to Herat, he might get killed because of me, I should've –

JACKIE: It's alright. I've got the Toyota keys.

JALALUDDIN: The motorbike keys aren't here. Where's the motorbike?

JACKIE: Shit. At the embassy compound. With the keys in the ignition. Herat is four hundred miles. You don't go four hundred miles in Afghanistan on a motorbike.

JALALUDDIN: He went across South America by motorbike when he was ten.

JACKIE: Did he? Why don't I know that?

JALALUDDIN: Yes, and he did that trip with his mother.

JACKIE: He what?

JALALUDDIN: He went across South America with his mother on a motorbike when he was ten, and you have insulted his honour, very badly, about his mother.

JACKIE: Shit! Come on!

They leave in haste.

SCENE FOUR

The Croydon office. A tea chest is set in the middle of the floor. Next to it the exercise bike, partly wrapped as if for transit, but recognisable as an exercise bike. FIONA is standing looking at mock-ups of a newsletter. JONATHAN is on the exercise bike, pedalling it.

FIONA: Can you get off the exercise bike please Jonathan?

JONATHAN: Eh? What's the problem?

FIONA: That was Jackie's bike.

JONATHAN: Alright. Cool. Fuck, is this her stuff. I'm sorry.

Slides off.

FIONA: Do you think we do any good? Ever. Anywhere.

JONATHAN: Oh for God's sake Fiona. Have you forgotten whose side we're on, we're on the side of the fucking angels!

FIONA: I don't think it's as simple as that. I think we do good, and simultaneously we do harm. Wherever we go, we take a virus.

Every time someone just looks at one of us, we change them, maybe even destroy them.

JONATHAN: If you're having an existential dilemma, maybe we ought to cancel the trustees meeting. Can you look at my proofs please.

FIONA: OK.

FIONA studies the proofs.

She's beautiful.

JONATHAN: Girls school. Afghanistan. Mazar i Sharif. What a photo, eh? It's the bandage isn't it. Brilliant. Almost fetishistic.

FIONA: The hope in her eyes. Beautiful eyes.

JONATHAN: Yup, she's saved us. Rescued us. Credit crunch? Qu'est-que c'est?

FIONA: How old is she?

JONATHAN: Dunno. Nine. Ten.

FIONA: Who is she? Where is Mazar i Sharif?

JONATHAN: Fiona, this is not the girl Jackie died trying to rescue. Mazar i Sharif is in the far north, Jackie and Graham were killed in Herat. You need a break.

FIONA: It's brilliant.

JONATHAN: What's the matter with you, it's fantastic! But I'm telling you it's the little injury. A legacy of violence, the burden of history carried by an innocent walking forwards into a hope filled future.

FIONA: OK. Let's go with it.

JONATHAN: I've never seen a photograph deliver a more perfect narrative. It's that perfect, you'd think I'd photoshopped it.

FIONA: Did you?

JONATHAN: Would I? I didn't no. (*Beat.*) 'cept the eyes.

TO BLACK

CANOPY OF STARS

by Simon Stephens

First production

The Tricycle Theatre, London, 19 April 2009

The following cast performed in the remount in July 2010 at the Tricycle Theatre prior to the USA tour:

Characters / Cast

JAY WATKINS, 31	Tom McKay
RICHARD KENDALL, 20	Karl Davies
CUTTY	Rick Warden
MURRAY	Danny Rahim
LLOYD	Daniel Betts
MEDIC	Jemma Redgrave
CHERYL WATKINS, 27	Cloudia Swann

Director Nicolas Kent
Designer Pamela Howard
Lighting James Farncombe
Sound Tom Lishman

Setting

The play takes place in the present.

Scene 1: is set in an underground mud and wattle bunker on the peripheries of the Kajaki dam.

Scene 2: Is set within the walls of Mazdurak.

Scene 3: Is set in the front room of a house in Levenshulme, south Manchester.

I.

SERGEANT JAY WATKINS, 31, infantry soldier of Helmand, Afghanistan and PRIVATE RICHARD KENDALL 20, share a room in a below-ground mud and wattle walled bunker on the peripheries of the Kajaki Dam. RICHARD is on watch. He glances very occasionally through infra-red glasses that look out of a hole in the upper rear of the bunker.

Its 4.20 am.

They speak quietly. There is the sound of a generator throughout quietly but present. RICHARD looks through the glasses. JAY watches him watch.

JAY: I like them.

RICHARD looks at him briefly, says nothing.

The terry.

The. Mullah.

Sorry. The Enemy Insurgents.

RICHARD goes back to his watch.

I respect them.

There is some time.

I'd shoot every last one of them in the mouth as soon as look at 'em mind you.

JAY smiles to himself. RICHARD continues to watch. Says nothing.

But you can't knock 'em.

RICHARD looks at him. Half smiles. Looks away.

A pause. JAY thinks.

I don't think my two positions are mutually exclusive by the way.

There is some time.

How long they been here?

RICHARD thinks. Before he has time to answer JAY continues.

There is some time.

We'll never beat 'em.

Fucking impossible.

RICHARD looks at him. Says nothing. Looks away again to watch.

These hills.

All that good brown.

Can't stop 'em shifting it. Watch 'em go by, fucking convoys of it and there's nothing we can do. Burn the shit out of it and it only sends the price up, yeah? Yes, Kendall?

RICHARD: Yes searge.

JAY: All that money.

Be buying out the Royal Bank of Scotland next. Make all their money selling smack to gormless teenagers down Manchester Piccadilly and spend it all on big fuck off multi-national refinancing initiatives.

RICHARD half smiles at this idea.

Just you watch.

Some time.

You know what this is don't you?

RICHARD: What's that searge?

JAY: This is the new Northern Ireland, Kendall. We'll be here for fucking years and years.

Some time.

You mark my words.

RICHARD looks again through the glasses.

Nothing?

RICHARD looks back. Shakes his head.

And now there is a longer time.

Best get set then lad.

RICHARD looks at him. He comes down from his watch. Checks his pack. His rifle. JAY remains rather relaxed looking.

They know it's the end of our tour and all.

RICHARD continues to prepare.

And they properly loved the blue on blue. Believe you me. Fucking lapped it up.

RICHARD continues to prepare. Says nothing. He checks his watch.

How long?

RICHARD: Fifteen minutes.

JAY: Do you mind me doing this?

RICHARD: Searge?

JAY: Talking like this to you.

RICHARD: No Searge.

JAY: It's one of the things I do. You'll get used to it. People do.

RICHARD: Yes searge.

JAY nods. RICHARD returns to his pack. He starts dismantling and cleaning his rifle.

JAY gestures out of the small exit of the bunker.

JAY: See fuckhead. He's one hell of a shot.

RICHARD looks. Pauses in his cleaning. Thinks.

RICHARD: With Private Higgins?

JAY: Peeyowng! Bullseye. Yer gotta hand it to the boy Kendall, eh?

RICHARD isn't sure how to respond to this.

RICHARD: I'm sorry about Higgins. The other lads told me he was a good man.

JAY: Oh fuck yes. Goes without saying. He did your job for the last three tours Kendall. On the lookout. Listening to me gabbing on.

RICHARD: I heard he was a good soldier.

JAY: Bit of a whining fuck

RICHARD doesn't know what to say.

His shit never stank eh?

RICHARD looks away. Returns to cleaning his rifle.

Some time.

Bet they don't need life insurance. Bet they're not getting emails from the Prudential.

JAY fixes on RICHARD cleaning his rifle for a while.

Your second innit?

RICHARD: Yes sir.

JAY: It gets better.

Last time I was back home I was properly, what?

RICHARD looks up at him, he chooses his word with care.

RICHARD: Bored, searge?

JAY clocks him for a beat.

JAY: Yes. Properly fucking bored. All them lot.

Our Mam gave us a bit of a party. I says to her 'Mam. Don't.' All me mates. Our kid. Rabbiting on. Cheryl. Billy. Fucking giving it.

He's six. Billy. Very, what, mouthy?

RICHARD smiles at him.

Oldham in't yer?

RICHARD nods, working again on the rifle, which, cleaned, he now begins to reassemble.

Bet Oldham's a bit quiet after a night out in downtown Musa Qala, eh?

RICHARD finishes his reassembly and then looks at JAY.

RICHARD: It can be.

JAY: Full of Haji?

RICHARD smiles.

You get a kind of instinct for it don't yer? Your hand reaches for your AK-47.
Stick an onion bhaji on this one you fuck.

JAY enjoys the joke for a beat.

Do you miss it?

RICHARD: What's that Searge?

JAY: Fucking Oldham you dense get.

RICHARD: Sometimes.

JAY: Do you?

RICHARD: Yeah, I do.

JAY: Well that's us fucked then.

RICHARD: How come?

JAY: If the calibre of infantry we've got sitting up at the front is the calibre of soldier that misses Oldham then what hope have we got against these hard-arsed motherfuckers.

RICHARD smiles at the joke.

What do you miss about it?

RICHARD: You what?

JAY: If you could bring one thing, one bit of Oldham out here what would you bring?

RICHARD thinks.

RICHARD: My bird.

JAY: Yeah?

RICHARD thinks a bit more. JAY approaches his own kit and rifle and effortlessly, with the kind of expert proficiency that means he can appear more carefree, gets himself ready for his tour.

RICHARD: There's a chippie at the bottom of our street that I quite like.

JAY: Fuck yes.

RICHARD: Chips and gravy.

JAY: Ha!

RICHARD: If I have one more ready made beef stew I'll take my bayonet and smash it up Dexter's arse.

RICHARD waits for JAY's response. It takes a beat and then JAY breaks into a broad grin. RICHARD laughs with relief.

JAY: How old is she?

RICHARD: Who?

JAY: Your bird?

RICHARD: 19.

JAY: What, blind is she?

Special needs. Bit of a spacca.

RICHARD smiles, ignores the tease. JAY is ready.

What's she called?

RICHARD: Gillian.

JAY: Gillian?

RICHARD: Yeah.

JAY: Sounds like a right slapper.

RICHARD laughs. Takes the joke. RICHARD is ready.

How's it going for you, Kendall?

RICHARD: What, Searge?

JAY: Tour 2. Of a series of eight thousand and fifty I promise you.

RICHARD goes to answer then changes his mind. Some time.

RICHARD: You know.

JAY: No. That's why I'm asking you.

RICHARD: It's easier than the first.

JAY: South Helmand weren't you? B Company?

RICHARD: Yes Searge.

JAY: Captain Winslow.

RICHARD: That's right searge.

JAY: Was he as much as a fuck as Dexter?

RICHARD smiles.

RICHARD: It wasn't what I was expecting at all. One bit.

Some time.

When I was a kid I used to have these little toy soldiers. Second World War soldiers. First world war some of them. *They* had bayonets and all. There were nothing different between them and us.

JAY: They probably had better helmets.

RICHARD: It took me by surprise a bit.

JAY: Yeah. (*Beat.*) I quite like that about it.

RICHARD: I'm not saying I don't.

JAY: It's quite old fashioned. Screw the bayonet on. Here y'are Osama, yer fuck. Get this under your rib cage. Twist.

Some time.

How much you on this tour round?

RICHARD: £1833 a month. Before tax.

JAY: Seventeen grand a year?

RICHARD: Yeah.

JAY examines RICHARD. RICHARD is aware of being examined.

He plucks up the courage to say something.

I've got a mate working security in the Trafford Centre gets paid five grand a year more than me. He doesn't have this kit, either. Last time I was at home I went out with him and a couple of his pals. You should have seen the looks on their faces. They asked me if I'd met Saddam Hussein. Straight up. They haven't got a clue, you know?

JAY smiles. RICHARD looks at his watch.

JAY: What time is it?

RICHARD: Twenty to five.

JAY: Ten minutes. Did Dexter tell you lot where we're going tonight?

RICHARD: No details Sergeant.

JAY: No. Safer, eh?

RICHARD: Yes Sergeant.

A silence. Both men are waiting now to move.

JAY: There's a village half a fifty miles north north east of Ghereshk called Mazdurak. It's deserted as far as we've known but is now considered a possible insurgent base. It's been unconfirmed for two weeks. We get in. We check it. We clear it. We get back up with air strike if we need it. We claim it. We get out.
Yes?

RICHARD: Yes searge.

JAY: They all ready?

RICHARD: Sorry Searge?

JAY: Everybody ready for that do you think? We up to the scratch of B Company? In your opinion?

RICHARD: I reckon.

JAY: How are they all keeping up do you think Kendall? From your perspective?

RICHARD looks at JAY before he confesses something.

RICHARD: I think well Sergeant. I think some of them are keen to get back to base.

JAY: That makes sense.

RICHARD: I just want a shower, me.

JAY: Fuck, well, yes. Fair dos.

A short time.

RICHARD: I didn't think we'd get nine. In one regiment. That took me by surprise.

JAY: Was Cracknall your first from our lot?

RICHARD: What?

JAY: Danny Cracknall was he your first from our lot?

RICHARD looks away before he answers.

RICHARD: Yes searge.

Some time.

I was a bit surprised that his helmet came off.

JAY: Yes.

RICHARD: That his legs were bare, he'd lost his fucking trousers Searge.

JAY laughs a touch at this idea.

The bruises on his chest by the way. Blue.

JAY: That's his ribs broken.

RICHARD nods.

RICHARD: They're closing in aren't they? On the dam?

JAY: Seems it.

RICHARD: Think we'll stop 'em? Push the FLET back.?

JAY: Maybe.

RICHARD: Think it'll make any difference?

JAY thinks.

JAY: If we keep it safe it will. If they can get the fucker working it'll sort out the lecky for the whole of the fucking South. You'll see their funny little faces light up then believe you me. They'll be sending their daughters over to us for a bit of a thank you chomp.

RICHARD smiles.

Some time.

I'm going on a lilo.

RICHARD: Sorry Searge?

JAY: Clarkey's got a lilo. I'm gonna borrow it when we get back. Go and have a bob about on the dam.
Catch a few rays. I'll lend you a go after I'm done.

They smile at this idea.

RICHARD: Reckon we'll gab to 'em, Searge?

JAY looks at him.

JAY: Who?

RICHARD: Taliban.

JAY looks away. Broods for a second or two.

JAY: We better hadn't.

RICHARD: That's what they're saying though, innit?

JAY: I'm not going to any road. No matter what Dexter says. They can all be sitting round having a fucking blather. A fucking Shura. I'll still be killing the twats. I'll charge their meetings. Fucking Rambo style.

RICHARD smiles.

Get this down your throat yer lollipop ragheads.

Pause.

It'd break my heart.

Pause. RICHARD looks at him.

If we can gab to 'em then what are we shooting them for? Yer ever think on that?

RICHARD thinks.

RICHARD: I'm fighting for my mates. I don't really care much about the, what? The Queen? No. The Government? No. I'm fighting to stop that lot from killing our lot.

JAY: That's not enough.

RICHARD: You what?

JAY: Its not. That's, forgive me for saying this and everything Kendall, lad, but that is one of the stupidest things I've heard in my whole life lad.

If the only reason you're killing them is because they're killing us lot then, then fucking hell, Kendall, let's just all join hands and stand in a big circle and go 1,2,3 stop and we can all fucking stop, yeah?

You want to know what I'm here for? I'm here 'cause I want to take the face of every single last Taliban and grind it into the rock of the desert.

RICHARD looks at him.

RICHARD: All of 'em Searge?

JAY glares at RICHARD for doubting him.

JAY: Some of the things that they do! They'll fucking break yer hands if yer trying to fucking, to read. They'll take a schoolteacher. They'll skin the fucker alive. They'll hang him on a telegraph pole. They'll set fire to his school.

As long as there's that then, no, I don't think we can just say 'no ok tery here yer go. Fair play to yer son.'

What they do is wrong. What they did is wrong. I am gonna draw a line.

RICHARD watches him some more.

Give the dumb-arsed ragheads a vote. Bob 'em tinternet. Bit of YOUPORN'd sort them cunts out good and proper. Bit of Jenna Jameson. Nice bit of smack. Sun's out. Have a bit of a swim. Everybody's happy. That's what I'm fucking here for.

RICHARD smiles.

I am a little unusual in that respect I have to confess. Have you ever heard of moral relativism?

RICHARD: No, Searge.

JAY: It's the new rock and roll. I'm getting it printed on my helmet.

RICHARD looks away. There is some time.

Three minutes.

RICHARD: Yes Searge.

JAY: Remembered your lines, Kendall?

RICHARD: Oh yes.

JAY: Best get into fucking character eh?

Some time.

RICHARD: I like this bit.

JAY: Yeah?

RICHARD: You can taste it. I always get.

JAY: What?

RICHARD: Very nervous.

JAY: My heart beat goes like a fucking drum.

RICHARD: Yeah?

JAY looks at RICHARD. Nods.

JAY: Best give 'em the beginner's call Kendall.

RICHARD: Yes Sergeant.

JAY: Two minutes to the stage.

The two men look at one another. There is a brief time.

244

II.

The stage is suddenly completely dark. It must be pitch black.

There is very sudden, very loud machine gun fire.

There are men's voices from the darkness. They should be almost indistinguishable from one another.

Maybe there is one or two red torch lights but extreme darkness and extreme and sudden noise should dominate the stage.

One of the men's voices is JAY. One is RICHARD.

CUTTY: Air Strike in thirty seconds.

LLOYD: Fire

JAY: Go five zero.

RICHARD: Firing

    A louder machine gun blast from closer proximity.

JAY: Keep down.
    Keep down.

LLOYD: Remainder let's go.

MURRAY: Clear the alleyway.

RICHARD: Clear the fucking alleyway.

MURRAY: Get out of the fucking alleyway

JAY: Come on.

RICHARD: Grenade

JAY: Just get the gun in there yeah?

    A grenade blast is incredibly loud and incredibly close by. It should be deafening and sudden.

JAY: Cutty what's going on with the air?

RICHARD: Grenade

    There's another immensely loud, immensely close grenade blast.

CUTTY: Twenty seconds sir.

    Another blast of gun shot from slightly further away. The men clearing the alleys are being shot at.

JAY: Fuck that's –

RICHARD: Compound clear

MURRAY: Fucking hell

JAY: Keep low

More machine gun fire from the troop.

More shots fired at the troop.

Just get your eyes to the right

LLOYD: Keep down

VOICE ON RADIO: 4 times enemy pax to north p.i.d

CUTTY: Air strike ten seconds sir.

JAY: Watch the tracer

VOICE ON RADIO: 4 times enemy pax to north p.i.d

LLOYD: Get up there

There is the sound of a rocket being launched. This has the familiar whiz and scream of a firework rocket but the noise of its launch is ferocious and close and casts some light on parts of the stage.

VOICE ON RADIO: 4 times enemy pax to north p.i.d

LLOYD: Rapid Fire
    Rapid Fire
    Rapid Fire

JAY: Move forward

MURRAY: Go go go go

CUTTY: Five seconds till air

JAY: 50 Cal Go

They are shot at again. This time the shots are closer and more unsettling than they've been before. In the darkness we struggle to make out that there is a man shot. It is MURRAY.

LLOYD: Contact Front
    Contact Front!
    Contact Front!

RICHARD: Man down, Man down

JAY: Who is it?

RICHARD: I don't know yet.

JAY: Get him to me now.

There is the sudden massive noise of an air strike from above. This should be far louder and far more sudden than you think you can get away with.

RICHARD: Through there

JAY: Get the casualty to me.
Get the casualty to me now

RICHARD: It's Murray.

JAY: Medic Medic – get me a fucking Medic now!
Where's he hit?
Come on.
Get his kit off him.
Get it off of him.

RICHARD: He's gone. T-1.

More machine gun fire from the unit and shots at the unit. Two more rockets are fired out of the base.

LLOYD: No. He's alive.

JAY: Right get him back.
Get him back.
And his kit Kendall.
Get him back.

More shots at the unit.

CUTTY: Support!

JAY: Just go. Just go.

More shots at the unit.

Needs to be quick.
Come on.
Where's his body armour?
Get me his body armour now.

LLOYD: Let's go! Two section
Extract!
Fast extraction

JAY: Where's the medic?
Where's the fucking medic?

MEDIC: I'm here.

JAY: I want him.
He's still breathing.

247

MEDIC: Yes seargeant.

JAY: I fucking want him.
    You hear me?

The scene should end as suddenly as it began.

III.

The front room of JAY WATKINS' house in Levenshulme, South Manchester. He is sitting on a sofa with his feet up in front of him. He is watching television He is drinking from a cup of tea.

We watch him for a while.

CHERYL, 27, his girlfriend enters. She's wearing pyjamas. She takes him by surprise.

JAY: Hiya.

CHERYL: Hi.

JAY: What you doing up?

CHERYL: Couldn't get to sleep.
    You gonna be long?

JAY: Don't think so.

CHERYL: What you watching?

    A beat.

JAY: It's Belgian football.

    A beat. He smiles at her. She doesn't smile back.

CHERYL: Billy's asleep.

JAY: At last.

CHERYL: He's just excited to see you home.

JAY: Yeah.

CHERYL: I am too.

JAY: That's good.

    She doesn't move. Stays looking at him in her pyjamas.

    What time is it?

CHERYL: I've no idea.

JAY: Do you want a cup of tea? I made a pot.

CHERYL: I'm all right.

Shouldn't drink tea at this time. Keeps you awake.
You rang your Mum?

JAY: I'll ring her tomorrow.

CHERYL: You better.

A brief pause. He glances at her.

JAY: You all right?

CHERYL: I don't know.

A beat.

JAY: What's wrong?

CHERYL: It doesn't matter.

Some time. He looks at her.

JAY: He's got bigger hasn't he?

She nods her head.

He looks like you.

CHERYL: He doesn't. He looks like you.

He looks at her for a beat. She still stands looking at him.

JAY: You're being.

CHERYL: What?

JAY: I don't know. You keep looking at us. You're being a bit –

CHERYL: You could *talk* to him.
Billy.

JAY: You what?

CHERYL: Your son. You could talk to him.
Or just, you know, look at him a bit.
If you looked at him a bit you might clock how much he looks
nothing like me at all and is basically so much the spit of you
he's practically your mini-me.

JAY: I did talk to him. I do talk to him.

CHERYL: You didn't Jay. You talked about him. You talked to me.
You talked to the television. You looked right over his head
mate.

JAY: Where did this come from?

CHERYL: He was so excited to see you.

JAY: Chez I'm a bit tired for this.

CHERYL: Well why don't you come to bed then? If you're a bit tired for this. If you're a bit tired for it Jay why don't you come to bed with me instead of sitting down here drinking a pot of flipping tea and watching Belgian flipping football?

He looks at her, slightly stunned.

I had this idea.

You could not go back. You could stay here. You could hand in your notice. You could come back home and you could live with me and with Billy and it could just be normal again.

Some time.

JAY: Are you being serious?

CHERYL: Doesn't it look like I'm being serious?

JAY: I don't believe this.

CHERYL: No.

JAY: I've not slept for thirty-four hours. I've barely had time for a fucking shit –

CHERYL: Don't you swear at me.

JAY: I'm sorry.

CHERYL: You should be.

JAY: I am. All right?

CHERYL: I watched you giving him a kiss. You didn't even look at him when you were doing that. I tried to give you a hug and it felt like I was hugging a bit of just wood, Jay.

JAY: I'm not listening to this.

CHERYL: No. Course you're not.

JAY: What's that supposed to mean?

CHERYL: You should just stick your fingers in your ears. Stick your fingers in your ears and sing 'God Save The Queen'. That'll make it a bit easier not to hear me Jay, eh?

JAY: Chezz. Please. Can we talk about this in the morning.

CHERYL: We won't.

JAY: What?

CHERYL: We never do, Jay, do we? No. Not really we don't. It's been six years of you going out to those places Jay and I think you've done enough and I hate it and I want it to stop.

JAY: And you need to tell me this at two o'clock in the morning?

CHERYL: What are you even doing out there?

What are you even doing out there?

What are you even doing out there Jay?

JAY: You wouldn't –

CHERYL: (*She roars at him.*) Don't tell me I wouldn't understand Jay, really don't. You don't have the slightest idea of the things that I understand only too flipping well.

Nobody thinks you should be out there. Not anymore. I can't turn the television on without somebody telling me that you should be coming back home. The place is a mess. It's always been a mess. It always will be a mess. But you're making it a thousand times worse.

And if all you're doing is shitting on the place and its shitty people then I want my husband back and Billy wants his Dad back and we want him back now please.

JAY looks at her.

Can we have him back now please?

Some time.

Can we have him back now please?

JAY: There's a village about 80 kilometres west of Kandahar called Pir Zadeh.

CHERYL: Can we have him back now please?

JAY: It was south of the dam that I spent most of my time on the last tour trying to protect from Taliban insurgents.

CHERYL: Can we have him back now please?

JAY: There's a school in the village. Which in itself is frankly amazing. I spent a few days on patrol there. You take your helmet off. You wander round a bit. Take the shades off. Hand out a few sweets. Got to know, actually, we got to know some of the kids.

CHERYL: Can we have him back now please?

JAY: One of the kids that I met there was a girl called Delaram. She was ten.

CHERYL: Don't.

JAY: And what was just astonishing about Delaram was that she was going to school.

CHERYL: Don't Jay. I don't want to hear this story. I don't want to know this.

JAY: She was learning to read. And she was able to learn to read and to write and to do sums because we were there stopping anything from happening to her. Or to her school or to her teachers.

CHERYL: This is just stupid sentimental –

JAY: On our last afternoon there she was coming home from school when a forty year-old man stepped from out of one of the houses in the west of the town near where the school was with a water pistol in his hand and he sprayed it at Delaram. Laughed a bit. Giggled a bit. Sprayed the water pistol in her face. And it might have looked a bit strange because here was this forty year-old giggling and spraying a water pistol at a ten year-old kid. Only what was in his water pistol, of course, wasn't water, was it Chez, it was acid. He burnt her eyes out because she was ten and she was going to school.

Don't you dare tell me that I'm making *that* a thousand times worse.

Beat.

CHERYL: Do you think that doesn't happen here? Seriously Jay, do you mate? You want to go up Moss Side Jay it's an initiation rite for thirteen year-old girls that up there.

JAY: If we leave now then that'll be everything fucked.

CHERYL: Everything's already fucked. There's nothing you can do about that.

JAY: There are people in that country who are vicious bastard monsters and they're full of just hate and they need to be stopped.

CHERYL: There are people on our street like that.

JAY: And the ones over here are creaming a fortune selling smack from a Helmand Poppy farm that we can burn down.

CHERYL: It won't change anything.

JAY: We can open up the power supply. We can protect the water supply. We can oversee the infrastructure. We can build roads there. We can build accommodation there.

CHERYL: (*Talking over him.*) What is it about that place that means that my husband can wander off five thousand miles away and shally around like he's some kind of action hero when he's not got the courage to come home and look his own son in the face?

You are changing nothing, Jay. You *can* change nothing. All you're doing is making yourself feel better about how useless you all are.

JAY: Don't.

CHERYL: You're a coward Jay. You think you're being a hero. You're not. We're so way beyond that now. It's gone on for too long. We're not helping. We're just smashing it all up. And every time you try to make it better you do the absolute opposite.

JAY: Stop it Cheryl.

CHERYL: Or what? Or what Jay? Come on.

People shouldn't survive in places like that. People shouldn't survive in heat like that. On land like that. It makes no sense. Everybody gets so upset about people dying. It's stupid. People die all the time. It's one of the things we do. It's good. There are too many of us in the first place. We just need to decide where. And that's a good fucking place to start if you ask me. It's a hole in the bottom of the world. You should let them burn. They deserve it.

Some time. He looks at her. The football continues to play.

JAY: You should go to bed.

CHERYL: I don't want you to go back there. Every day I think that it's going to be you they talk about on the radio as being the person the Ministry of Defence are informing the family about. I hate that feeling. It exhausts me.

JAY: You. You should do. You'll be knackered in the morning.

She doesn't move.

The television carries on playing.

Sudden black.

THE GREAT GAME

The Great Game was first performed as a trilogy on 24th April 2009.

Between the plays in performance there were verbatim pieces from public figures giving their views on the future of Afghanistan – these were from interviews conducted and edited by Richard Norton-Taylor; there were also monologues by Siba Shakib telling some of the stories of Afghanistan before 1842.

Naomi Wallace's play was performed separately before each of the political discussions which formed part of the Afghanistan theatre, film and visual arts festival which ran at the Tricycle from 17th April to 14th June.

NO SUCH COLD THING

by Naomi Wallace

Characters

MEENA (a young Afghan, 15 years of age)

ALYA (a young Afghan, 13 years of age)

SERGIO (US Army soldier, Chicano, twenties)

Time

Late Autumn, 2001

Place

Just outside Sar Asia at the edge of a possible desert, near Kabul, Afghanistan.

'Grief melts away
Like snow in May,
As if there were no such cold thing.'
– George Herbert

SCENE

Lights up on an almost empty stage/desert. Night. Two sandbags, one slightly smaller than the other, lie upstage, some distance apart. ALYA, wearing a burka, stands center stage, looking up into the sky. ALYA carries a small, hard, old fashioned suitcase. Suddenly her sister MEENA appears. MEENA is wearing a headscarf covering her hair, and a long coat, covering her more Western-style dress. ALYA is startled to see MEENA. They stare at one another for some moments in silence.

MEENA: Hedgehog? Is it you, hedgehog? Alya, is it you?

ALYA: (*Quotes.*) 'He is the lord of sleep/lord of peace/lord of night'

MEENA: (*Quotes.*) 'on whose arm your hair is lying.'

MEENA claps her hands with joy.

You still have a good memory for verse!

ALYA: Ahmed Faiz gets sentimental when it comes to his Lord. Allah doesn't like sentiment. He likes lemons, hard rain and hedgehogs.

MEENA takes a small book of verse from her coat.

MEENA: I've still got the book.

MEENA holds it out to ALYA but she doesn't take it.

ALYA: You stole it when you left. That was our one book of verse that Uncle Khan brought back from his studies in Pakistan.

MEENA: What do you care if I took it? You don't like Faiz.

ALYA: But I like to read. Mother taught us from that book.

MEENA: Show me your face.

ALYA: Not here. I'm not supposed to be out of the house.

MEENA: Look at my hair.

MEENA pulls her scarf off and shakes her hair free. ALYA gasps and looks about her nervously.

ALYA: I can see your ankles. They'll kill you.

MEENA: They're on the run. The Americans have sent them running.

ALYA: Not all of them are running.

MEENA: Let me see your ankles.

ALYA: (*Backing away.*) No.

MEENA: Please.

ALYA: It is forbidden.

MEENA: Let me see your hair.

ALYA shakes her head 'no'.

All right. But I can see your shape through the cloth.

The little hedgehog has become a woman. (*Beat.*) That's your suitcase then? It's not much. I've so many things now I would need six suitcases! But we have to go. The taxi is waiting at the end of the road.

ALYA: We have no one to travel with us. If the Taliban see us travelling alone, they'll beat us.

MEENA: I told you they've left the area. It's all clear.

MEENA moves to take ALYA's suitcase but ALYA won't let it go.

ALYA: I can't go to England with you.

MEENA: Don't be silly. Father is waiting for us at the airport. They wouldn't let him pass but he is waiting. The airport is in the hands of the Americans. It's safe.

ALYA: I can't speak English. They'll laugh at me.

MEENA: You're speaking English now.

ALYA: Mother still pulls me out of bed at 2 a.m. I try to bite her because I am so tired. We do math, geometry, English.

MEENA: If my exams are good I'll go to University. I'm going to write a brilliant essay on Faiz Ahmed Faiz and –

ALYA: the idea of hell and heaven. You already wrote us about that.

MEENA: Oh. (*Beat.*) The taxi won't wait for long. He warned me. Father is anxious.

ALYA: Mother says she'll follow us soon. I don't believe her. She limps. In England they won't like a limp.

MEENA: Don't be stupid, everyone limps in England.

ALYA suddenly eyes MEENA.

ALYA: You've lost your tarbia.

MEENA: No. I haven't lost my manners.

ALYA: You go without the burka.

MEENA: Father agrees. In England no one cares. I wear the hijab. Sometimes just a scarf.

ALYA: What size bra do you wear now? When you left you only had buds. I see melons now.

MEENA: (*Delighted.*) Not melons. Maybe oranges, yes. But I think yours are bigger and I'm older than you! Can I see them?

ALYA: No. Do you let men touch you?

MEENA: Of course not. But I make a noise when I walk.

MEENA opens her coat and walks in a circle, purposely clicking her heels as she walks. ALYA is nervous.

ALYA: Shhh. Shhhh. Someone will hear you.

MEENA just laughs and makes louder clicks as she walks.

Remember Fauzia?

MEENA: Fauzia with the black, black hair.

ALYA: Black as oil.

MEENA: I think I'm prettier than she is now.

ALYA: Fauzia was walking with her father to see family. It was two years ago. She had on her best shoes and they made a click, click, click. Not loud but too loud. The Virtue Police heard Fauzia clicking and they shot her.

ALYA watches MEENA walk. Then MEENA stops 'clicking'.

It's true. Now you are prettier than she was.

MEENA: Let's go.

ALYA: We've been alone, mother and I, and outside, the Taliban. We cannot leave the house. Mother had to stop her teaching; she is forbidden to work. Uncle Khan keeps us alive with scraps from his table. Our cousin Nargis laughed too loud at the market and the Virtue Police hit her and now she is missing three front teeth and is ugly. Girls are not allowed to go outside at all. I'm forbidden to learn to read and write. There is no one to collect the water. Uncle brings it. And all this. All this and you and father are far away in England, clicking.

MEENA: The plan was for Father and I to get out first. You know that. We couldn't get back here 'til now.

ALYA: (*Calmly.*) Pig. I want to slap you.

MEENA steps close to ALYA, within her reach.

MEENA: Then slap me.

The two sisters just regard one another.

ALYA: Does it rain in England all the time?

MEENA: It rains. But it's not hard rain.

ALYA: Then Allah doesn't like England. Will you take me to buy earrings?

MEENA: Yes.

ALYA: Mother says they have hedgehogs there. But with little ears, not like here with the long ears.

MEENA: You can buy a bird at a shop on the high street and teach it to sit on your finger. You can't do that here.

ALYA: Do the English like their hedgehogs?

MEENA: There is a hedgehog society. You can join.

ALYA: But they'll laugh at me. All the children in the new school will laugh at me.

MEENA: You're just a girl. That's not so funny. No one will laugh.

ALYA: Liar. I'm not just a girl. My back hurts. It hurts so much I can hardly move.

MEENA: What's wrong with your back?

ALYA: Quills. I'm growing quills.

MEENA laughs but ALYA is serious.

Along my spine.

MEENA: Let me see.

MEENA grabs at ALYA but ALYA dodges her.

ALYA: No! You might cut yourself. The quills are sharp. I can't go with you.

MEENA: You're just scared. Take my hand.

MEENA holds out her hand but ALYA doesn't take it.

ALYA: Don't tell anyone. It's a secret.

ALYA thinks she hears something, whispers.

Shhh. Footsteps!

Both of the girls listen, alert.

MEENA: It's nothing. The streets are clear tonight. We're safe. Alya, I have a secret too.

ALYA: Tell me.

MEENA: I've been held in the arms. Of a man.

ALYA slaps her sister's face. MEENA touches the sting with her hand.

ALYA: You are dirty. You are disrespectful. You shame me. You shame father.

MEENA just stares at her sister.

Tell me more.

MEENA: It was night. Dark. I couldn't find my way home. I got lost. Such a big city. I was tired and he put his arms around me, and carried me.

ALYA: (*Eager.*) Did he squeeze your boobs?

MEENA: Now you are dirty! No. He just carried me and then put me down again. His hands were warm. He touched my neck.

ALYA: You've been touched by a man not of your family. That's a death sentence for you here. Whore. Whore. I have missed you every hour. I smell your clothes to remember you. Your bed is silent and your pencil cold on the table. (*Beat.*) We'll come back here when we're teachers?

MEENA: Yes. And we'll teach in the daylight. And girls will be allowed to go to school.

ALYA: And we'll scrape, scrape the paint from the windows.

MEENA: And we'll open our doors, skip out any time,

ALYA: And we won't need a man to be with us.

MEENA: And we can click and shout as loud as…

ALYA: cannons! And we can eat till our bellies are round…

MEENA: as buckets!

ALYA: And we'll have radio and singing

MEENA: and so many apples we can fill our mouths

ALYA: till they burst!

The girls are enjoying their reunion, but then suddenly they find their composure again. ALYA glances around nervously, fearing their discovery.

Shhhh. Okay. I'm ready to go with you, sister. My back hurts and I can't move but my shoes are strong.

MEENA notices now that ALYA's shoe lace is hanging loose.

MEENA: Your shoe lace is untied. Let me tie it.

ALYA doesn't move for a moment. Then she slowly lifts the hem of her burka to reveal that she is wearing US Army boots, far too big for her.

MEENA: Oh my.

ALYA: That's what I said when I found them. But at least they're warm on my feet.

The sisters continue to stare at ALYA's shoes. Elsewhere on stage SERGIO wakes on a small bed that has no mattress. He's been sleeping on the springs but he doesn't seem to notice. A sandbag is his pillow. The bed is rusty and old. SERGIO is wearing boxer shorts and is barefoot. He shakes his head and moans, confused.

SERGIO: Fuckin' Kubick. Jeez that guy can put 'em away. Put 'em away. Kubick. And Tony, and Mike, and… Shit. We were all there at…Joe's Place, yeah bunch of drunks and I didn't even drink that much.

SERGIO's words roll steady out of him.

And I said I'm going to have one of those dogs Yeah I'm going to eat one of those dogs That one Yeah I was hungry and my gut hurt. I'm still hungry and my gut hurts. Mama's gonna make me french toast when she gets up. What time is it?…

SERGIO rubs his head and eyes.

Give me one of those jumbo-sized hot dogs I said last night they all laughed Fuck you I said and your mother and your sister even if she is only ten the hot dogs were turnin' and turnin' the heat lamp burnin' them almost black and then. She was there, alone at the bar.

He runs his hands out along what he thinks is a mattress.

And she was so pretty and her mouth was… Her hair was so… Her neck was so… What? What? I can't remember. Her hair was… Her mouth was… And then she was gone.

He suddenly feels the metal of the springs. He jumps up.

What the…fuck –

He suddenly looks around him and then under the bed. He finds his pyjamas and starts to put them on. He still seems to be missing something.

Shit where are they? Where are they? (*Shouts.*) Must have been one hell of a night hell of a night At Joe's Place.

SERGIO is now dressed in his pyjamas. He surveys his bed. He notices something odd about his pillow. He takes a closer look.

Kubick, Tony, Mike and…

SERGIO discovers that the pillow is a sandbag. He pulls it off the bed and holds it, his arms out stretched. It strains him to hold it like this.

Fuck this for a pillow. (*Calls out.*) Mama? Mama you up yet?

Hearing no answer from his mother, SERGIO flings the sandbag away. It lands at the feet of the girls. Now the girls look at the 'pillow' that has landed between them. Then they simultaneously see SERGIO and he sees them.

God damn.

SERGIO speaks in a rush of words to the sisters.

I wasn't I forgot I didn't I'm sorry but I must have been too drunk but hey it's all right it's all right. (*Beat.*) Two, huh. Two of you? Man I must have been wasted cause I can't remember picking you up. I can't remember bringing no chick home. Chicks home.

MEENA: We are sisters.

SERGIO: Hermanas. Jesus, sisters. (*Laughs.*) Wait till I tell Kubick, Tony, Mike and. They won't believe it.

SERGIO notes ALYA's suitcase.

Uh. I guess you need a ride home?

ALYA: We have a taxi, thank you.

MEENA: Waiting at the end of the road.

SERGIO: Great. Cause I don't got a car.

SERGIO looks hard at MEENA.

Now you I kinda remember your face

He looks at ALYA in her burka.

Don't suppose I'd remember yours anyway. But hey, to each his own. To each his own, yeah.

ALYA: The airport is safe now? Meena says its safe?

SERGIO: Last time I checked. I flew Delta home. Did my Mama see you come in last night?

The sisters are confused by his question but shake their heads 'no'.

Good. Good. I mean my Mama she's open minded and she knows I got needs but she just doesn't want me fillin' them in her house. How 'bout you go out the back door?

ALYA looks around perplexed.

MEENA: We're going to England.

ALYA: We're going to get our diplomas.

SERGIO: Even better, would you mind going out the window? I think the back door's locked.

The sisters glance around, uncertain.

ALYA: Where is your uniform, soldier?

SERGIO: Mama has it at the dry cleaners. Hey, hope you don't mind but I forgot your names.

MEENA: I am Meena. This is my sister, Alya.

ALYA: Put on your uniform please. We are young women. We don't want to see your feet.

SERGIO: You want me in my uniform? A little kink? I like a little kink. We going to do it again then?

ALYA: Do what again?

SERGIO just grins.

SERGIO: Sisters, huh? I never did two at a time before. How did I do?

MEENA: Where is your gun?

SERGIO: I mean you came home with me so you must think I'm hot.

ALYA: Where is your helmet?

SERGIO: I mean I kinda hope you think I'm a little bit hot...

MEENA: How many Taliban did you kill today?

SERGIO: Hey. Don't get personal.

ALYA: Can you read?

MEENA: Can you write?

SERGIO: What do you think? A year at the U of Indiana but then I joined. Thought they'd make me a pilot. Ha. No fucking luck cause they put me on the ground.

MEENA: But you're American.

SERGIO now really looks at the sisters for the first time, as though his hangover is clearing.

ALYA: We'll be able to work now. We'll be able to read and write

MEENA: and calculate, because of you.

ALYA: But if they see Meena's hair they will kill her.

SERGIO: (*To ALYA.*) Let me see your face, honey.

ALYA steps back.

Come on. I seen more than that last night.

MEENA steps in front of her sister.

MEENA: Pick up your suitcase, sister. We must go now.

ALYA emits a sharp scream, and puts her hands to her back. Then she's just as suddenly still.

SERGIO: (*Panicked.*) Shush. Shush. Shush. Shush. Shit.

ALYA: My back hurts.

SERGIO: If my Mama hears you and comes in here, I am fuckin' toast. Out the window. Both of you. Now.

Both sisters look around.

MEENA: What window?

SERGIO: The only fuckin' window in my bedroom.

ALYA: There is no window. Do you have quills?

SERGIO: What?

ALYA: Quills.

SERGIO: No, no, no. I don't do the hard stuff. A little dope. Jack on the weekends. But no quills.

ALYA: They're growing on my back.

MEENA: You said it was a secret.

ALYA: He's just an American. He won't tell anyone. Will you?

SERGIO is uncertain but shakes his head 'no'.

SERGIO: Nah. Where you girls from?

ALYA: We were born here.

MEENA: Our father was born here. And his father's father.

SERGIO: Huh.

ALYA: Same piece of land.

MEENA: Grapes, mulberries, pomegranates.

SERGIO: Pomegranates? Shit. You grow pomegranates here?

MEENA: Our pomegranates are famous in India and Iran.

SERGIO: Bullshit, chica. Only thing that grows in Gary, Indiana is unemployment.

ALYA: Who is Gary Indiana?

MEENA: (*To ALYA.*) I think it's a movie about temples of doom. (*To SERGIO.*) Are you married?

SERGIO: No…

MEENA: Engaged?

SERGIO: No… Now wait just a minute. If you two are trying to trick me it won't work. I use a wrapper. When I hose a girl I wrap up real tight so no babies. No babies from me.

ALYA: (*Looking at SERGIO's toes.*) Oh my. It's a shame to say it but you have ugly toes. Doesn't he, Meena?

MEENA: Well, they're almost as ugly as Uncle Khan's.

All three look at SERGIO's feet.

SERGIO: Well, I'm sorry about the feet but last night, as you most likely remember, I lost my boots.

ALYA: I don't think you are a good soldier.

SERGIO: You watch you mouth. I did my service. Got a purple pulling a buddy out under fire.

MEENA: You shouldn't lose your boots. It's bad luck.

SERGIO: Shit.

MEENA: Don't you like being a soldier?

SERGIO: I didn't say that. Army's paying me to finish school. I started last week. I'd lick their ass if they ran out of toilet paper.

ALYA: You have bad tarbia.

MEENA: She means manners. A man without good tarbia won't find a wife.

SERGIO: Great. Cause honey I don't want to marry. Certainly neither of you.

ALYA: They you're still chaste?

SERGIO: Yeah. Chaste as the fuckin' dew.

MEENA: That's my favourite verse in the book, 'There's no dew/ anywhere, so/strange that there's no dew/anywhere

ALYA: (*Quotes.*) 'not on the forehead/of the cold sun,'

SERGIO: Huh?

ALYA: She's got a thing for Faiz Ahmed Faiz.

SERGIO: Well if he thinks he can move in on my chick, my chicks, without talking to me first, I'll take out his lights.

MEENA: (*Quotes.*) 'And the roses of your hands, the –'

ALYA: (*Quotes.*) 'the decanter and the glass,/were like the outline/of a dream.'

SERGIO: (*To ALYA.*) Baby, baby.

MEENA: (*Stomps her foot.*) Stop doing that, Alya.

ALYA: What?

SERGIO: I like the way you talk to me.

MEENA: Finishing the lines. I hate it.

> *ALYA sticks her tongue at her sister and continues.*

> Stupid Hedgehog.

ALYA: See, I'm not even in England yet and already they're calling me names.

SERGIO: Who's calling you names?

ALYA: (*To SERGIO.*) Everyone. Because of my quills. Down my spine, I only have three hundred of them. But the hedgehog has seven thousand. I have a long way to go. They're ugly but I need them. They're not solid, the quills. Each one is filled with a complex network of chambers, so they're lightweight and strong, so they won't buckle and break.

MEENA: (*To SERGIO.*) All she knows is about those quills. (*To ALYA.*) You ignorant brat.

> *While the girls face off, SERGIO moves around the stage curiously, uncertain now as to his surroundings.*

ALYA: You shit English girl who leaves her sister and mother behind, with nothing but a fart and a smile.

MEENA: You're right. They won't like you in England. Your mouth is full of dirt.

ALYA: Your head is full of worms.

You left us to rot. Father left us to rot.

MEENA: I'll pull out your hair.

The girls raise their fists at each other, ready to fight.

ALYA: I'll tell the village you're a whore.

MEENA: I'll tear out your quills!

Suddenly SERGIO is between them, pushing them apart.

SERGIO: Stop it! Both of you. There will be no ass-kicking in my space. You should be ashamed.

The sisters quit, but turn their backs to one another.

You don't fight family.

The sisters remain with their backs to each other, angry.

Hey. Hey! You two make up now.

ALYA/MEENA: Never!

SERGIO: Listen you guys. When it's *la familia.* The family. You never say never.

SERGIO takes ALYA's hand. She tries to pull away but he holds on. She calms. Then he takes MEENA's hand. MEENA resists less but it's still strange to hold a man's hand. SERGIO squashes the sisters' hands together.

Because when there's no one else there anymore. Not even a sound. Nothing. Nada...

For a short moment all three of them are holding hands but then SERGIO quickly lets go, uncomfortable.

Okay, you two are good again? Right.

MEENA and ALYA glance furtively at each other and nod.

So as Rafael Nadal the king of clay would say: Vamos. As Sergio Vasquez, that's me, would say as nicely as possible: Please, Get. The. Hell. Out. Of. My. House. Now.

ALYA: We're not in your house. How dare you suggest it? This is a desert.

SERGIO: Well, yeah, there's not much here sure, but who needs more than a bed, right?

ALYA: Let's go, Meena. I don't like his mouth.

ALYA turns to leave. MEENA is reluctant.

MEENA: But Alya, we must have compassion for his bad tarbia.

SERGIO: Sure, whatever. Just get going now and haul ass out my window.

SERGIO looks around but can no longer see his window.

Hey. Where's my window?

ALYA: In our home we had to paint the windows because it's forbidden for men to look inside the house and see us.

SERGIO: It was right here.

SERGIO is disoriented.

MEENA: This is the desert. We are in the desert.

ALYA: Bye, bye soldier.

SERGIO: I could see the oak tree from my bed.

MEENA: There are no trees here.

SERGIO: Hey, where the hell am I?

ALYA: I don't think I like you. Do you like him, Meena?

MEENA: Only a little. Maybe. But I'm glad we won't have to look at his toes anymore.

ALYA: Let's go then. But Meena, my other shoe lace is untied. Help me.

MEENA bends down to tie ALYA's other shoe lace. ALYA lifts the hem of her burka. SERGIO sees his boots.

SERGIO: Hey. Those are my boots!

MEENA: Don't be stupid.

SERGIO: I been lookin' for them all over.

ALYA: Finders keepers.

SERGIO: That's US Army property.

ALYA: Not anymore.

SERGIO: Where did you get them?

MEENA: (*Finishes tying.*) Good-bye, Soldier.

ALYA: (*Chants to SERGIO.*) Watch your back. Watch your back.

Taliban, Taliban might come back!

MEENA makes a 'whooo' scary sound, then ALYA continues chanting at SERGIO, taunting him.

Taliban, Taliban, Taliban
Come to chew you

Come to swallow you

The sisters laugh and chant together, staggering the song, as though this song were their childhood 'Row, row, row the boat', but far darker.

MEENA/ALYA: Taliban, taliban, taliban
Will take your eyes
And make apple pies.

ALYA and MEENA move to leave. SERGIO purposely steps on the hem of ALYA's burka to stop her. ALYA can't walk further. She strains against the cloth to walk forward but can't. SERGIO picks up the hem and slowly pulls the burka off of ALYA. When ALYA is revealed, it is as though she is waking from a dream. ALYA is dressed in slacks and a long sleeved shirt. She looks down at her 'nakedness' and as she kneels she cries out in fright, as though she is falling.

MEENA rushes to her side but it's as though ALYA can't see her.

MEENA: Alya? What is it? Alya?

Now ALYA begins to chant again, as though to comfort herself.

ALYA: (*Whispers.*) Will come to chew you
Come to swallow you.

MEENA: Alya!

ALYA: (*Chants.*) Will take your eyes
and make apple pies.

SERGIO: Don't ever separate a man from his boots.

SERGIO moves to pull the boots off of ALYA's feet but MEENA gets there first and takes the boots. ALYA does not resist. MEENA clutches the boots to her chest defiantly. SERGIO moves towards her, she evades him.

MEENA/ALYA: (*Chant.*) They'll slip into your home
and eat you to the bone.

SERGIO: Come on, honey. Don't tease me.

MEENA/ALYA: (*Chant.*) They'll slip into your bed
and hump you till you're.

ALYA finishes the chant by herself, now alert to her surroundings.

ALYA: Dead. Dead. (*Beat.*) Dead.

MEENA turns and starts to walk away. SERGIO no longer acts like he's in pyjamas but in a battle zone. He flips the bed on its side so it's a barrier he's standing behind. He starts out speaking calmly but then gets more frenzied.

SERGIO: Stay where you are. All of you. Hey. Get back in line. That's right. Get back in line. Hey. Stop right there, kid. Hey. I mean you.

SERGIO has no gun but he seems to be holding something in his arms, perhaps the memory of a gun. All the while he shouts at MEENA, she keeps slowly walking away.

Stop. I'm warning you. I'm warning you! You stop. You stop! Hey. Fucking stop or I shoot!

MEENA now stops walking and stands very still for some moments. As though she were suspended. Then MEENA turns around and looks first at SERGIO, then at her sister. The boots fall from her arms.

ALYA: Soldier, soldier.

SERGIO comes out of his 'state', and looks himself over.

SERGIO: I don't have a gun.

ALYA: But you did today.

MEENA: (*To ALYA.*) Where, Alya?

ALYA: In the yard.

MEENA: Where on my body do you think he shot me?

ALYA: In your neck.

SERGIO: No, no, no.

SERGIO violently kicks the bed out of the way.

I fucked you I didn't shoot you. Right here in my bedroom.

The sisters ignore SERGIO.

MEENA: I don't believe you, Alya.

ALYA: Okay.

SERGIO: Well you better believe me.

MEENA: This is one of your stupid tricks, hedgehog. Isn't it?

SERGIO: Yeah. This is one of her stupid tricks. I got drunk last night. In my home town bar. With Kubick, Tony, Mike and. With Kubick, Tony, Mike and… (*Shouts.*) Mama? Wake up. Come in here.

ALYA: (*To SERGIO, calmly.*) Meena was running in the yard. Everyone was standing in line. You told us to stand in line.

SERGIO: Be quiet. (*Calls.*) Mama!

ALYA: There were twenty of you, maybe thirty. We raised our arms. My mother, my father.

SERGIO: (*Calls.*) Hey!

ALYA: My father's arms were trembling and he was ashamed so he raised his arms higher. And you were in command.

SERGIO: You're out of your mind.

ALYA: You said

SERGIO: (*In Dari.*) Raise your arms. Don't move.

ALYA: (*Translating.*) Raise your arms. All of you. Don't move.

MEENA raises her arms in the air.

SERGIO: (*In Dari.*) And keep them up or we'll shoot.

ALYA: (*Translating.*) And keep them up or we'll shoot.

ALYA looks at MEENA as she speaks.

ALYA: Meena broke out of the line and ran.

SERGIO: I told her to stop.

ALYA: She didn't stop.

SERGIO: I was scared.

ALYA: She was scared.

SERGIO: (*To himself.*) Fuck.

While the sisters continue to speak, SERGIO very softly talks to himself and to his mother in Spanish as he sits on the bed, gets up, sits again, trying to force himself into another reality, trying to make himself believe that he is at home.

MEENA: I was afraid. Because…

MEENA slowly lowers her arms, trying to remember.

ALYA: You were afraid because I broke out of the line. I ran so fast the soldiers couldn't stop me. I ran round the back of the house.

MEENA: You ran round the back of the house?

ALYA: I could not breathe. (*Beat.*) I cannot breathe. Father tells us not to move. Mother is shushing us. All of us in line. The whole village. You grip my hand so tight, so tight and tell me to be still. You hum my favorite song to keep me quiet.

ALYA hums the song MEENA hummed to her.

That's how it goes. But your throat is dry with fear and the tune will not come out. So I pull. I pull and pull 'til my hand comes out from your hand. And then I run. I run so fast you almost can't see me. But I trip and fall, down the well. And as I fall I grow quills so quick because while hedgehogs are skilled climbers, they are not good at getting down. When they come across a drop they roll into a ball and just. Drop. The quills cushion the fall. To keep the quills from being damaged, the thin stem just above the skin flexes on impact. Wild hedgehogs have been seen to drop twenty feet with no apparent signs of injury. (*Beat.*) Down the well I fall and when I hit the bottom, because I don't have enough quills, my back breaks. Crack. I cannot move. I lie on my back in three inches of water.

MEENA: (*Remembering.*) You ran first. Yes. I was afraid for you so I ran after you. Didn't I?

ALYA doesn't answer.

MEENA: (*Shouts.*) Didn't I?

ALYA: Yes.

MEENA: So it's your fault I got shot.

ALYA: I had to run. I couldn't stand still.

MEENA: (*Angry.*) It's your fault. It's your fault! You let my hand go.

ALYA: From where I lay on my back in the well I could see a round circle of sky above me. (*To SERGIO.*) And then I heard you fire. And then I heard my sister –

SERGIO: (*Interrupts, to ALYA.*) I gave her warning. I had to stop her. I gave her half a dozen warnings. But she kept on running. She dropped so fast to the ground. I couldn't believe how fast she dropped. I knelt beside her. I picked her up and carried her into the shade.

MEENA: You carried me?

SERGIO: Yes.

MEENA: How?

SERGIO: How? What the hell does it matter?

MEENA: It matters to me. It matters to me!

SERGIO looks around, locates a sandbag and picks it up in his arms. He adjusts his arms to hold the sandbag better.

You held me in your arms like that?

SERGIO: Yeah.

ALYA: He touched your neck.

MEENA: (*To SERGIO.*) You touched my neck?

SERGIO: I tried to stop the bleeding but

ALYA: there was too much of it.

SERGIO: There was too much of it. I'd never shot someone before. Your neck was so small and. So small and. My bullet was in there. My bullet was in there, inside, and I couldn't get it out. I couldn't get it out. Your skin. Your skin was so –

ALYA: (*Interrupts.*) Don't you shame my sister!

SERGIO: Your mouth was so –

ALYA: (*Interrupts.*) Don't you talk about Meena like that.

MEENA: Let him speak.

SERGIO: Your hair lay across my arm, black and –

ALYA: Shut your mouth!

MEENA: Alya, please!

SERGIO: Your hair lay across my arm, black and…

MEENA: My hair was black and what? What, soldier?

SERGIO now turns away and will not answer.

My mouth was what? Speak! My skin was what?

Sergio can no longer remember. For a moment he just looks at MEENA.

SERGIO: You were alive when I carried you.

SERGIO and MEENA regard one another.

MEENA: I was alive? (*To ALYA.*) He says I was alive, Alya, so I didn't die. I didn't die!

ALYA: You are alive, Meena. Right now. For a few more minutes. And I am alive for this same time. And the soldier too. For a few more minutes.

SERGIO: Hey. Hey. This is your shit, don't bring me into it. I got out. I got out.

ALYA: Yes. You and your buddies get out. You get out fast because the Taliban have circled back and Kubick, Tony and Mike are with you and you're gunning the truck and spinning away from our village and then BANG, guess what?

SERGIO: Guess what? Guess fucking what? I'm going back to bed. I ate a hot dog long as my leg last night.

ALYA: Indigestion.

SERGIO: Like you wouldn't believe.

ALYA: (*Loud.*) Bang!

SERGIO: I'm going back to sleep.

ALYA: (*Louder.*) Bang!

SERGIO: I was out drinking last night. With Kubick, Tony, Mike and. Kubick, Tony, Mike and.

ALYA: You. Kubick, Tony, Mike and you. Hit a land mine. Your friends are unharmed but you fly up in the air, high, high and your boots fly off your feet, one with a foot still attached and Uncle sees your boots lying a hundred feet from your body. He throws your boots in the well to hide them. He is afraid the village will be blamed. He doesn't even know I'm down there.

SERGIO: (*Threatening.*) You are a dirty girl.

ALYA: Yes. At this very moment I am covered in dirt and slime at the bottom of a well and I'm dying. And my sister Meena is in the yard and she is also dying. And you are lying on the road and Kubick, Tony and Mike are leaning over you and you are dying.

SERGIO: (*Fiercely.*) No. No way. I'm in bed.

ALYA: (*Shrugs.*) I think we got caught in each other's…

SERGIO: (*Interrupts.*) I'm in bed and my mother's making french toast in the kitchen and I can smell it burning at the edges, just the way I like it.

ALYA starts to laugh. She laughs and laughs. Then she points to the largest sandbag.

And I'm in my pyjamas. I'm in my pyjamas. (*Shouts.*) I'm in my fucking pyjamas and I'm home. In Gary, Indiana. I made it home!

Now they are all silent some moments. ALYA just stares at SERGIO till he looks away. Now he knows he didn't make it home.

MEENA: (*Quietly.*) Alya, I'm sorry to say this but you are a liar. I went to England. I studied Faiz Ahmed Faiz.

ALYA: You didn't go to England. We can't even speak English.

MEENA: But we are speaking English.

ALYA: Yes. Father and Mother would be impressed.

MEENA: Father is waiting at the airport. We've come back to get you. We're going to university!

ALYA: We've never left our village.

MEENA: But the taxi is waiting.

ALYA: There is no taxi.

The sisters regard one another some moments.

MEENA: If I were dying, I would remember. I don't remember.

ALYA: But you do. You just don't want to. (*Beat.*) What is real is that we are usually hungry. We are usually afraid. We are usually more hungry than afraid for years now. And we don't grow pomegranates anymore. Father sells scraps. Me and you, we can't leave the house so we dream of apples. Of clean water. Of the sweetness of meat and rice.

MEENA: No.

ALYA: We dream of electricity, of our fingers moving on pages, of baskets full for picnics.

MEENA: No.

ALYA: We dream of escaping the Taliban, of going to England,

MEENA: No.

ALYA: of you and father leaving first, of your coming back to get us.

MEENA: No! It's that simple: to you, Alya, I say no. (*Beat.*) Where is my body?

ALYA hesitates.

Where is my body?

ALYA points to the medium sandbag.

That's me?

ALYA nods 'yes'. MEENA stands over the bag, looking at it for some moments. Then suddenly she kicks it.

Get up.

She kicks it again.

Get up!

She kicks it again and again.

Get up, girl! You will live. You will be a teacher. Do you hear me? You are free now. You will travel. Get up! You will write a brilliant paper on Faiz Ahmed Faiz. Get up! You will kiss a man. Get up. Get up! You will live! You will live!

MEENA kicks the bag till she's worn out, then she quits. The three of them are silent some moments.

ALYA: It's not your fault, Meena.

MEENA: Why did you let my hand go, Alya? I held on to you so tight, so tight I was afraid I'd break your bones.

ALYA: But I pulled and pulled and finally we came apart.

ALYA looks at her own hand.

You used to draw the alphabet on my palm under the table when we sat with the elders. (*Beat.*) I'm sorry, Meena.

The sisters are silent some moments.

MEENA: It's all right, little hedgehog. It's all right now. Listen. My throat's no longer dry.

MEENA now hums the song that ALYA hummed earlier. Now MEENA hums it clear and strong. ALYA listens with delight. Then the two of them hum the song together. When its over they just stare at each other.

SERGIO: How much more time do we got?

ALYA: (*Calmly.*) Just a few seconds, I think. I'm going now. I'm the first to go.

ALYA approaches her sister, takes MEENA's hand and kisses it.

Meena.

Then ALYA releases MEENA's hand and takes a sandbag by its corner. ALYA begins to drag the sandbag behind her as she exits. But then she stops and looks at the bag, and speaks matter-of-factly.

Oh. This isn't mine. I'm the small one.

ALYA now takes hold of the smallest sand bag and drags it away. She glances back once, just for a moment, at MEENA, then disappears off stage. MEENA and SERGIO watch her leave in silence. Then MEENA realizes her sister is truly gone. She calls for her.

MEENA: Alya? Alya!?

MEENA listens for a reply. No reply comes.

SERGIO: Well, I guess I'm next. Damn it's cold. So damn cold.

SERGIO starts to drag his sandbag back to his bed. MEENA is still watching the place where her sister disappeared. She hears the sound of SERGIO's sandbag dragging and now regards him.

MEENA: Soldier.

SERGIO: Yeah?

MEENA: Wherever Joe's place is, you shouldn't have left it.

SERGIO just looks at MEENA.

MEENA: Soldier.

SERGIO: Yeah?

MEENA: If you were not dying, I would wish you dead. (*Beat.*) Are you sorry?

SERGIO: (*Sincerely.*) I wish I had the time to be.

SERGIO drags the sandbag.

MEENA: Soldier.

SERGIO stands still.

SERGIO: Yeah?

The following is hard for MEENA to ask but she makes herself ask it.

MEENA: Am I pretty? (*Beat.*) Were we pretty? My sister and I.

SERGIO: You were just kids.

MEENA: But if we had grown up?

SERGIO studies MEENA some moments, trying to figure out what she wants. MEENA straightens her shirt, shifts her hair. Then they stare at one another.

SERGIO: Well, I wouldn't kicked you out of bed, that's for sure.

MEENA: Bastard. (*Beat.*) Thank you.

SERGIO nods to MEENA, then lays the sandbag on his bed as a pillow and lies down on it and closes his eyes. He is shivering badly. MEENA watches him shiver. Then she picks up the burka and nears SERGIO. She looks down at SERGIO. Then she slowly pulls the burka over SERGIO, completely covering him like a shroud. SERGIO stops shivering and is still.

MEENA returns to 'her' sandbag. She nudges it gently with her foot. No sign of life. MEENA looks around her, sees the suitcase. Calmly, surely, she picks the suitcase up, feeling that it fits well in her hand. Then she stands on the sandbag, holding the suitcase to her chest, readying herself for her journey. She closes her eyes. She hums clearly, strongly the lines of the song she hummed earlier.

Then suddenly MEENA opens her eyes, no longer humming but looking straight out over the public. Black out.

END OF PLAY

Biographies

STEPHEN JEFFREYS

Stephen Jeffreys is an internationally acclaimed playwright whose work includes *Valued Friends*, Hampstead Theatre (1989), winner of the Evening Standard and Critics' Circle Award for Most Promising Playwright; *The Clink*, Paines Plough (1990), for whom he was Art Council Writer in Residence from 1987-1989 and *The Libertine* (1995), which was staged at the Royal Court Theatre to great popular and critical acclaim and went on to produced at Steppenwolf Theatre, Chicago (1996), directed by Terry Johnson and starring John Malkovich. Stephen's screenplay version of the play was released in 2005 starring Johnny Depp. Other plays include *A Jovial Crew* (RSC); *A Going Concern* (Hampstead Theatre); *I Just Stopped by to See the Man* (Royal Court Theatre); *Lost Land* (Steppenwolf Theatre); *The Art of War* (Sydney Theatre Company) and *Bugles at the Gates of Jalalabad* (Tricycle Theatre). Stephen is currently writing feature films for Ecosse and Fortune Films.

RON HUTCHINSON

Ron Hutchinson was Writer In Residence at the Royal Shakespeare Company and has had plays performed at the Royal National Theatre, The Royal Court Theatre, the Goodman, the Public Theatre, the Mark Taper Forum and The Old Globe. His plays include *Topless Mum* and *Moonlight and Magnolias* (both performed at the Tricycle Theatre 2007/2008), *Says I Says He* and *Rat In The Skull* and an adaptation of Mikhail Bulgakov's *Flight* and *The Master and Margarita*. A winner of the John Whiting Award and other awards including the Dramatist's Circle Award, he is an Emmy winning feature and television writer whose credits include *Murderers Among Us*, *The Simon Wiesenthal Story*, *The Josephine Baker Story*, *The Burning Season*, *The Ten Commandments* and *Traffic*. He lives and works in Los Angeles and teaches screenwriting at the American Film Institute.

AMIT GUPTA

Amit Gupta's first play *Touch* was a winner of the Royal Court Young Writers' Competition. As Writer in Residence at Leicester Haymarket Theatre he wrote and directed *Heroes*. He has written for stage, screen and radio and last year wrote and directed an award-winning short film, *Love Story*. He is currently working on feature film adaptations of his Radio 4 play *Jadoo* and Owen Sheers' novel *Resistance*. Amit is a member of the Tricycle's Bloomberg Playwrights group.

JOY WILKINSON

Joy Wilkinson's play, *Acting Leader*, opened at the Tricycle in June this year as part of 'Women, Power and Politics'. Joy's other writing credits include: *Fair* (Finborough Theatre and Trafalgar Studios); *Felt Effects* (Verity Bargate Award-winner, Theatre 503) and *The Aquatic Ape* (Edinburgh Festival). She has recently completed an attachment at the National Theatre Studio and is writing a new play for the Liverpool Everyman/Playhouse. She also writes for radio and was a graduate of the BBC's inaugural Writers' Academy.

DAVID EDGAR

David Edgar is one of England's foremost political playwrights and has longstanding relationships with the Royal Shakespeare Company and the National Theatre. His play *Testing the Echo* for Out of Joint, played on tour and at the Tricycle Theatre in 2008. He is the recipient of numerous awards including the Arts Council's John Whiting Award for *Destiny*, the Laurence Olivier and Tony awards for Best Play for his adaptation of *Nicholas Nickleby*, Plays and Players' Best Play Award for *Maydays* and the Evening Standard Best Play Award for *Pentecost*.

LEE BLESSING

Broadway and London's West End: *A Walk In The Woods*. Off-Broadway: *When We Go Upon the Sea*, *A Body of Water*, *Going to St. Ives*, (Outer Critics Circle Award, Best Play, OBIE for ensemble performance); *Thief River* (Drama Desk nomination, Best Play); *Cobb* (Drama Desk award, best ensemble); *Chesapeake*, *Eleemosynary* and *Down the Road*. Notable world premieres: *Great Falls* in the 2008 Humana New Play Festival of the Actors Theatre of Louisville; *Lonesome Hollow*, *Flag Day* and *Whores* all at the Contemporary American Theatre Festival; *The Scottish Play* at La Jolla Playhouse; *Black Sheep* at Florida Stage and *The Winning Streak* at George Street Playhouse. Other plays include *Riches*, *Independence*, *Oldtimers Game*, *Nice People Dancing to Good Country Music*, *Perilous Night* and *A User's Guide to Hell*, featuring Bernard Madoff. Recent adaptations: *Heaven's My Destination,* from Thornton Wilder's picaresque 1935 novel, commissioned by the Cleveland Play House, and *Courting Harry*, commissioned by the Weissberger Group in

New York from a non-fiction work by Linda Greenhouse. Additional awards: The Steinberg/American Theater Critics Association Award and Citation, the L.A. Drama Critics Award, The Great American Play Award, The Humanitas Award and the George and Elisabeth Marton Award among others. Nominations for Tony and Olivier awards, as well as the Pulitzer Prize.

DAVID GREIG

David Greig's award winning work includes *Dunisinane* (RSC at the Hampstead Theatre); *Midsummer* (Traverse Theatre and Soho Theatre); *Creditors* (Donmar and BAM), *Damascus* and *Miniskirts of Kabul* (Tricycle Theatre) *Brewers Fayre, Outlying Islands* and *Europe* (Traverse Theatre); *The American Pilot* (RSC, Soho & MTC); *Ramallah* (Royal Court); *Pyrenees* (Paines Plough) and *The Cosmonaut's Last Message to the Woman He Once Loved in the Former Soviet Union* (Donmar Warehouse). Adaptations include *The Bacchae* (Edinburgh International Festival and Lyric Theatre, Hammersmith); *Tintin in Tibet* (Barbican and The Playhouse); *When the Bulbul Stopped Singing* (Traverse Theatre); *Caligula* (Donmar Warehouse) and *Peter Pan* (NTS, Traverse/ Barbican).

COLIN TEEVAN

Colin Teevan's plays include *How Many Miles to Basra?* (West Yorkshire Playhouse); *Amazonia* (with Paul Heritage, Young Vic); *The Diver* and *The Bee* (both with Hideki Noda, Soho Theatre and Setagaya, Tokyo); *Monkey!* (Young Vic); *Missing Persons: Four Tragedies and Roy Keane* (Assembly Rooms and Trafalgar Studios); *Alcmaeon in Corinth* (Live! Theatre); and *The Walls* (National Theatre). His adaptations include *Kafka's Monkey* (Young Vic); *Don Quixote* (West Yorkshire Playhouse); *Peer Gynt* (National Theatre of Scotland and Dundee Rep); and *Svejk* (Gate and The Duke 42nd Street). His translations include *Bacchai* (National Theatre); *Iph...* (Lyric Theatre, Belfast); *Cuckoos* and *Marathon* (Gate Theatre). All his plays are published by Oberon Books. Teevan is an Artistic Associate of West Yorkshire Playhouse.

BEN OCKRENT

Ben Ockrent's first play, *The Pleasure Principle*, was produced at the Tristan Bates Theatre in 2007. In 2008 he developed *Khoa San Road* for BBC3/World Productions, and *Kidnapped* for BBC3/Company Pictures. In 2009 he wrote an episode of *Material Girl* for BBC1; and was nominated as a Broadcast Magazine "Hotshot". He is currently developing a new comedy series for BBC3/Hartswood Film and a new play for the Tricycle Theatre.

ABI MORGAN

Abi Morgan's plays include *Skinned* and *Sleeping Around* (Paines Plough); *Tiny Dynamite* (Traverse); *Tender* (Hampstead); *Splendour* – which won a Fringe First at the Edinburgh Festival in 2000, and *Fugee* (National Theatre). Her television work includes *My Fragile Heart, Murder, Sex Traffic* - the multi award-winning drama for Channel 4, *Tsunami – The Aftermath, White Girl* and *Royal Wedding*. She is currently working on her new series for Kudos and the BBC called *The Hour*. Her film writing credits include *Brick Lane*, an adaptation of Monica Ali's bestseller. She also has a number of films in development including *The Invisible Woman* for BBC films, *Suffragettes* for Film Four, Focus and Ruby Films, *Little Mermaid* for Working Title and *Iron Lady*, for DJ Films and Pathe.

RICHARD BEAN

Richard Bean's version of *London Assurance* premiered at the National Theatre in 2010. His play *Big Fellah* tours in 2010 (Out of Joint/Lyric Hammersmith). His other writing credits include *England People Very Nice* (National Theatre), *The English Game*, produced by Headlong Theatre Company; *In The Club* (Hampstead Theatre); an adaptation of *The Hypochondriac* (Almeida); *Smack Family Robinson* (Newcastle Live!); *Harvest* – Critics' Circle Best New Play 2005, *Honeymoon Suite* – Pearson Play of the Year 2003, *Under The Whaleback* – George Devine Award 2003; and *Toast* (Royal Court); *The God Botherers* (Bush Theatre); *Up On Roof* (Hull Truck); *The Mentalists* (Lyttelton Loft, National Theatre); and *Mr England* (Sheffield Crucible Theatre). Radio plays include *Yesterday, Of Rats and Men, Unsinkable,* and *Robin Hood's Revenge*.

SIMON STEPHENS

Simon is an award-winning playwright whose work includes *Bluebird* (Royal Court, 1998); *Herons* (Royal Court, 2001); *Port* (Manchester Royal Exchange, 2002 - Pearson Award for Best New Play); *Country Music* (Royal Court, 2004); *On the Shore of the Wide World* (Manchester Royal Exchange/National Theatre, 2005 - Olivier Award for Best New Play); *Motortown* (Royal Court, 2006); *Harper Regan* (National Theatre, 2008); *Sea Wall* (Bush Theatre/Traverse Theatre, 2008-2009); *Pornography* (Deutsches Schauspielhaus, Hanover, 2007, Edinburgh Festival/Birmingham Rep, 2008 and Tricycle Theatre, 2009); *Punk Rock* (Lyric Hammersmith/Manchester Royal Exchange, 2009); *The*

Trial of Ubi (Schauspielhaus, Essen/Toneelgroep Amsterdam, 2010), *A Thousand Stars Explode in the Sky* written in collaboration with David Eldridge and Robert Holman (Lyric Hammersmith, 2010) and *Marine Parade*, a play with songs written by Mark Eotze (Animalink for the Brighton Festival, 2010). Simon also writes for radio and the screen. TV includes a short film adaptation of *Pornography* for Coming Up (Channel 4, 2009) and *Dive* (Granada/BBC, 2009).

NAOMI WALLACE

Naomi Wallace's work has been produced in the United Kingdom, Europe and the United States. Her major plays include *One Flea Spare*, *In the Heart of America*, *Slaughter City*, *The Trestle at Pope Lick Creek*, *Things of Dry Hours* and *The Fever Chart: Three Short Visions of the Middle East*. Her work has received the Susan Smith Blackburn Prize, the Kesselring Prize, the Fellowship of Southern Writers Drama Award, and an Obie. She is also a recipient of the MacArthur 'Genius' Fellowship. Her award-winning film *Lawn Dogs* is available on DVD. Her new film, *The War Boys*, co-written with Bruce Mcleod, will be released in 2008.